As the income gap between the ultra-rich and the other 99 percent grows, many are questioning whether capitalism has to be so inequitable. Others challenge the viability of capitalism as we know it. This book presents an alternate economic reality, drawn from European economic thought. Specifically, it refutes the common belief that the sole purpose of work is profit, which we might call socially irresponsible capitalism. In socially responsible capitalism, work is to serve employees and society as well as owners. This book will be hated by people motivated by greed, and embraced by those who practice servant leadership or rejoice in the economic teaching of Pope Francis.

—John Conbere, University of St. Thomas, USA

In this time of increasing ecological problems, technological revolution, and change in the workforce, the focus of businesses is shifting from solely being on the profit to how businesses develop their people and contribute to the society. The Millennials are challenging and scrutinizing the common premises of traditional business and management. We need to develop socially responsible organizations that would invest in their people and communities. Socioeconomic management helps to grow socially responsible organizations, but also changes a mental model of traditional business and management. Socially responsible organizations by employing socioeconomic management can bring together profit-oriented capitalism and care for human beings.

—Alla Heorhiadi, University of St. Thomas, USA

Socially Responsible Capitalism and Management

In the current crisis context, capitalism is questioned by its detractors or defended by its partisans. The concept of socially responsible capitalism (SRC) is based on the entrepreneurial spirit. It encourages exemplary behaviors, such as effective, efficient and ethical behaviors, by stimulating social responsibility of companies and organizations. This is combined with the development of economic empowerment and legitimate efforts of each citizen-actor.

Socially Responsible Capitalism and Management does not confuse financial capitalism and entrepreneurial capitalism. The first one improves the creation of artificial value which leads to financial bubbles that periodically burst and bankrupt the real economy. Quite the reverse, entrepreneurial capitalism creates both solid economic value and employment. This is justified by the production of goods and services that meet legitimate needs of consumer-citizens.

This book shows that putting human beings at the heart of action enables them to produce sustainable economic value and anthropological values that are inseparable. The innovative aspect of this book lies in its analysis, starting from the macro-economic level to the individual one, by presenting a detailed analysis of the micro-economic level of companies within its managerial issues. *Socially Responsible Capitalism and Management* is dedicated to presenting the different aspects of SRC for the society, companies and organizations and also individual actors, as citizens, producers and consumers.

Henri Savall is an emeritus professor at the Institut d'Administration des Entreprises, University Jean Moulin Lyon, France, where he is the founder of the EUGINOV Centre (École Universitaire de Gestion Innovante) and the Socioeconomic Management Master's programs. He is also the founder and president of the ISEOR Research Center, where he supervised 78 doctoral theses.

Michel Péron was an emeritus professor at the University of Paris III Sorbonne Nouvelle, France. A lexicographer, he published several English–French dictionaries. He unfortunately passed away three weeks before the French version was published.

Véronique Zardet is a professor of management sciences and director of EUGINOV (École Universitaire de Gestion Innovante) Center, IAE Lyon Business School, Jean Moulin University, France.

Marc Bonnet is professor of management at EUGINOV Center, IAE Lyon Business School, Jean Moulin University, France.

Routledge Studies in Management, Organizations and Society

For a full list of titles in this series, please visit www.routledge.com

This series presents innovative work grounded in new realities, addressing issues crucial to an understanding of the contemporary world. This is the world of organised societies, where boundaries between formal and informal, public and private, local and global organizations have been displaced or have vanished, along with other nineteenth century dichotomies and oppositions. Management, apart from becoming a specialized profession for a growing number of people, is an everyday activity for most members of modern societies.

Similarly, at the level of enquiry, culture and technology, and literature and economics, can no longer be conceived as isolated intellectual fields; conventional canons and established mainstreams are contested. **Management, Organizations and Society** addresses these contemporary dynamics of transformation in a manner that transcends disciplinary boundaries, with books that will appeal to researchers, student and practitioners alike.

Recent titles in this series include:

**How Speech Acting and the Struggle of Narratives
Generate Organization**
Thorvald Gran

Governance, Resistance and the Post-Colonial State
Management and State Building Social Movements
Edited by Jonathan Murphy and Nimruji Jammulamadaka

The Work of Communication
Relational Perspectives on Working and Organizing
in Contemporary Capitalism
Tim Khun, Karen Ashcraft, and François Cooren

Socially Responsible Capitalism and Management
*Henri Savall, Michel Péron, Véronique Zardet,
and Marc Bonnet*

Socially Responsible Capitalism and Management

Henri Savall, Michel Péron,
Véronique Zardet, and Marc Bonnet

Original 2015 French version "*Le Capitalisme
Socialement Responsable existe*" published by
EMS Publishers, Paris, France

Routledge
Taylor & Francis Group

LONDON AND NEW YORK

First published 2018
by Routledge

2 Park Square, Milton Park, Abingdon, Oxfordshire OX14 4RN
52 Vanderbilt Avenue, New York, NY 10017

Routledge is an imprint of the Taylor & Francis Group, an informa business

First issued in paperback 2019

Library of Congress Cataloging-in-Publication Data
A catalog record for this book has been requested

ISBN: 978-1-138-28200-1 (hbk)
ISBN: 978-0-367-88560-1 (pbk)

Typeset in Sabon
by Apex CoVantage, LLC

This book is dedicated to the memory of our co-author and close friend, Prof. Michel Péron, who passed away three weeks after finishing the manuscript of the French version. He did not see the published book that he contributed to so greatly.

.

Contents

Tables

Foreword

In the context of the current crisis, traditional capitalism is questioned by its detractors or defended tooth and nail by its partisans. The proposed concept of *socially responsible capitalism* (SRC) is based on the entrepreneurial spirit. It encourages exemplary behaviors, such as effective, efficient and ethical behaviors, by stimulating the social responsibility of companies and organizations. This is combined with the development of economic empowerment and legitimate efforts of each citizen-actor.

Socially responsible capitalism does not confuse financial capitalism and entrepreneurial capitalism. Financial capitalism encourages the creation of what we call *artificial value*, which leads to financial bubbles that periodically burst and bankrupt the real economy. Quite the reverse, entrepreneurial capitalism creates both solid economic value and sustainable employment. This is justified by the production of goods and services that meet legitimate needs of consumer-citizens.

Socially responsible capitalism is not an idealistic form of utopia. It already exists in the factual accounting of the world's economic and social history. It is currently viable. It includes a set of effective and proven practices, referring to the socioeconomic approach of management, implemented in 1,854 companies and organizations, in 72 industries and over 44 countries.

Socially responsible capitalism, in the economic sphere, amounts to democracy for political, social and anthropological ends. It relies on companies as the engines of economic, social and cultural activity insofar as they create value in the proximity of human relationships benefitting employees, customers, users and stakeholders. The entire book shows that putting human beings at the heart of action enables the production of sustainable economic value and anthropological value, the two of which are inseparable.

The innovative aspect of *Socially Responsible Capitalism and Management* lies in its analysis, moving from the macroeconomic level to the individual level, and presenting a detailed examination of the microeconomic level of companies with managerial issues. The entire book is dedicated to presenting the different aspects of SRC for society, companies and organizations, as well as individuals as citizens, producers and consumers.

Preface

Global Capitalism Is Unsustainable, but Perhaps Savall and Zardet's Socioeconomic Sustainable Responsible Capitalism Can Help

I have been traveling to Lyon, France, each year for 17 years to learn their approach to resolving the many problems of global capitalism. I teach sustainability, chair the sustainability council at New Mexico State University and teach what Savall and Zardet call the socioeconomic approach to management (SEAM). I therefore am in a position to write about their approach and to tell you why it is not the usual socially responsible capitalism (SRC) idealism one finds taught in the business school today or used to legitimate current global capitalism practices of companies and their governments.

The Savall and Zardet approach is not at all like the typical SRC models because they start from fundamental reforms of socioeconomic practices of companies and propose to curtail runaway speculation markets that have all but drained productive markets of their capacity to build viable companies capable of anything like sustainable business practices. I call their approach socioeconomic sustainable responsible capitalism (SESRC) in order to differentiate it from the apologetic and insubstantial SRC models so popular in schools of business these days.

In this preface, I will divide my remarks into four parts. In Part I, I will first give you some idea of the magnitude of the sustainability problems that 'global capitalism' has created in recent decades. These have to do with depletion of natural resources due to population explosion and its growing footprint on the plant, the CO_2-driven climate change crisis tied to the human diet and transportation that increases levels of pollution globally. In Part II, I will explore why the various approaches to 'socially responsible capitalism' sound good but are unable to resolve the magnitude of sustainability problems that 'global capitalism' has created. In Part III, I will explore ways that Savall and Zardet's SESRC can succeed where global capitalism has failed. Finally, in Part IV, I will end with some suggestions for ways SESRC can get global capitalism beyond its fourth epoch of unsustainability and allow it to move along to the fifth epoch of a sustainable global capitalism.

Part I: Major Unsustainability Problems of Global Capitalism

Before I describe the multiplicity of global capitalisms and their histories, let me answer a basic question: *How bad is the worldwide sustainability crisis?* Global capitalism today is in the worst crisis of its 500-year history. It is far worse than the Great Depression of the 1930s, the oil crisis of the 1970s and the chaos of the 2008 banking collapses that tanked national economies around the globe. There are several important consequences that are unsustainable to all nations.

The world population is now 7.4 billion, and by 2100, it will reach 11.3 billion. Half of the 7.4 billion people live on less than $2.50 a day, and 80 percent live on less than $10 a day.[1] One billion children live in poverty. With the population increasing so dramatically by 2100, famine will be far worse than today, and more people will live on less than $2.50 a day. It's not just about population; the real problem is that the current form of global capitalism is bringing about climate change and is engaged in forms of speculative market gambling and misappropriations of company funds that degrade national socioeconomic performance.[2] There is a particularly perverted global capitalism in 2016 that is wreaking havoc upon the forms of global capitalism that occurred in three former epochs. Global capitalism has now entered its fourth epoch, and it's not able to forestall, much less reverse, these systemicity problems.[3]

The Four Epochs of Global Capitalism

1. Mercantile capitalism
2. Classical state capitalism
3. National corporate capitalism
4. Transnational Regulatory Superstructure of WTO, World Bank, IMF and UN

The first three global capitalism epochs were led by nation states, but the fourth epoch is driven by transnational corporate power. By transnational corporate power, I mean the group of organizations attempting to govern global capitalism: the World Trade Organization (WTO), International Monetary Fund (IMF), World Bank and the United Nations. Global capitalism is currently stuck in this transnational corporate power epoch. Global capitalism has been experiencing recurring cycles of recession and attempted recovery since the 2008 global financial system crisis. And it's stuck in ways that do not address the population explosion from 7.4 billion today to an anticipated 11.3 billion by the year 2100. Keep in mind that it took older ways of doing capitalism until 1804 to reach the first billion people. After the Industrial Revolution took root, the second billion were reached around 1927. More billions were added in cycles as short as 12 and 13 years between 1987 and 2016. During this time, the total greenhouse gases measured in tons of carbon dioxide (CO_2) created climate change, which has been especially dramatic since the Industrial Revolution and passed the point of no return in the third epoch of global capitalism. In the United States, for example, the average citizen's carbon footprint is 20 tons of CO_2 compared to, for example, India, which has a footprint of 1.1 tons per citizen. The United States accounts for only 5 percent of the world's population, yet it is responsible for 20 percent of CO_2 emissions and consumes 30 percent of the world's natural resources. Clearly, the U.S. form of state capitalism is unsustainable. Beyond a certain per capita energy footprint, the global capitalism practiced today—its manner of production and consumption and its entire political system of transnational corporate governance—is unsustainable. We are witness to the fourth epoch of global capitalism, which many believe is endless warfare, increasing famine and a rise in temperature from CO_2-producing climate change that will result in human catastrophe, if not the extinction of the human race.

Many believe CO_2 production is merely the product of transportation based in gas and oil combustion engines (cars, trucks, trains, ships and planes). However, all these forms of transportation account for only 13 percent of annual CO_2 production, while an additional 18 percent is from cattle. Cattle consume more water and more food than the entire human population of 7.4 billion people.

I am a vegan, and I don't anticipate the world population becoming vegan or vegetarian. However, it is true that the footprint from our choice of diet and its CO_2 emission from food production methods, supply-chain losses, consumer waste and so on affects the 3,900 kcal of food supplied (per person per day) just to the United States.[4] Worldwide, if people went from meat-lover diets to no beef, the CO_2 footprint could reduce dramatically. Going vegetarian would be about half the footprint of the meat-lover's diet. My point is that most people are not going to give up cars to go to work or shop by bicycle (except in places such as Copenhagen, where 45 percent of the people bike to work), but if they could, the CO_2 footprint would change. Since most of the people on the planet are not going to trade their gas-consuming cars for bikes, the biggest change we can make to our footprint on earth is to change our diets. However, riding a bike and changing to a half-meat or meatless diet is still not going to change the other unsustainable practices of third-epoch global capitalism.

Global capitalism in its first epoch was mercantile capitalism, during the time of Adam Smith's (1776) book *Wealth of Nations*. During the Industrial Revolution, mercantilism put the world population over the one billion and multibillion threshold. Yet it did so without producing the kinds of carbon footprints or the kind of ecological collapse we see today.

Global Capitalism in Its Second Epoch Was Classical State Capitalism. There are several types of state capitalism. Here we emphasize the French and American versions that have done their fair share to create unsustainable state capitalisms.

In 1962, when I first started going to France, I was 14 years old. French capitalism was resistant to US capitalism in demonstrations I saw on the streets of Paris. Until a decade ago, globalization in France translated to American capitalism. Let's jump forward to the end of WWII, when both U.S. and French capitalism took different turns.

Since WWII, France has engaged in a form of state capitalism (in the Colbertist tradition, it supports entrepreneurial spirit to create industrial giants and world-class companies). The problem is that France's state capitalism is no longer compatible with global capitalism, which has resulted in France's state capitalism reducing its footprint in the global economy. State capitalism has reached its limits.

Global capitalism in its third epoch is a corporate capitalism still tied to nation states. Since WWII, US national capitalism engaged in creating more international debt:

> The net American international debt in the late 1990s stood at approximately $1 trillion; as a consequence, a sizable portion of the federal budget must be devoted to interest payments on this huge and increasing debt. Furthermore, throughout the 1990s, Americans had emptied their personal savings accounts to fuel "seven years of good times", leaving too little for the "seven years of bad times" that many and perhaps most economists believe loom ahead; the spending spree left 20 percent of American households net debtors. And the "good times" of the 1990s left many behind as the income of the least skilled lagged." Americans appeared to be unaware that one day the nation's huge accumulated debt will have to be repaid and serious adjustments in the American standard of living will be necessary.
>
> (Gilpin & Gilpin, 2000, p. 6)[5]

> In the United States, it is no longer fashionable to admit you are a capitalist. In the richest and most market-oriented country in the world, only 42% of that group said they "supported capitalism". The numbers were higher among older people; still, only 26% considered themselves capitalists. A little over half supported the system as a whole.
>
> (http://time.com/4327419/american-capitalisms-great-crisis/)

Global capitalism in its fourth epoch: Transnational Regulatory Superstructure of WTO, World Bank, IMF and UN. Half of the world's wealth is in the hands of 1%, who are mostly billionaires (total $42.7 trillion). Eighty-five billionaires have more wealth than half the world's population.[6] In the last decade of fourth-epoch global capitalism, it has morphed (especially after the 2008 crisis) into a new form for producing billionaires of extreme self-interest who are able to stand by while half the world's population lives on less than $2.50 a day. Many eat only one meal a day, and some can only eat one meal every other day. The 2008 crisis was more than a recession, it was the beginning of a larger cycle of recessions and attempts at recovery that collapsed economy after economy in nation after nation, and it continues to do so. The cyclical crises, recurring about every ten years, are expected to continue into the future. The really bad news is that there is no structural or fundamental change to fourth-epoch global capitalism on the horizon that will be positioned to change the situation and become its successor or replacement. It is an existential crisis. Our ways of being-in-the-world (Heidegger, 1962) have resulted in alienation for half the 7.4 billion people living on less than $2.50 a day, who can only aspire to become a source of cheap labor and cannot afford any of the global trade goods they might produce. The fourth epoch is bigger in scope and deeper in its ontology; it is an entire crisis of the human experience of our world. It is a socioeconomic crisis of global capitalism. As we shall see, Savall and Zardet have proposed a viable alternative, a fifth-epoch successor that promises solutions to the problems summarized here.

The rise and fall of American capitalism becomes apparent when we consider that it took a hit in the 1970s and again in the 2008 crisis, which brought back the memory of the Great Depression. The trade of nations is now linked to transnationalism of production, finance and capital accumulation, and the rise of the transnational state: a loose network of supra-national corporations (with some national states included) that exploits inequality of economic and social class on a global scale. Changing this network from transnational corporate control to an interest in socioeconomic sustainability for more than the wealthy 1 percent who are mostly billionaires is what Savall and Zardet's socioeconomically responsible, sustainable capitalism must be able to do in order to meet the needs of 7.4 billion people attempting to survive during planetary destruction with endless warfare, drones, bunker-buster cluster bombs, star wars lasers and all kinds of surveillance technologies that make us believe George Orwell's 1984 prophecies have come true.

Failed U.S. presidential candidate Bernie Sanders claims that the top 0.1 percent of Americans have almost as much wealth as the bottom 90 percent. In other words, the top 0.1 percent or just 160,000 families with an average wealth of $72.8 million now own 22 percent of U.S. wealth and the bottom 90 percent (144 million families averaging $84,000 own 22.8 percent of wealth).[7] Income inequality and overpopulation are the moral issues of our time. Michael Moore says 400 Americans have more wealth than half of all Americans combined ($1.37 trillion exceeds the wealth of 69 percent of U.S. households). The wealth of Sam Walton's heirs is $89.5 billion and equal to the bottom 42 percent of American families. The world's wealthiest 1 percent, almost entirely billionaires, own $42.7 trillion more than the bottom three billion residents of Earth. The gap between the income of the average CEO and that of the average U.S. worker is 325 to 1. This is not a SRC, and without socioeconomic interventions, not only in the way corporations operate, but also in curbing the runaway speculative (gambler) markets, none of the SRC approaches to change organizations, one at a time, will be able to deal with the scale and magnitude of the global capitalism crisis.

Global capitalism in the fourth epoch is creating an ecological downward spiral due to limits of its reproduction being passed. Mass extinction of species and the degradation of the earth system environment (climate change, nitrogen cycle, biodiversity loss) are past what reputable scientists worldwide call tipping points that, once reached, are irreversible. Global capitalism has not only passed the tipping points of ecological recovery, but its expansion into new geographical territories and spaces of their commodification has reached a limit point as well. Now global capitalism must depend on a global state police force to enact militarism from the right and left, which was unprecedented in the first, second and third epochs. This is accompanied by an increase in racism, xenophobia and homophobia worldwide.

Global capitalism in its fourth epoch is disembodied from nations, and the new regulatory superstructures of WTO, World Bank, IMF and UN are not able to control the transnational corporations' rape of planetary resources, nor their control of ownership by the super-wealthy 1 percent. The transorganizational network governance solutions that Hardt and Negri (2001) promised would create postmodern rhizomatic control over global capitalism have not only failed to come to pass but are also an unmitigated disaster.[8]

This global interorganizational governance approach cannot even change car consumption, let alone reverse the CO_2 footprint per person. We have moved along in consumption practices from 1 to 1.5 cars for every American and 53 million total cars on the world's roads, with forecasts of 2.5 billion cars worldwide by 2050 (Voelcker, 2014).[9] We are past the threshold to avoid global warming of two degrees centigrade that will have such dire long-term consequences that no tech-fix miracle is going to reverse it. There is no technical solution to bring us into green energy, reduce the billions of cars on the road worldwide or bring back the forests and reverse the population explosion. Meanwhile, the world's 7.4 billion people want a higher material standard of living. Econ 101 textbooks do not include the word "overconsumption."

The situation is critical for human survival. In the fourth epoch of global capitalism, we humans are "sleepwalking to extinction" (George Mongiot, Guardian). Large multinational and transnational corporations are destroying the biodiversity of life on Earth. There is now no way to overthrow this global economic social system, because the top 1 percent of the population has amassed the wealth equal to the bottom 90 percent. The 1 percent has won the global game of monopoly and is not letting go of its board spaces. The bottom 90 percent can starve, not pass 'go' and head straight to monopoly jail (or into the private prison system).

Global capitalism is destroying all other forms of capitalism, despite unleashing one world economic crisis after another (including the 2008 collapse of one nation after another into recession due to the mortgage and bank deregulation that began in the Reagan administration). The 1 percent of super-successful global capitalists are pumping out lakes, clear-cutting forests, leveling mountains for minerals and sucking out the planet's oil and natural gas. They are also responsible for the extinction of species. Monsanto, DuPont, Syngenta and so on are addicting the planet to their pharmaceutical medications. In the United States, for example, 45 percent of its citizens are on at least one medication, and 35 percent are taking two or more medications each day.

The nation states are spiraling downward in their crises of legitimacy and failing to meet social grievances of local working conditions. The middle class is in a cycle of downward mobility, and billions of people are facing unemployment and insecurity. Meanwhile, global elites are unable to counter the erosion of the system's authority or create a global moral economy. This is a great collapse of the world civilization akin to that which occurred during the Dark Ages.

The top 1 percent wealth owners have wiped out bees, monarch butterflies, birds, entire animal species and crop diversity. In Adam Smith's day, mercantile capitalism did not have much impact on global environment resources, but in its fourth epoch, global capitalism is responsible for climate change due to patterns of overproduction and overconsumption. We are unable to curtail overconsuming natural resources and revise the desertion of biological diversity. We are locked into a global capitalism that is killing the planet. The situation is catastrophic.

In this fourth epoch of global capitalism, corporations can distribute (disperse) production systems around the world into a variety of geographic areas (Apple, Walmart, Nike and so on go to China, Africa and Southeast Asia for production, human and natural resources). Global capitalism is no longer limited to one home nation, nor is it controlled by the collaborative effort of nation states. The financial speculation system is global, with financial instruments that subvert nation-states' efforts to exert direct control. The capitalists in global capitalism have social lives on a global scale, while half the world's population lives on less than two dollars a day. The United Nations, WTO, Group of Thirty, World Economic Forum, IMF and World Bank all provide transnational governance. These governing organizations set the agenda for global production within their system of wealth accumulation, which causes inequities between the top 1 percent (or tenth of a percent) and the remaining 99 percent of the world's populace.

During the fourth and current epoch of global capitalism led by the IMF, World Bank, GATT, NAFTA, UN and so on, Ronald Reagan tore down the regulations of banks and finance established by Franklin D. Roosevelt to return to a free-market ideology, and Bill Clinton continued this when he signed NAFTA. The WTO was launched in 1995 to replace GATT. The WTO in concert with IMF and World Bank govern the global trade.

What is it all for? Why does 1 percent need the wealth of 90 percent of the world's population? If we have our iPhones and iMacs, will that save the environment? Will it solve inequality of wealth, bring back the rain forests and put healthy fish into the oceans? Three hundred years of global capitalism development and the gap between rich and poor is wider than ever, with 85 percent of total global assets in the hands of the wealthiest 1 percent. We are losing nations for copper and cobalt and coltan (conflict minerals) for iPhones when half the population only eats once a day and one-fourth eat less often than that.

If global capitalism is destroying the world socially, economically and environmentally, then what can SRC (as it is currently defined) really accomplish? It's a smokescreen to legitimate the status quo of inequality. SRC cannot put the brakes on overpopulation, depletion of oil, war for bottled water, industrial logging, overfishing the oceans and military-surveillance-police states to give security to the 1 percent profiting from exploration, destruction and inequality. SRC is *not* sustainable, cannot restrain the destruction or overconsumption or provide health care or jobs or food for the bottom half of the population

With the triumph of the fourth epoch of global capitalism, the financial system is out of the control of regulation and the standardization mania that tetranormalization (Savall & Zardet, 2005a; Savall, Zardet & Bonnet, 2009; Boje, 2014) is attempting to counteract. There occurred an elimination of capital controls in the global financial system. Global capitalism has been targeting all welfare state systems for deconstruction—the new imperialism. The sustainability movement is split into two. One faction believes that the ills of global capitalism can be contained. The other faction believes we have passed all the tipping points and are on a downward spiral into famine, more wars and total environmental destruction. With the latest major crisis of global capitalism in 2008, there is a breakdown in accepted consensus methods for social and economic control. Global capitalism attempts to counter the 2008 crisis and its ecological and social deterioration by investing in propaganda. Meanwhile, the transnational capitalist class (TCC)—the 1 percent owning the wealth of global capitalism—tries to use global communications media to convince everyone that the situation is under control, that the tipping points are an illusion and that sustainability is possible to achieve. Meanwhile we have become what Truthout (2007) calls a 'planet of slums' alienated from the wealth of globalizing economy, excluded from food, shelter and quality of life.[10] TCC uses the militarized mechanism to continue accumulation, within the cycles of destruction and reconstruction, in the military-prison-industrial-security-energy-financial complex (Truthout, 2007). TCC uses financial speculation power and influence to impose austerity on the working poor and world's poor. Global capitalism is the biggest casino in the world—with speculation in the trillions of dollars—that collapse the global financial system into cycles of crisis and recovery, which are escalating out of cycles into spirals of downward momentum into the abyss. Instead of upward mobility, for the 99 percent there is only downward mobility, social violence, military service and the global police state. Resistance is futile. In the twenty-first century, fascism by the 1 percent TCC is riding on the backs of everyone who has been alienated in global capitalism. Global capitalism is a system that needs the police state to sustain transnational capital and maintain its representatives' continued political elections. Criminalization of drug use so that private prisons can stay populated is the new concentration camp of our time, perpetuated under the siege of global capitalism. Global capitalism invests in warfare, social violence and private prisons, as well as surveillance technologies to achieve wealth objective, evermore.[11]

Wars make money for transnational corporations. The flurry of wars (Vietnam, Afghanistan, Iraq, Gazam Lebanon and so on) by the military-industrial-global complex serves to expand the geographical reach of markets for cheap products made from cheap raw materials and wage slave labor. This expansion involves spending funds on weapons, preserving nations' economies by making weapons for global capitalism while the elite concentrate their wealth at the expense of everyone else who lives amid crisis after crisis and war after war, to sustain the 1 percent standing on the shoulders of the 99 percent.

We are in a downward spiral, with speculative capitalism, made worse by the Trump election. By achieving deregulation, capital has broken free of its national boundaries and is increasing its speculation capitalism at greater and greater risk of economic collapse. The 1 percent do not need or want a welfare state. The 1 percent (e.g., Koch brothers) use their ownership of the media to resocialize the masses to hate health care, fair wages, and protection of shirking environmental resources. With the Trump election, the 1 percent are having their way. America is now a two-party system in which most Americans would rather not vote for either of the current candidates (Clinton or Trump). Transnational oil companies have made the Middle East the site of war and global conflict, after Vietnam. Global capitalism is relaxing one social-welfare capitalism territory after another in the new form of global imperialism. Social-welfare capitalism cannot sustain military production activities and military service recruitment without scuttling higher education, public schools and health care.

The fourth epoch of global capitalism is no longer grounded in the logic of Fredrick Jameson's or David Harvey's cultural logic of spatial identities. Rather, the spaces of localities, cities, nations and communities are not subsumed by the logic of warfare and 'multiple forms of state and transnational violence; and surveillance in what Hardt and Negri call the 'technologization of death'—what the WTO, World Bank and so on were supposed to use Deleuzian rhizomatics to counteract. Hardt and Negri's 'Empire Thesis', how transnational networks of corporations and regulatory organizations WTO, World Bank, and so on) would contain exploitation and war, has not worked out. Now global war accompanies global capitalism, which Hardt and Negri predicted were supposed to use transnational organizational and corporate governance mechanism to counteract. Despite locality, global war is the parent in the new global marketplace. Hobbes's prediction has come to pass, "Continual fear and danger of violent death, and [where] the life of man [is] solitary, poor, nasty, brutish, and short." As global capitalism marries global war in the new fulfillment of Hobbes's *Leviathan*, what happened to postmodernity? It has displaced the permanent state of global war and economic cycles of crisis and recovery.

Part II: Various Socially Responsible Capitalism (SRC) Approaches Will Not Come Close to Resolving the Sustainability Gap Created by Global Capitalism

Various SRC approaches have been suggested. I would like to review them briefly to show why they will not close the sustainability gap's mega-problems of overpopulation, Earth's resource depletion and the CO_2-driven climate change crisis created by the human diet and transportation in the fourth epoch of global capitalism.

Is SRC Possible? Given the downsides of global capitalism, is SRC possible? My short answer is no. The SRC movement has been unable to combine its social focus with an economic approach that achieves sustainability that can get global capitalism unstuck from its fourth epoch of recurring recessionary crises.

Part III: How a Socioeconomically Sustainable, Responsible Capitalism (SESRC) Can Succeed Where Global Capitalism Has Failed

SESRC is an approach developed by Henri Savall in collaboration with Véronique Zardet, Michel Péron and Marc Bonnet. It began with Savall's education in accounting and economics. He did not study just any kind of economics but the work of Spanish economist Germán Bernácer. Bernácer's reforms of Spain's economic system focused on regulating 'speculative financial systems', particularly in banking, and stimulating productive economics. Savall assumes that the reason for the 2008 world financial crisis was runaway, unregulated speculations markets that drained productive markets of resources to invest in building entrepreneurial and intrapreneurial activities in companies. As we explored in Part I of this preface, global capitalism is stuck in its fourth epoch—the endless cycles of recession and attempts at recovery. It is stuck in the sense that there is not a successor to global capitalism that can actually resolve the sustainability problems created by explosions in the world population that will lead to 11.3 billion people on this planet by 2100 and the CO_2-related climate changes brought on from the human diet and transportation choices.

How do Savall, Zardet, Péron and Bonnet plan to implement their approach to SESRC as the fifth-epoch, the successor to global capitalism?

Part IV: Ways Socioeconomic Sustainable Responsible Capitalism (SESRC) Can Move Global Capitalism Into the Fifth Epoch

If we are to have a fifth epoch of global capitalism, we must get unstuck from the fourth epoch—that is, the recurring cycles of recession and attempts at recovery that have the world economies unable to address the major problems of global capitalism's rampant unsustainability. Savall, Zardet, Péron and Bonnet propose, in this book, ways that their SESRC can address the problems of unsustainability that escape the grasp of typical SRC models. I believe that SESRC can succeed where the SRC models fall short because the authors start with fundamental socioeconomic reform of companies, government agencies and nonprofit organizations. They assume that a new form of organization is possible, one that builds the human potential of workers and incentivizes workers to achieve innovation and efficiency, while developing sustainable strategies.

Savall et al. propose both a bottom-up corporate reform strategy and a top-down transnational reform of company financing that move away from the speculative market (gambling of JP Morgan, Lehman Brothers, Enron, World Com and so on) and can take worldwide governance and control back from the WTO, IMF and World Bank hegemony over nation state sovereignty. If people listen to Adam Smith's maxim, 'look out for No. 1', then the global public good is to take back the wealth that the 1 percent have amassed at the expense of the 99 percent and all other life on earth. Wealth redistribution must, in my opinion, be part of the socioeconomic strategy.

Savall, Zardet, Péron and Bonnet's SESRC cannot be just another ideological approach, but rather must develop a socioeconomic approach that is global in scale and sustainable in ways that address problems identified in Part I of this preface. This means it must develop an ethical action in part of the citizens of the world to close the gap between the 1 percent and the 99 percent living on what is left over. In the authors' SESRC, corporate decisions are made under democratic governance, and in negotiation with labor and community stakeholders; investments are made for building sustainability and entrepreneurial (and intrapreneurial) production rather than for speculators' gambling addictions in speculation markets and the greed to have it all, no matter if people do not have enough money for food, shelter, health or dignity worldwide. People are going hungry and the transnational governance network is rigging the game for the speculators, while giving nothing but junk goods and services to the populace. Regulation of banks is constantly under attack by the speculators and gamblers of the self-interested 1 percent who own and run global capitalism. Global capitalism is responsible for ocean acidification, global warming, deforestation, biodiversity destruction, world famine and war.

What is socioeconomically sustainable responsible capitalism (SESRC)? It is not the same as *SRC*, because the latter is without sustainability and is destructive of environments and human potential, or it's a philanthropic capitalism of the good-hearted 'super capitalism' billionaires (Gates, Buffet, Sores, Koch brothers, Ma and Guangbiao) who make sociopolitical-legitimacy investments. Savall, Zardet, Péron and Bonnet, by contrast, are focused on socially and economically sustainable, responsible capital, as both a theoretical and practical framework of socioeconomic development of a democratic project—a way to contain destructive technology and excessive regulation, in a framework of socioenvironmental value.

We must now ask the big question: *what kind of global capitalism are Henri Savall, Véronique Zardet, Michel Péron and Marc Bonnet professing?* It cannot be a repeat of SRC models or we might as well stop reading. Typical SRC cannot reverse the perverted global capitalism of speculation markets or unchecked corporate and government corruption, nor the widening of the gap between the 1 percent and the 90 percent.

The reason we think their eco-socioeconomic alternative to the crisis of global capitalism is possible is that it is rooted in the works of Spanish economist, Germán Bernácer's work (see Boje, 2015 for a review). It will take a mass uprising against today's kind of global capitalism (*Capitalism and the Destruction of Life on Earth: Six Theses on Saving the Humans*, Richard Smith [Institute for Policy Research & Development, London], 2013).[12] It is time to bring back Bernácer's project of regulating speculative capitalism, in order to give productive capitalism and Savall and Zardet's socioeconomic tetranormalization a chance at world-making.

SESRC is not the same as social capitalism: a means to get social management under state control and supervision to protect market functioning, while instituting programs to help the poor or building quality-of-life perks into organizations. Social capitalism is an ally of close state collaboration with regulation, while optimizing economic growth. SESRC, on the other hand, takes into account SEAM's well-being improvement interventions and programs that accomplish both human potential and sustainable overall performance of the company, while transforming dysfunction that results in hidden costs and untapped revenue potential. The SESRC investment in human potential is a negotiation of hidden-cost reduction by taking care of the collaborators in bringing about human and social performances. The expectation of SEAM is that there is a negotiation of shared rewards for negotiated commitment to creating economic value. Therefore, to create social and economic performance, the company must sustain cooperation of all its members.

What can we do about the collapse of global capitalism? How can we reduce the damages of global capitalism? When the state is the servant of the global corporation and the global owners of wealth, the 1 percent, then it is obligatory for states to intervene and to regulate speculator's gambling habits. But how can a bottom-up movement of sustainable socioeconomic intrapreneurship counter the collapsing global capitalism and its governance structure—that is, World Bank, WTO, United Nations and so on?

SESRC is not a Marxist historical materialism of opposition of capital and labor; rather, in SESRC, the only genuine wealth is the development of human potential, which the speculative market cannot accomplish. It is rather accomplished by socioeconomic intervention to bring about new corporate practice and by a move away from global speculative markets by the financial gamblers. Savall is a fan of the Spanish economist Germán Bernácer.

Bernácer confronted speculative capitalism in order to develop the 'real' economy. Speculators on Wall Street brought down the economies of nations in 2008, resulting in bailouts for banks and the destruction of pensions. Perhaps we need a world without Wall Street's financial values, with speculators gambling on stock prices, and the financial instruments of the money lords of short-term speculation (hedge funds, subprimes, mortgage bundling and so on). Savall et al. follow Bernácer in focusing on socioeconomic performance and markets that make investments in production—the 'real' economy. At the heart of SESRC is the entrepreneur doing start-ups and building industry after industry, even when immediate profit is not guaranteed in the short run, but is rather the product of long-run success and value from developing human potential of the entire enterprise. Human potential investment is a prime mover of economic value creation. This is not the Schumpeterian entrepreneur of creative destruction but rather a purveyor of the continuous improvement of human potential that adds value to materials.

SESRC is a specific intervention in a place, and each territory/place is a socioeconomic space of an organization, transorganization, and a metaorganization. Speculative capitalism, by contrast, is without place and without accepting the risks of activities that realize profit from real activities of the Schumpeterian entrepreneur. SESRC is also in a time (or temporality of a socioeconomic history and future). SESRC is a smattering of production, economic activities, exchanges and social practices. As we know from quantum physics, you cannot separate space (s), time (t) and (m) mattering, so we can follow Karen Barad (2007) in using the construct of *spacetimemattering* (*STM*) of actual activities of work, not just speculation (Boje & Henderson, 2014; Henderson & Boje, 2015). Savall contends that Bernácer eliminates (deletes) the "time preference, and that interest is not treated as the price of time." The downward spiral from excessive speculator construction of speculative markets has created worldwide economic crises again and again. This means that each organization interfaces with other organizations within its environment (transorganization), and with metaorganizations (industry, market, profession) within a socioeconomic *spacetimemattering* of globalization where communities need companies to preserve jobs, create wealth and do so in a supportive environment. History gives warning signs that 'speculative' capitalism is not sustainable or responsible. Domestic economies shifted to become market economies and created strange and dangerous financial instruments for hyper-speculation markets, which in turned trained productive markets. Then, to make matters worse, today an *ultraliberalism* promulgates a maze of standards to control company activities. These historical practices have undermined SRC.

A SESRC is not entangled in the perverted practices of speculative financial markets, which only keep short-term focus on quarterly returns and are disconnected from the 'real' economy.

SESRC in its *spacetimemattering* is a forerunner to Michael Porter's 'creating shared value' by promoting human happiness and well-being, but SESRC is more than intention. On the other hand, it is directly opposed to Milton Friedman's self-sufficient enterprise in the autonomy of markets with lots of financial speculation and Jeremy Rifkin's Internet of things in collaborative commons, which does not address ways to develop human potential within organizations.

—*Preface, August 10, 2016, David M. Boje, PhD*

Notes

1. '11 Facts about Global-Poverty' www.dosomething.org/us/facts/11-facts-about-global-poverty, accessed April 14, 2017; Income is not the only measure of poverty. White (2013: 60), for example, argues for a multidimensional assessment of poverty, where such factors as education, having a dwelling separate from animals, and well-being are important. White, H. (2013). The measurement of poverty. Pp. 60–67 in Desai, V., & Potter, R. B. (Eds.). *The companion to development studies*. New York/London: Routledge.
2. See for example, Robinson, W. I. (2014). *Global Capitalism: Crisis of Humanity and the Specter of 21st Century Fascism*, online at www.worldfinancialreview.com/?p=1799
3. Systemicity is a word I use in my writing to define the common situation of organizations, where most systems are partially implemented, and preceding systems are only partially discontinued. This results in a myriad of partially implemented, unfinalized and disintegrating state of organizational systemicity. See Boje, D. M. (2014). *Storytelling organizational practices: Managing in the quantum age*. London: Routledge.
4. These statistics and assessments come from my April 2016 presentation to my university (NMSU) on the impact of population, CO_2 footprints on the world situation of sustainability.
5. Mentan, T. (2016). *Neoliberalism and imperialism: Dissecting the dynamics of global oppression*. Langaa RPCIG.
6. Source of this statistic is the Guardian, 'Oxfam: 85 richest people as wealthy as poorest half of the world', online at www.theguardian.com/business/2014/jan/20/oxfam-85-richest-people-half-of-the-world, accessed April 14, 2017.
7. Source of Bernie Sanders Remarks, online at www.politifact.com/wisconsin/statements/2015/jul/29/bernie-s/bernie-sanders-madison-claims-top-01-americans-hav/, accessed August 5, 2016.
8. Hardt, M., & Negri, A. (2001). *Empire*. Boston, MA: Harvard University Press.
9. Source of these statistics, Voelcker, J. (2014). 1.2 Billion Vehicles On World's Roads Now, 2 Billion By 2035. Greencarreports.com/www.greencarreports.com/news/1093560_1-2-billion-vehicles-on-worlds-roads-now-2-billion-by-2035-report accessed April 14, 2017.
10. Truthout re-published this article titled 'Baghdad 2025: The Pentagon Solution to a Planet of Slums' by Nick Turse. TomDispatch.com. Monday 08 January 2007.

http://truth-out.org/archive/component/k2/item/67959-nick-turse--baghdad-2025-the-pentagon-solution-to-a-planet-of-slums, accessed April 14, 2017.

11. The above section relies on work done by Robinson, W. I. (2013). Truth Out, online at www.truth-out.org/news/item/18280-global-capitalism-and-the-crisis-of-humanity. Crisis of Humanity: Global Capitalism Breeds 21st Century Fascism.

12. See more on this point: Smith, R. (2013). Capitalism and the Destruction of Life on Earth: Six Theses on Saving the Humans, in Truthout, online at www.paecon.net/PAEReview/issue64/Smith64.pdf accessed August 5, 2016.

Acknowledgments

Our initial research in the field of the macroeconomics helped us discover the pioneering and extraordinarily original theory of an underestimated Spanish economist who was the neglected inspirer of the famous Keynes. In an article from 1922, Germán Bernácer proposed an explanation of the recurrent crises, which are congenital to the existence of speculative, real estate, art, financial and trade (materials, energy, etc.) markets. We thank his family for facilitating our access to his personal correspondence with most of the famous contemporary economists of his time.

We had the privilege of working with François Perroux, our second inspirer in economy, from 1973 till 1987. Gilbert Blardone founded the François Perroux Association, which is currently chaired by Henri Savall. It is thanks to the unorthodox posture, acquired by studying Bernácer's works and consolidated by our encounter with François Perroux and Maurice Allais, that we had the strength and the boldness to defy the risks of refuting those 'historical monuments': production function and the theory of two factors, capital and labor.

The socioeconomic theory and SEAM approach to management acquired their *belles lettres* both in national and international spheres. From the national sphere, the main recognition markers of our works are the Rossi Award given to Henri Savall and Véronique Zardet in 2001 by the Académie des Sciences Morales et Politiques (Institut de France, Paris); the publication of our book in 2000 by the ILO (International Labor Organization, Geneva) in English, French and Spanish (co-authored with our colleague Marc Bonnet), and its republication in 2008; and the special issue of the *Journal of Organizational Change Management* (March 2003) dedicated to Institute for Socio-Economy of Enterprises and Organizations ISEOR works.

The books edited with Anthony Buono and published by Information Age Publishing (IAP) in 2007 and 2015 (Buono & Savall, 2015) on socioeconomic intervention and also the translation and the English publication of eight of our books are proof of American interest in socioeconomic theory. Furthermore, the Academy of Management gave ISEOR, from 2001 to 2016, 14 colloquiums delocalized from North America. In a universe dominated by Anglo-Saxon thought, these events constitute recognition of the innovative, original and robust aspects of research steered by ISEOR for more than 40 years.

After eight years of Henri Savall's research in macroeconomics, 1973 marked the beginning of work dedicated to socioeconomic analysis. That work had been individual up until the creation of our Institute for Socio-Economy of Enterprises and Organizations (ISEOR) in 1975.

This book reveals and clarifies the macroscopic framework that has guided socioeconomic management implementation for the past 40 years. This innovative method helps in the development of simultaneously sustainable social and economic performance. This is why we are grateful to the companies and organizations that have agreed, for many years, to be ISEOR partners in order to experiment with new methods of management. These CEOs, managers, employees and unions have always accepted the constraints that an external, demanding and rigorous intervention necessitates.

We thank the 1,854 enterprises and organizations that have been our partners and totally financed our research, which was realized without any public subvention. Small and medium enterprises (SMEs), big industrial and services corporations, public enterprises, administrations and territorial collectivities and health-care establishments in a great variety of industries (72) have participated. Most of the intervention research was carried out within companies and organizations in Belgium, France, Morocco, Mexico, Portugal, Lebanon, Switzerland, United States and Saudi Arabia. Some of the intervention research played a prior role in developing and enhancing socioeconomic management and theory: Brioche Pasquier Group (32 years), La Poste and Banque Populaire in France, Technord (22 years) and the FOREM in Belgium.

The Fondation Nationale pour l'Enseignement de la Gestion des Entreprises (FNEGE) regularly supported us from an institutional point of view, especially Philippe Agid and Jean-Marie Doublet. We consider the decisive action of Prof. Pierre-Louis Dubois, general delegate, and Éric Lamarque as even more useful to enterprises and society than scientific research. Since the creation of ISEOR, the Agence Nationale pour l'Amélioration des Conditions de Travail has facilitated and diffused ISEOR results. The Institute of Chartered Accountants, the National Superior Council of Notary and the French Architects Association recommended this management method of quality and strategic development to their affiliates.

Roger Delay-Termoz, deputy director of Groupe École Supérieure de Commerce de Lyon (became EM Lyon) until 1994, with the organization's faithful support, which was essential for ISEOR development, deserves a preponderant expression of our gratitude.

Maurice Bernadet, Philippe Lucas, Michel Cusin and Brunos Gelas, successive presidents of Université Lumière Lyon 2, as well as Dean Paul Rousset, founder of IUT Lumière, actively supported our research and the development of innovative diplomas that we created from them.

This book is the fruit of considerable teamwork from the researchers, who, by their direct intervention in companies, by their academic works and publications, are contributing to, according to a proven experimental démarche, the socioeconomic theory on a scientific basis. Michel Grivel was the first doctorate recipient from ISEOR.

We especially want to thank our permanent team members: Marc Bonnet, Olivier Voyant, Frantz Datry, Laurent Cappelletti, Nouria Harbi, Emmanuel Beck, Françoise Goter, Renaud Petit, Alexis Roche, Cécile Ennajem, Amandine Savall, Miguel Delattre, Nathalie Krief, Jeannette Rencoret, intervener researchers in charge of intervention programs; Andry Rasolofoarisoa, Thibault Ruat, Jérémy Salmeron, Pierre François, Maïté Rateau, Carole Bousquet, intervener researchers; and Michelle Bonnard, Delphine Fauré, Karile Morel, Émilie Bernard, Nathalie Rebut, Rhida Ziani, Anthony Harbonville and Amélie Guérineau, members of administrative, communication, IT and management control departments.

More than 600 young researchers and doctoral candidates who spent some years of their careers at ISEOR are now academics with positions in universities. This is the case for many associated professors and tenured professors, including Isabelle Barth, Thierry Nobre (Strasbourg), Jean-Michel Plane and Florence Noguera (Montpellier), as well as Laurent Cappelletti, who holds the chair of Management Control at CNAM (Paris) in France as well as numerous professors in Tunisia, Brazil, Morocco, Burundi, Angola, Mexico, Great Britain, Switzerland, United States, etc.

Regarding our adventure in the United States ('La Fayette Operation'), our gratitude is first addressed to our historical French teammate Michel Péron (Paris, Sorbonne), followed by Monique Péron, Rickie Moore (EM Lyon) and Georges Trépo (HEC). Our actions in the United States during all the presentations of ISEOR's works to the Annual Meeting of the Academy of Management since 1998 would not have been as rapid and effective without the support of our American colleagues Randy Hayes and Lawrence Lepisto (Michigan); Anthony Buono (Boston); David Boje and Grace-Ann Rosile (New Mexico); Peter Sorensen and Therese Yaeger (Chicago); Robert Gephart (Edmonton, Canada), John Conbere and Alla Heorhiadi (Minneapolis and Duluth), Christopher Worley (Los Angeles) and Murray Lindsay (Lethbridge, Canada, former president of the management control section of the American Accounting Association.

To ILO, we are indebted to Pierre Trémeau, Eric Maertens, Jean-François Retournard, François Eyraud and especially to Pierre Hidalgo, vice president of the International Scientific Committee of ISEOR, for their constant support in promoting socioeconomic management in the ILO members' countries.

Last but not least, we thank Gilles Guyot and Guy Lavorel, successive presidents, and Jérôme Rive, general director of IAE Lyon, who opened the doors of the Jean Moulin University Lyon 3 in order to welcome 15 professors and associate professors from ISEOR and EUGINOV (École Universitaire de Gestion Innovante), who asked for their transfer in 2001. They allow us to follow up our creative action in favor of innovative training and research in management science and to contribute to the international development of our university. We thank also the current president, Jacques Comby, for his support.

We would like to express our gratitude to the CEOs of 1,854 companies, organizations and administrations, including Serge, Louis-Marie and Pascal Pasquier; Jacques Morin, M.-A. Lanselle and Henri Talaszka; Jean Pichon and Loïc Daniel; Michel and Philippe Foucart; Gérard Pigaglio; Jean-Pierre Méan; Jean Caghassi; Michel de Trogoff; Christophe Fargier; Issac Sánchez; Grégoire de Préneuf and Franck Gotte; Eric Vergne; and Georges Devesa, who trusted in us, as well as all the managers and staff members of the companies from 44 countries with whom we coproduced the concepts, the tools and methods that it is convenient to call the socioeconomic management of companies and organizations.

In fine, we renew our acknowledgment of the unstoppable craftsperson of the international diffusion of our work, the revered Michel Péron, emeritus professor at Paris Sorbonne Nouvelle University, for his expertise in English lexicography and American civilization, as well as his extraordinary involvement in the success of the international diffusion of SEAM in the United States. Martha Fernández Ruvalcaba and Pedro Solís Pérez, professors at the Universidad Autónoma Metropolitana in Mexico, have realized remarkable work for 20 years, proof of their engagement in SEAM diffusion in Mexico and in the Mexican Academy of Administrative Sciences (ACACIA). The economic and accounting side of our SEAM benefited from the constant and effective support of Miguel Bacic (Brazil) and Daniel Carrasco (Spain), former presidents and Carlos Diehl, current president of the Latin-American and Latin-European Network Instituto Internacional de Costos for the last ten years.

Henri Savall, Michel Péron,
Véronique Zardet, and Marc Bonnet

About the Authors

Henri Savall is an emeritus professor at the Institut d'Administration des Entreprises, University Jean Moulin Lyon, where he is the founder of the EUGINOV Centre (École Universitaire de Gestion Innovante) and the Socioeconomic Management master's programs. He is also the founder and president of the ISEOR Research Center, where he has supervised 78 doctoral theses. Henri and Professor Véronique Zardet were awarded the famous Rossi Award by the Academy of Moral and Political Sciences (Institut de France) for their work on the integration of social variables into business strategy. Henri created, designed and developed the socio-economic theory and SEAM approach to management with the ISEOR research team. He is also the editor of the Revue Sciences de Gestion—Management Sciences—Ciencias de Gestion (Journal of Administrative Science). He has published many books and articles in French, Spanish and English and is the president of Association François Perroux (www.iseor.com).

Michel Péron passed away two weeks before the French version of this book was published. He was an emeritus professor at the University of Paris III Sorbonne Nouvelle. As a lexicographer, he published several English-French dictionaries. He received his PhD from the University of Lyon with a dissertation on William Petty's economic thought. He was a researcher at the ISEOR and the CERVEPAS research centers. He was the chairman of the International Scientific Committee of ISEOR. Over a period of 24 years, Michel was the mayor of St. André la Côte (France), where he was influential in the development of the rural city.

Véronique Zardet is a professor of management sciences and director of EUGINOV (École Universitaire de Gestion Innovante) Center, IAE Lyon Business School, Jean Moulin University. She is the director and, along with Professor Henri Savall, the founder of the ISEOR Research Center. She heads the 'research in socioeconomic management' master's program. She is president of the Association for Development of Corporate and Social Responsibility. She holds a PhD in management sciences from the University of Lyon. In 2001, she received with Henri Savall the Rossi Award from the Academy of Moral and Political Sciences (Institute of France) for their work on the integration of social variables into business strategies. She published many books, articles and papers in French, English and Spanish on change and strategic management of tetranormalization.

Marc Bonnet is professor of management at EUGINOV Center, IAE Lyon Business School, Jean Moulin University. He is deputy manager of IAE Lyon and in charge of the 'industrial security, environment and normalization management' master's degree. He is also deputy manager of ISEOR Research Center. Formerly the president of the Academy of Management Consulting Division, Marc Bonnet has also been the president of the French Human Resource Management Association (AGRH). He has written many books, articles and papers on socioeconomic theory and human resource management.

Introduction

In this crisis period, capitalism is disputed by its detractors or defended tooth and nail by its partisans. Proof of this is found in the increasing number of colloquium presentations, books published, and papers gathered by editors. Why write another book on this theme while audiences study and comment on the mutation and the diversity of capitalisms until they have drunk their fill? A TV channel broadcasted six documentaries that outline a wide saga from the origins of capitalism to the current day. From this profusion of representations and interpretations there emerges a certain confusion about the origin of capitalism and what it covers without speaking about the term itself. A French book (Michel Leter Le capital, 2009) reduced capitalism to a myth when, earlier in 2009, Paul Fabre delivered a severe blow to a capitalism without capital in his eponymous book *Capitalism without Capital?*

"What is that capitalism we are talking about?" was Henri Savall's question in 1979. According to the development of our socioeconomic analysis of companies and organizations, there is no empty space for doubt in 2015. This is not an ideological approach that corresponds to a simplistic definition of a market economy system built on the private property of both production and exchange means with pursuit of profit finality. Our objective is to define the characteristics of the framework that will allow socially responsible companies and organizations, public or private, to develop and support the implementation of the so-called socioeconomic approach to management (SEAM) so that it is involved in jointly improving the economic performance of the company and its social performance. This framework is a socially, economically and sustainably responsible capitalism founded on the entrepreneurial spirit, which tends toward the exemplarity of behaviors and puts forward the social responsibility of companies and organizations combined in the economic empowerment and the ethical exertions of each citizen (actor).

Our current research contributes to building the concept of socially and sustainably responsible capitalism, which is the theoretical and practical framework of the socioeconomic theory of company and organization development. It reconciles the two levels of analysis that have been excessively differentiated: the company and the social and economic environment. We highlight that the essential contribution of the ISEOR (Socioeconomic Institute for Enterprises and Organizations) management model not only focuses on social responsibility limited to companies because the company is only a capitalist microcosm according to François Perroux, but also that sustainability can be found in the structures of a territory. Each territory or economic space could be nearly considered as an organization, a transorganization, a tangled organization or a metaorganization (Henri Savall & Véronique Zardet, *The Dynamics and Challenges of Tetranormalization*, 2005b, p. 7).

Michael Porter and Mark Kramer advocate conscious capitalism in an article republished in *Harvard Business Review* entitled "Creating Shared Value". They discover, as we did in 1973 (Savall, 1973), that we have to "Reshape Capitalism and its relationship to the society" and to "promote human happiness and well-being". Consequently, by uncovering the specific framework of the company, we have been able to establish that here is a certain isomorphism of the different territory levels that produces norms. Those levels are infra-micro or microscopic (inside the organization), micro (the enterprise: interface within its environment), meso (an industry, a market), macro (a profession), megascopic (a world region composed by several countries) and gigascopic (the economic and social globalization space) (Savall & Zardet, 2005b, p. 7). According to Anne Krupicka and Benjamin Dreveton's contribution (*Les rôles des collectivités locales dans l'adaptation d'un projet relatif à la responsabilité sociale des entreprises* [Local Administrations Role in Adapting a Project of Social Responsibility of Enterprise] in Savall, Bonnet, Zardet and Péron (eds.) *Actes du 3ème Congrès de l'ADERSE*, 2015) on the role of local administrations in adapting a social responsibility policy, Di Maggio and Powel could be at the origin of this concept in their article entitled "The Iron Cage Revisited: Institutional Isomorphism and Collective Rationality in Organizational Fields" (*American Sociological Review*, 1989). As Krupicka and Dreveton notice, the concept of isomorphism presents as the homogenization process of organization.

We are interested in this concept insofar as it expresses the different territory levels as an application field for the socioeconomic approach to management (SEAM). Di Maggio and Powel (1989) stated as a principle that a community needs companies that gather in order to preserve jobs and to create wealth for all its members, as well as companies' need for a prosperous community and a supportive environment. In this scope, our concept of socioeconomic management is opposed to a monolithic conception of the enterprise as an entity that is self-sufficient, as presented by Milton Friedman.

We will not try to distinguish the good capitalism from the bad capitalism as a book published in the United States does (Baumol, Litan & Schramm, 2007). Unlike the Nobel Prize laureate Joseph Stiglitz, we dare not establish a prognostication on capitalism's early ending. We will not ask ourselves about the crisis as an engine of this political, economic and social system. We will not interest ourselves in capitalism as an ideology but as the motor of the economy, among centuries and also as a human energy catalyst, which aims at fostering growth and development. We refuse to put it on standby on behalf of a collaborative economy as Jeremy Rifkin, an American futurologist, invites us to do in his last book, *The Zero Marginal Cost Society: The Internet of Things, the Collaborative Commons, and the Eclipse of Capitalism*, in 2014.

We are looking to draw some trails in order to propose a model of a social and sustainable capitalism, the history of which gave us some warning signs without offering us clear solutions that come from real stakes rather than utopia (Rifkin, 2015).

We will show through examples the practicability of our propositions at the macroeconomic level as well as the microeconomic level under the view of **entrepreneurship** (persons' and teams' behaviors regarding the external environment) and **intrapreneurship** (persons' and teams' behaviors regarding the internal environment inside a company). Thus without intending to, in a two-level analysis, we modify the behaviors of companies through new rules or additional norms—that is to say, external constraints but rather from a position of acting from the internal perspective by a most consensual approach. That is what *socioeconomic management* fosters in companies and organizations. We are explaining the difference between entrepreneurship and the liberty of undertaking such behavior inside the organization (Savall, *Réussir en temps de crise. Stratégies proactives des entreprises* [Be Successful in Crisis Period. Enterprises Proactives Strategies], 2010, pp. 3–6). But we don't distinguish the creative and innovative behaviors of persons and teams inside the company and the external environment because they obviously interact.

This first clarification allows eliminating planned, official and centralized economic systems, which can only lead to totalitarian regimes, which are nondemocratic and condemned by history for enslaving people and tolling the knell of free entrepreneurship.

In addition, it is not surprising, as we will further explain, to see in the same perspective a debate being established on liberalism marked of all the evils either for its insufficiencies, or for its excesses and the necessity to make the market controlled and semi-official or on the contrary, ultra-liberal and without lawful obstacle. According to Gilbert Blardone (*François Perroux Conference: Acting in a New World*, 2013), John Maynard Keynes, Maurice Allais and François Perroux were the promoters of a "realistic liberalism" founded on rules of the game elaborated from a thorough observation of society and actors themselves". The new pope, François, also raises objections when he advocates, "With the ideologies that highlight the absolute autonomy of the markets and the financial speculation, thus denying the States' right to control" (Guénois, J.-M. 2013). In truth, the terms *capitalism* and *liberalism* are inextricably linked as Joseph Stiglitz suggests that we understand in an interview granted to the *Journal du Dimanche* on September 2, 2012, when launching his book on the French market (Joseph Stiglitz, *The Price of Inequality*, 2012a). He declares, "In today America . . . the most wealthy ones have only one obsession: to increase their share of the cake". He also attacks the "all-market approach" with the excesses that this system generates, without forgetting the disastrous impact of a resigning government.

Nevertheless, history teaches us that the market has always been a primordial arena to show moral responsibility. It also teaches us that during the eighteenth century, plenty of books abounded in discussions on the moral quality of the market and its responsibility in respect to the well-being of individuals and society ("The Moral Crisis in American Capitalism", Robert Wuthnow, *Harvard Business Review*, 1982). It is particularly instructive to consider the development of former, present and future capitalism to better perceive its rise to power in all the fields.

For example, one could not accredit the thesis according to which Adam Smith would be at the origin of capitalism under the angle of the market economy. Admittedly, Smith was the witness of a formidable expansion of trade exchanges on the worldwide scale. However, this expansion has always been blocked by a protectionist system decreed for competition and reason of state. Above all, it is advisable to take into account his penetrating critical analysis of the prevalent economic doctrines throughout sixteenth and seventeenth centuries in Europe and which persists at the beginning of the Industrial Revolution within the framework of states' centralization—what he named the 'mercantile system'. The liberal approach (often considered synonymous with capitalist, as we will see hereafter) that Smith defends in opposition to the mercantilists' principles appears primarily evoked in his attacks against them.

What it is necessary to underline in the optics of a non-utopian presentation of a SRC is the absence of any ideological consideration of the profit of very concrete new economic and commercial concerns. Thus it would be a heavy error to believe that the authors of economic lampoons, as well as supporters as adversaries of mercantilist practices, were 'idle philosophers' whereas under their names often appeared the mention 'merchant', like a title raised with pride. It is in this remark that we find the justification of our work. Smith's opposition to the mercantile system was not due to theoretical considerations. He appointed theoreticians like "very speculative philosophers" but with abundant and concrete observations: without forgetting a new vision of the market, following the globalization of the large companies and with the opposition or the development of groundbreaking scientific techniques, in the field of production as well as the exchanges. Who else is from the Middle Ages? The economic and social organization from the Italian and Rhenish commercial cities (Venice, Genoa, Florence, Bruges, the Hanseatic League) had already been made effective by an entrepreneurial management, without which the setting up of far-off expeditions and the development of companies just for the financial instruments would not have been possible.

Thus it is in day-to-day or long-term management that it is necessary to seek the premises of a socially and economically responsible capitalism and not fall prey to the analyses, as brilliant as they were, of economy ideologists. We can support that our conception of a socially responsible capitalism does not find its source in a sidereal vacuum but rather in the evolution of the society, the production and the exchanges. Its roots come from the progressive passage of a domestic economy to a market economy and the creation of new financial instruments are stuck to the field reality, without evolving toward a virtual analysis from an economy which one says on the way to become to it very as much.

Among centuries, we thus move from a *beggar thy neighbor policy* and die-hard protectionism, from all state to less state, from a claimed *ultra*liberalism with *no holds barred*, to the application of international standards and norms, plethoric and constringent in order to end up with a world disoriented where we delocalize to relocalize and de-industrialize to find the way to revive the industrial activity by following discourses that sound like incantations from one and the other. Various reactions that marked different stages in the evolution of the economic history, today should attend to the uninterrupted progression toward a socially and sustainably responsible capitalism. This, consequently, led to the progress or the crises, and to the sudden starts as the durability of economic activity, and are the historical practices that have presided over a perpetual change dynamic driving the simultaneous expansion of commercial, industrial and financial industries. As for service industry, it was in gestation in London *coffee houses*, first in Lloyd's coffee house where important shipping insurance contracts were signed in 1688.

These two systems received their *geographical appellations* well after the fact: the mercantilist system (which has always been referenced in periods of protectionists' temptations, a turning inward or a nostalgic evocation of Colbertism) and the capitalist system, which we could not resume to the maximization of profit (that does not represent the unique finality of businesses but that which is necessary to the accomplishment of their social utility). These systems have supplied a structure to the metamorphosis inspired by the vision of man, economic progress engines, the projectors of the eighteenth century and pioneers of today's entrepreneurship ready to play the cards of creativity and innovation.

Our incursions into history have to be completed by the study of some philosophical doctrines, simultaneously with the evolution of the liberal approach of the economic world, in order to reveal the symbolic in the social contract and the attachment to human values. Thus a lexical study of certain terms, whose interpretation could pose some problems, is necessary to avoid the semantic soft focus effect, as, for example, in the case of the social and sustainable responsibility, the misguided assumption that it is possible to analyze the components separately.

All these evolutions lead us to ask ourselves questions regarding socially responsible capitalism's contribution to **democracy**, the **state** role, **technology** importance and the educative role of the **press**.

This book wants to be invigorating and a bearer of **hope**. *This is not another discourse on ambient* **gloominess**.

Some Lexical and Methodological Considerations

Michel Marchesnay, in the paper entitled "Who Is Afraid of Its Social Responsibilities" (Qui a peur de ses responsabilités sociales, 2005), asks himself about the fact of being 'responsible'. He reminds us (by referring himself to the Robert dictionary and to the "Power of Words" ["Pouvoir des Mots"] written by Judith Butler) that the Latin origin *respondere* of the word responsible points out that the concerned entity is able (suffix ible). This could signify to the ability, the authority, to answer for his actions (including discourses), especially when those receive a damaging effect from a tierce person (*ADERSE Conference*, 2008).

The use of the word *responsabilité* in France and *responsibility* in England comes from the eighteenth century, more precisely 1787. This is the moment when "the social contract has been established in Europe as the founding paradigm of Public Law and Political Philosophy" (Jean-Jacques Rosé, *Introduction to CSR: For a New Social Contract*, [Introduction à la RSE: pour un nouveau contract social]). Speaking about social responsibility seems to be ambiguous or limitative to some authors (Van Marrewijk, 2003). This expression is often compared to a context of social assistance and can logically be replaced by societal responsibility. This last term indeed covers all dimensions in which the impact of the activities of the companies is seen, pertaining to both relationships to the company as a whole and the responsibilities that result from this. We can consider a first circle of stakeholders (shareholders, salaries consumers, suppliers, renters and managers) that have their roles to play in corporate social responsibility. However, in the broader context of socially responsible capitalism, it is necessary to take into account the involvement of companies and organizations in the whole society and its repercussions on the environment and the catchments areas.

It is interesting to notice that the English language affords us a second term to express the idea of responsibility: the notion of accountability. This term introduces the supplementary notion of owing an explanation with the possibility of being penalized or indemnified for the damages caused. This term is often employed in the context of a sustainable economy. This translation does not evoke the ethical and religious bedrock of the word that we find, when we are referring to man's moral accountability in the face of God's omnipotence. To the article's page of *Webster's Dictionary*, we also find as reference a quote from Robert Hall (1764–1831), a Baptist theologian, who talks about the awful idea of accountability.

According to the dictionary *Le Robert*, the adjective *social* comes from the end of the nineteenth century, while *societal* and its wide acceptance appeared in the 1970s. According to the *Oxford English Dictionary*, this term has been in common usage since 1898 and employed since 1938 in ethnography, as in the expression *societal system*. Today, the OED defines this term as "*pertaining to, concerned or dealing with society or social conditions*" and illustrated by the expression *broad societal change*. The term **sustainably bearable** may offer a better understanding of the multiple significations of the English of *sustainability.*

The generalized translation of '*lasting*' as equivalent to *sustainable* is too restrictive and deserves to be reconsidered with respect to the different notions that this adjective (borrowed to the French) covers, in order to better grasp its wealth and its semantic range. The *Webster English Dictionary* gives as a definition "capable of being sustained", while the *Le Littré* dictionary defines it as "that (which) could be endured". We notice that in *Webster*, the verb *to sustain* gives four senses, which contribute to a more complex interpretation of the expression's meaning such as *sustainable development, sustainable enterprise, sustainable performance*, etc.: 1) to support, as the foundations that support superstructures or the pillars of an edifice; 2) to keep alive, to hold somebody or something in reserve such for army support, population or family; 3) to hold without collapsing; and 4) to go on. The *Oxford English Dictionary* makes the definition more specific by adding "to sustain to the level or to the appropriate norm" clearly a partisan approach to the definition of this approach.

We will show in our socioeconomic holistic approach of sustainable development, how departments and industries of companies could be considered in their whole in order to facilitate the emergence of a common representation. This may help modern industry to find a sustainably bearable solution that can be elaborated in an integrative démarche by eliminating the well-criticized presentation of individual problems as unrelated silos. This will end to the same representation by articulating the existing oppositions. This point of view corresponds to our definition of the concept of an *enterprise* as **a dynamic set of structures and human behaviors in interaction**. Only a holistic approach could, on one hand, explain the level and the mechanisms of economic performance, and on the other hand, inspire sustainable improvement actions of this performance (Savall & Zardet, 2005a).

In France, the **stability** notion seems to be considered to be part and parcel of an overly reductionist approach, while in the English literature *sustainable* aims to be more and more assimilated to **socially responsible**. On the one hand, we say that a sustainable company is creating long-term value for shareholders by catching opportunities and by managing risks associated with economic, environmental and social development. And on the other hand, sustainable management is described in Brundtland report (former President of World Commission on Environment and Development) as the *capacity to manage and drive the direction of an enterprise, a community, an* *organization or a country so that reestablish or increase all forms of capital (humane, natural, industrial and financial) in order to generate value for its stakeholders and to contribute to actual and future generations well-being* (Brundtland, 1987).

The concept of sustainability applied in this new approach to managerial responsibility implies the integration of economic factors and environmental concerns, along with social and societal considerations. This concept has long been taken into account in the United States. Tom's of Maine's declaration of faith in 1993 perfectly personifies our own belief: "We believe that the enterprise could be financially successful, sensible to its environment, and socially responsible" (Chappel Tom, *The Soul of a Business*, 1993). The French company EDF (Électricité de France), whose operational and financial results were strong in 2014, communicates (www.edf.fr) on its entry to the fourth place of 100 most responsible companies in the *Most Sustainable Corporations in the World* (*Global 100 index*) that assimilate performance and responsibility. In order to be better, one must understand the broader meaning of the adjective **bearable**. To do so, one just has to refer to the sustainable development definition proposed by the *Dictionary of Modern Economics* published by McGraw-Hill in 1965 "a bearable economic growth situation means that the economic stagnation will not occur". Recent evolutions made the word **sustainable** a term with a pregnant advantage because it gets a dynamic coloration and conveys meaning as explains Collins and Kearins (2010), in the framework of a constructivist social strategy.

In such a context, environmental concerns do not limit to ecology and are in perfect coherence with a definition made by the OED in 1827: "conditions in which lives or develops itself; the totality of influences that contribute in modifying and determining the development of life or personality". A sustainable development strategy needs the implementation of an **internal and external strategic action plan** (IESAP) and improvement objectives on key drivers. These overstep the simple notion of the so-called green company. We define the IESAP as a management tool that synchronizes all the strategic objectives, in three- to five-year terms, wherever external objectives focus on customers and suppliers or internal objectives, e.g., the increasing of **human potential** level in terms of energy, behaviors and competencies or the innovation capacity of the company and its employees. These objectives are clarified as prior objectives and as concrete actions which could be implemented by the different levels, including staff.

The IESAP is upgraded each year to better take into account environmental changes and the objective's degree of achievement with the use of a tool that helps with implementation of a socially and sustainably responsible capitalism, the **priority action plan** (PAP). Such plans establish priority-ordered activities by classifying actions in terms of time and constitute an effective management tool, not only to reach objectives that make sense in theory and in practice as well, but also to allow concrete operations by using the appropriated know-how. A valid PAP focuses on reducing the dysfunctions before taking action on growth or development of new activities that could appear as abstract objectives if those do not roll out in a realistic context of resource allocation (Savall & Zardet, *Ingénierie stratégique du roseau, souple et enracinée*, 2005b, p. 338).

Sustainable development may be likened to a change or a long-term **metamorphosis**. We insist on this last word because it expresses the importance of a development built on the internal organizational energies. The modifications of the structures and the behaviors take place inside the enterprise, and external influencers do not generally dictate them. There are essentially *endogenous* transformations conducted in co-creative intra-actions with the marketplace and planned inside the company. Our expert opinion must be interpreted as advice and an invitation to always keep on innovating (Savall & Zardet, 2010). In truth, the concept of *sustainable management* is not under the umbrella of pure and simple social responsibility of enterprises that stands on a long-term engagement but concerns the totality of its objectives. In order to survive in a globalized universe, the enterprises need to constantly innovate. **Sustainability** is an essential factor of survival and development, rather than an ephemeral "buzz word" that seems to dominate the economy nowadays. This is a complementary and interconnected notion as it pertains to social responsibility. Such a type of management does not imply focusing on immediate problems observed in specific contexts, but to be concerned about a company's problems within an overall, holistic and long-term process.

William Petty is an English economist from the seventeenth century. He was distinguished as an exceptional, successful manager, with a certain capacity to foresee the unpredictable and to overstep factual and numerical data (permanent root causes of change) in order to avoid being caught unawares—e.g., by modifications in consumer's behaviors or variations in the product supply in markets (contingent causes of change) that he/she should be able to anticipate (Hull, *The Economic Writings of Sir William Petty*, 1889). The term of *foresight* employed by Petty means planning and approaches anticipation, without actually being called a strategy, per se. As a good physician, Petty thought that it would be worth preventing rather than healing, in politics as in economy, thanks to the new science of Political Arithmetic paired with Political Anatomy that he created. It should not be acceptable to let a situation deteriorate due to a lack of information. All the details must be gathered to enable one to discern "*what manufactures & Trade can & cannot be maintained or introduced*" (Hull, *Petty Papers*, 1889, p. 173). The information obtained will facilitate the deployment of production factors in order to reach a better effectiveness and an optimized productivity in a global competition context.

Nowadays, in both the social and economic domains, the concept of **strategic vigilance** aims at implementing an active monitoring of companies' internal and external environments in order to obtain information with a strategic range and data useful for effectively steering the organization. This concept constitutes an a priori element in the strategic implementation of sustainable development. To lean on unique immediate results' indicators of classical accounting do not typically enable one to detect and outdistance latent problems that mortgage a company's future and ultimate survival. A development strategy implies the choice of **warning indicators** and both social and economic vigilance, aiming at a strategic three- to five-year landscape and in no way should be combined in a passive approach, opposite the socioeconomic approach to management (SEAM). The indicators addressed using SEAM enable one to effectively evaluate both short and long-term economic performance and social performance as well.

If one focuses on conjuncture, it dares to constitute a contemplative démarche, while the constructivist and proactive socioeconomic approach consists of implementing supervision and an organized system, in addition to its **decentralized synchronization** principle. This principle allows making a permanent and transversal diagnosis positioning the company facing its environment. This last term does not cover only ecological considerations, such as climatic disruptions, exhaustion of natural resources, diverse forms of pollution, etc., but also concerns all the repercussions that could occur; all those affect the *extremely complex* internal and external environment of a company on territorial, regional, national or international scope and in social, law, administration, education, tax policy domains. A perverted capitalism that leads without any scruples to exploitatively construct an oil rig or to bleed a big company after misappropriation goes against the grain of socially responsible capitalism that refuses the destruction of the environment, and each involvement in the profit run, in favor of the collective interest and human relationships. Environmental concerns should not lead to speculation or corruption and then forgetting our *entrepreneurship* model, but on the contrary, one must answer to the challenge of these environmental dramas by taking into account the innovative spirit that belongs only to humankind.

We prefer the reality of facts to visions, however tangible, delivered by brilliant economists who become futurologists. That is why we resort frequently to information circulated in daily economic journals. It is about exploiting those with prudence in order to eliminate the part of "social demagogy", fierce enemy of a certain type of truth.

We grant, of course, their place in the expressed fantasies from recent books, as wished for earlier in the seventeenth century by the English William Petty, founder of econometrics according to Schumpeter. However, our démarche is in some way archaeological because it involves highlighting the first simmering of a *socially responsible capitalism* (SRC) by dispersing fears about being considered utopian. In order to avoid this pitfall, it has been desirable, quite essential, to avoid each dichotomy between a purely economic approach and a "civilizationist" lighting.

When one juggles with the word *stock* or *capital* in order to design the result of well-steered accumulation, if one chooses the second term, one introduces a dose of cerebrality. Thus, this ceases to give to capital a static coloration. One could already observe what appears to be the notion of circulation, as invigorating blood. If one still sees it's a stock, the capital will still be the useless fat of the political community.

We will see along those pages the tutelary figure of the **entrepreneur** who restores its respectability to the capitalist by forbidding him/her to take pleasure in being a partisan of wait-and-see policy in a fossilized gentrification process. On the contrary, he/she will be here to stimulate each innovative and invigorative effort, by transcending the only field of enterprise in order to enlarge its intervention scope to the territory and even to the nation. In the framework of a parallel research carried out by ISEOR institute, research center associated to IAE Lyon, Jean Moulin University, and the CERVEPAS, research center associated to Sorbonne University Paris, we now offer a historical quick view of the entrepreneurship notion in a holistic view. This term had been studied across the prism of the advocated considerations of Cantillon and Say, or from the fresco designed by Schumpeter.

Such continuity was demonstrated in the actions led by Elizabeth I and Sir Richard Branson. We mention for their bracing lighting the books "*La Transdisciplinarité: fondement de la pensée managériale Anglo-Saxonne*" (*Transdisciplinarity: Anglo-Saxon management thinking fundament*) under the direction of Michel Péron (2002) and "*L'entrepreneur et la dynamique économique. L'approche Anglo-Saxonne*" (*The Entrepreneur and the Economic Dynamic: The Anglo-Saxon Approach*, 2003). In the 17th century, when William Petty (*Petty Papers*, p. 189) advocated that "*all kingdoms and states are all merchants*", he gave another dimension to the entrepreneurship function and accorded the idea to the real spirit of the Renaissance. Petty is tempted to explore the world with the taste of risk and the adventure in all domains while expecting from entrepreneurs foresight of the unpredictable.

This book is structured in three parts of unequal volume. The first one is the most expansive. It offers an economic regime for actual society: socially responsible capitalism (SRC). It also highlights that the history of facts and economic thinking across centuries carries traces of certain fundamental specifications of what we could call SRC. Socially responsible capitalism does **not** conflate financial capitalism and entrepreneurial capitalism.

The second part is focused on the enterprise and the organization as a crucible that fosters the creation of added value. It makes explicit the management contribution to the development of socially responsible capitalism and offers the socioeconomic management method, as it has been experienced for 40 years in about 2,000 diverse organizations in more than 40 countries all over the world, as a viable and pertinent response for developing prosperity and social responsibility among companies and organizations.

Last but not least, the third part is more concentrated and stresses individual social responsibility, the only real, physical and spiritual entity able to hold and stimulate socioeconomic responsibility, which guarantees both personal and professional well-being and contributes to the collective prosperity.

Part I

Socially Responsible Capitalism in Society

1   Financial Capitalism Versus Entrepreneurial Capitalism

The socially responsible capitalism (SRC) proposed in this book is a viable and pertinent alternative to the contemporary economy. It distinguishes itself clearly from the excessively financial capitalism that entails speculative practices and dries up the investment flows that would otherwise irrigate enterprises and organizations, all producers of value added. This capitalism contributes to solving contemporary social issues, linked to the employment crisis or to the degradation of societal, national and global performance. The second subsection presents a synthesis of the thought of several great economists, whose theories implicitly point toward SRC without naming it; Petty, Bernácer, Keynes, Schumpeter, Perroux and Allais then situate socially responsible capitalism and its concrete incarnation: the socioeconomic management (SEAM), with respect to Marxism and other capitalism detractors.

Social Economy and Solidarity Capitalism

It is not for us to extol the rejection of capitalism in favor of a social and solidarity-driven economy that relies only on great principles such as the human primacy on capital or the choice of global interest as an objective without describing any concrete implementation process. By the way, this evolution of the social economy concept was first defined in the *Oxford English Dictionary* in 1845 as "*laws that take directly into consideration the health, the comfort or the well-being of people*". Bruno Frère's book title is revealing to this point: *Économie sociale et solidaire: béquille du capitalisme* (Social and Solidarity Economy: Capitalism's Crutch) (Éditions Textuel, 2011). Pascal Salin (*Libéralisme* [Liberalism] 2000, Odile Jacob) also criticizes the social and solidarity economy, which does not allow a clear exercise of individual responsibilities, however essential they may be to him. The investor, or rather the saver, would give to this configuration a meaning of his/her placement without sacrificing profitability. His/her objective is to ensure that money really helps to promote projects in social industry or to finance urgent activities in matters of the environment. SRC inserts this démarche in the framework of its opposition to speculative finance in accordance with its objective to work on the return of these resources in the service of the real economy.

In the same general idea, we have to negatively answer the question asked by Virginie Seghers in her book title *La nouvelle philanthropie réinvente-t-elle un capitalisme solidaire* [Is the New Philanthropy Re-inventing a Solidarity Capitalism] (Autrement, 2009). Actual philanthropists are waiting for "*a return on investment*" for society, or maybe for themselves, without any doubt. Jean Baptiste Say (*Cours complet d'économie politique 1828–1829* [Completed Lessons about Political Economy 1828–1829], 1953, p. 194) noticed, "*The poor's hope does not have for basis rich's charity. It is based on his/her interest*". Carlyle was saying that even the term *philanthropy* is the most odious word of the entire English langue. But do not forget, after all, following the Industrial Revolution that pulled the common laborer down into poverty, some CEOs reacted by seeking to demonstrate the capital/labor relation as uncontentious (in the debate on complementarity or substitutability of those two factors, the last one won). As Robert Owen (1771–1858) or Josiah Wedgwood (1730–1795), they struggle to treat their employees as individuals and to build them a welcoming and stable environment that fostered of course the productivity. The notion of socially and sustainably responsible capitalism may be considered to have been in gestation when those visionary CEOs realized that ensuring employees' commitment in their organization was an essential approach. Ida M. Tarbell in her book New *Ideals in Business: an Account of their Practice and Their Effects upon Men and Profits*, published in 1916, pulled up this evolution of the CEO's state of mind during the 1910s.

We think that the notion of socially and sustainably responsible capitalism comes under the jurisdiction of philanthropists only by incidence. Certainly, according to *the Economist*, we are attending the birth of philanthro-capitalism at this moment when all the billionaires are considering themselves as social investors and entrepreneurs. Bill Gates, Warren Buffet and George Soros in the USA; Jack Ma and Chen Guangbiao in China all apportion billions of euros to foundations that they created themselves, or to public and private charitable organizations, as Andrew Carnegie and John Pierpoint Morgan did in their time. Nevertheless, they still are wise investors. The Bill and Melinda Gates Foundation spend fortunes in Nigeria to eradicate polio and measles, but put millions of dollars in regional oil companies. Warren Buffet encourages its richest fellow citizens for donating at least 50 percent of their fortune but gambles on IBM *via* its enterprise Berkshire Hathaway Inc., 10.7 billion dollars in an investment that has already gained 12 percent because the stock value is increasing on Wall Street market (NYSE values consulted on *Le Figaro Économie*, November 15, 2011).

Moreover, this gambling is still a productive investment, the fruit of "*an attentive lecture from IBM annual reports since 50 years*", and it is speculative only from the first meaning of this adjective with the Latin root *specula*, which indicated an observatory. Adam Smith used it to show philosophers and physicians (*physicians* is preferred to *surgeons*), whose "*business is to observe everything, without doing*". We find at this place Quesnay (Smith,

1776, p. 168), who gets into that supposed neutral position, free of the external contemplative approach derived from the flourishing positivism of the nineteenth century. Jack Ma advocates that using his money for a good cause could pay off, but he pretends that his company Alibaba.com exists in order to solve social issues instead of simply doing business (Chen & Miller, 2011). By submitting its enrollment to the stock exchange, Jack Ma has felt forced to reaffirm to his employees his principle of first serving the client, then the staff and at the least the shareholders (Desné, J. 2012). We notice that this laudable intention is expressed under the form of a linear sentence that is not significant because it results in a circular and indivisible process of three parts without any preference for one or the other. Georges Soros is the blazing financier who made his name through monetary speculations—the English pound in 1992 or Thai baht in 1997—while forging his reputation as a philanthropist by distributing considerable sums to charitable organizations worth billions of dollars in their own right. But facing this crisis and its risks, he revealed his intention to give back the funds placed into his company to his investors in order to make it a family business.

Muhammad Yunus, Nobel Peace Prize laureate has even been suspected of seeking to personally enrich himself using micro-credit development as an intermediary, because lending money to poor people could be considered a profit source. Yunus insists on the fact that beneficiaries should not be considered as recipients of donations, but rather as clients (*Building social business: The new kind of capitalism that serves humanity's most pressing needs*, 2010). This idea is not brand new because the tradition of offering loans to the industrious poor dates to a time far in the past. In England, in 1699, philanthropists founded a specialized institution called *"The Charitable Corporation for the Relief of Industrious Poor"* in order to assist poor citizens by granting small sums of money with "a loyal interest rate" (Lipson, 1958). Donors considered their donations as investments. This is not matter of charity, in the truest sense, because we insist on the fact that there is no dependence between the lender and borrower, but instead there is interdependence. Nowadays, the charitable industry may be submitted to the market laws with a new financial tool, the *social impacts bonds* (*New York Times International Weekly*, November 26, 2013).

Previous examples that we could enumerate do not match our vision of a socially and sustainably responsible capitalism. SRC is the closest and the most contributing economic regime to the *concrete local and daily democracy*. The project is not to save abstract capitalism, even less so the financial capitalism often called speculative, but instead to foster a concrete form of a socially and sustainably responsible capitalism that allocates value creation into social performance (anthropological, physiological, sociological and economic needs satisfaction) and economic performance (few resources creation and regeneration). Those examples fit into the generic vision of corporate philanthropy, perceived as altruistic interventions that answer those social exigencies not taken into account or not enough ensured by public authorities. McDonald's, for example, has created a charitable organization to help families with children who need hospitalization. This safe philanthropy improves the company's image in the external environment. In the same order, Michael Bloomberg, former New York City mayor, when confronted by social services' powerlessness regarding the situation of disadvantaged young people, decided to solve this deficiency by allocating a part of his personal fortune to the problem, perhaps in light of reelections.

It is fair to consider philanthropy not as the expression of altruistic solidarity but as a means for entrepreneurs to settle their sociopolitical legitimacy in the eyes of the public. It follows that they have to earn the support of people and from public authorities not only in the emerging countries but also in more advanced countries in which legislators and governmental agencies wield economic influence and could foster such and such industries with financial repercussions. It is interesting in this regard to refer to the analysis made by Heli Wang and Cuili Qian entitled *Corporate Philanthropy and Corporate Financial Performance: The Role of Stakeholder's Response and Political Access (Academy of Management Journal, 2001)*. Not only do we have to respond to ethical internal requirements of companies to their shareholders but also make all the "**stakeholders**" react well to politics. Stakeholders in the socioeconomic approach to management (SEAM) include both public and private institutions. But in a more general way, this philanthropy/performance relationship is supposed to come into play only for large companies whose CEOs are well introduced in political context. The socioeconomic theory of *tetranormalization* (see Part 2) highlights this game and explains how the game is different for different kinds of actors, by generalizing it to all kinds of stakeholders and not only for big companies (trade unions, cab unions and non-governmental organizations, for example).

Such an approach of enterprises' philanthropy recalls for us the "supercapitalism" denounced by Robert Reich, former labor secretary under Bill Clinton. For him, the big competitive companies seek not only to influence markets but also the political community in order to tip the scales in their favor under norms, decrees and regulations on their industry (Reich, 2008). A similar approach linking business evolution and democracy is evoked in *Supercapitalism: The Transformation of Business, Democracy and Everyday Life*, Reich, 2008). A recent article extracted from *Academy of Management Review* (Muller, Pfarrer & Little, 2014) and entitled *A Theory of Collective Empathy in Corporate Philanthropy Decisions* attacks the well-spread interpretation of philanthropy as a tool used by directors in order to reach strategic objectives (p. 1) in an approach that is essentially rational. He advocates that the excerpt results in taking into account social issues may lead to tax and financial advantages, coupled with an improvement of the brand image without reallocating the shareholders' money. Its authors, Muller, Pfarrer and Little, argue that philanthropists' decisions, which may only be matters of calculation, are influenced by empathetic motivations derived from employees' regard for people in need both inside and outside of organizations. Just because a company is interested in profitability, that does not make it blind to the emotional concerns of its employees. The socioeconomic theory considers that human behavior is a mix of **emotion** and **reason.**

Our conception of a socially and sustainably responsible brand of capitalism may lead one to consider that the philanthropist's interventions, from the etymological sense should be those aiming to contain within reasonable limits the destructive strengths of technology, excessive regulation and extravagant globalization with a main objective—**quality of life.** This aspect is taken into account to a certain extent in the sphere of economic activity at this time when reactions from public opinion need to be integrated with investment decisions from public and private institutions (in the framework of social and environmental value added seeking ambition) and on the other hand with entrepreneurship strategies. Therefore, it always prevails in the economic sphere that in order to survive on a market made increasingly competitive because of globalization, the most effective method is to reduce indirect costs (first, employees) and to enhance productivity (Datry & Savall, 2015). That is representing the "skeleton of the entrepreneurship approach" according to Eric Maertens (Henri Savall, Véronique Zardet et Marc Bonnet, *Management socio-économique: une approche innovante*, 2009a, p. 171).

Experience shows that by taking into account **hidden costs,** using the socioeconomic method helps avoid massive layoffs, which we refuse to support while negotiating our intervention contracts, because almost 40 years of experimentation show that method enabling wage increases to be self-financing. Hidden costs are costs not detected by the information systems of a company or organization. They are engendered by the accumulation of dysfunction that affects economic performance by entailing excessive functioning costs, an insufficient productivity, a loss of quality . . . Those dysfunctions lead to chronic overconsumption of technological resources, financial and human that is largely underestimated. To think of such costs as a necessary evil is irresponsible. To reduce or eliminate those hidden costs frees up sums that could allow the increase of remuneration, among other things. Measuring the hidden costs is an important task because they represent a potential deposit of overall and sustainable performance improvement. When those hidden costs are not identified, quantified or steered in accounting system, the company cannot elaborate objectives of reduction in order to ameliorate its immediate profitability (Savall & Zardet, 2005b).

We do not take into consideration preeminence to ethical action on a particular so-called economic behavior. If we wrote socioeconomic with a dash, it would assert that our method lies in the *articulation* and not on the *assimilation* between these two approaches. Increasing efficiency and productivity of a company and having as a secondary effect a progress on a societal plane is a fantasy because reaching the first objective lays on a restructuration plan mournfully renowned as "downsizing plan," rather than socioeconomic on an action plan based on the socioeconomic background and adopted progresses after *communication, coordination* and *cooperation* (3C) in a spirit of exchange. Such approaches only enable organizations to recycle existing dysfunctions. Achieving both objectives together is possible because this approach generates energy and constitutes an essential lever in a company's actor mobilization. Moreover, given that it exists in employers' representations as well as for employees' trade unions, it is vital that dialog run through a will stir project, based on a preliminary study.

We should not forget to mention the social capitalism that the Anglo-Saxons highlight, suggests a wild and depraved capitalism bent on getting social management under the state supervision that should allow a better market functioning (by protecting it from eventual manipulation) and the optimization of the production. The phrase *social capitalism*, which could appear as an oxymoron, does not imply antagonism between socialism and capitalism. We find the elementary principles since 1995 in Kees Van Kersbergen's book *Social Capitalism: A Study of Christian Democracy and the Welfare State*. This approach is clearly macroeconomic in light of the utilization of the word **poor** in order to notice the underserved workers and not the deprived persons. This sense has been used at the end of nineteenth century by *The Economist* in order to indicate the masses of Indian workers, whose inheritance were constituted as written by Adam Smith (*Wealth of Nations*, 1776, p. 110) only by the strength and their hands' dexterity. By using the word *dexterity*, Smith let us understand that besides raw strength, the only quality that Taylor (1911) should be recognized in workers, there still exists a practical intelligence form regarding an intellectual approach of work. We could not impeach ourselves by thinking that the mournfully famous English *Poor Laws* that were promulgated for the first time in 1620 and the return of a welfare state, which is an excessive recourse, are polemic.

In the social capitalism framework, the general help programs for the poor are supposed to ensure a better economic stability and support growth. But they aim at eliminating all those who represent dead weight for the economy without trying to force a certain actualization of workers, akin to green-washing types of activities on the macroeconomic level. The objective of social capitalism would enable enterprises to seek maximum profit in socially and sustainably compatible ways. Those foster a climate that enables production development and sustainable economic growth.

Social capitalism, without being hostile to a certain liberal view of the market, is imposing a close collaboration with regulations that are, in our view, a prior obstacle to socioeconomic development, as we will show later in this chapter. Social capitalism, as we define it, puts the emphasis on interventionism. We observe, in order to restore justice, that social capitalism (also called socio-capitalism) aims at optimizing the environment of enterprises in order to maximize sustainable economic growth. So to get this result, the need and will of all the *stakeholders* must be satisfied. This is the conclusion reached frequently by our researchers in all interventions.

Economic and Social Performances

This new approach to the work concept arouses new expectations nowadays. Workers of all categories seem to await certain recognition of their efforts with the consequence being a higher level of commitment in their function, which allows them to project themselves in companies that would reconcile professional exigencies and personal values. Among the issues of the French *Agence Nationale pour l'Amélioration des Conditions de Travail (ANACT)* (National Agency for the Improvement of Working Conditions), their CEO affirms that *"this improvement is there as a systemic approach aiming at improving the health of salaries, their quality of life and so their capacity to create and to involve them into the company"*. If enterprises suffer from difficulties in hiring for some different professions, the lack of skill is not the only one put in consideration but also the lack of skilled workers' attraction to the jobs available as underlined in the *Conseil d'Orientation pour l'Emploi* (COE) (Employment Guidance Committee) report from October 1, 2013.

One could quote, for example, the current article from Teresa Amabile, Harvard Business School professor and Steven Kramer, independent researcher, published in the opinion section of the *New York Times* dated September 3, 2011. One could read, *"As long as workers experience their labor as meaningful, progress is often followed by joy and excitement about the work. [. . .] Fully 95 percent of these managers failed to recognize that progress in meaningful work is the primary motivator, well ahead of traditional incentives like raises and bonuses. [. . .] Work should ennoble, not kill, the human spirit. Promoting workers' well-being isn't just ethical; it makes economic sense"*.

Socioeconomic theory has long shared this point of view: one could not realize as a main heading social actions for ethical purposes alone, but the message is well received when it is understood to be efficient. We could go further in this analysis by seeking the relations which could exist in one part between "joy and enthusiasm", and in another part with the well-being and ask, like Luc Ferry (Ferry, 2012) if happiness is reduced to the **well-being**. The employment section of the periodic *L'Express* (April 16, 2011) titled "Happy workers, prosperous companies" draws up a list of working condition improvements (catering, fitness center, nursery, concierge services . . .) which, indeed, bring an improvement of the working conditions but do not treat in-depth stress situations. In the *prêt-à-porter* company Kiabi, there is a *chief happiness officer*. It has been a long time that there was, in Air France, a corporate manager 'working life quality' who figures on the organization chart. The managers are trained in prevention of psychosocial risks, but the company has felt the necessity for moving beyond the preventive step in order to adopt a well-being approach, which is an important lever for performance, according to the observatory *Enterprise and Health* (http:// observatoireentreprise.lefigaro.fr). In terms of Euros dedicated to prevention and working life quality, the return on investment is factor 13, 62 Euros per euro invested according to the European Agency for Safety and Health at Work (ADEME). Air France responsibly echoes to a position held by the socioeconomic management enthusiasts when they conclude, "a sustainable policy of working life quality has to be translated in terms of social dialog" *["une politique durable de qualité de vie au travail doit se traduire en terme de dialogue social"]*. The untouchable *standard of living* is the symbol of the well-being in this country of capitalism (USA), that is to say the accumulation of material goods while the idea of happiness supposes that one takes into consideration the dimension of the meaning of life. However, socially and sustainably responsible capitalism goes further because it does not reduce the happiness to well-being, which is not "the final word of human existence" because the essential is this sense of self-accomplishment, this extra-professional surpassing.

It is impossible to build a *business plan* only on financial, taxes and organizational competencies. Only human consideration could inflate sense to an economic project. Danone's vice-president, Emmanuel Faber (Faber, 2012) expresses with confidence in his book *Chemins de traverse. Vivre l'économie autrement* (Byways. Some Other Way to Live the Economy) that "*an economic decision which does not take into account its social dimension is barbarism, a social action which not takes into consideration its economic dimension would be a utopia*". This is our point of view since 1973 when started our research on **socioeconomic approach to management (SEAM)**. In order to avoid any possibility that this praiseworthy declaration remains merely a dream and to ensure its sustainability, we **have to conceive workers' satisfaction as an aim and not as a means**, deeply incorporated at the heart of the enterprise. We are not thinking in terms of return on investment from a well-being improvement program. The workers' well-being notion as the corollary to economic performance seems to be integrated by executives in their strategies: let us take the example of CEOs' declarations that follow each other in the weekly TV broadcast show "Impressions d'entrepreneurs (*Entrepreneurs' Impressions*)" from BFM-Le Figaro.

Workers are not only expecting to live well as a result of their day-to-day jobs, but they would also like to better themselves in the process. According to François Perroux in his preface to Henri Savall's book, *Reconstruire l'entreprise, analyse socio-économique des conditions de travail* (Rebuilding the Enterprise, Socioeconomic analysis of working conditions), "*salaried employees are not robots and they are aware of it: they are judging their physical working conditions, they appreciate the content of work organization, they get an opinion on their contribution to earn their purchasing power and on the virtue that they are admitting (or denying) about developing their skills and abilities*". It is about time for us to take into account not only the economic performance of the enterprise (*survival* and *development* sources for the enterprise both in terms of immediate results—strong self-financing ability due to a solid financial health, to an increasing sales development with markets conquests—as in terms of *potential creation* with intangible and tangible strategic investments) but also its social performance, as both an individual and collective source of satisfaction for company actors in the domains of working conditions, work organization, time management, communication-coordination-cooperation, integrated training and strategic implementation. **Professional quality of life** factors result in a democratic consideration of individuals not only as companies add value but also as actual *growth potential*.

Socially and sustainably responsible capitalism rests on the preeminent complementarity of those two factors, on the fact that they may be substituted for each other as highlighted in SEAM and **not on their incompatibility**. Indeed, sustainable overall performance of a company is by nature socio-economic and is composed by the two previously mentioned elements. The social performance is measured by minimizing the *dysfunctions* that affect the organizational level of functioning quality. The economic performance includes immediate results, that integrate **hidden and costs performances** and *creation of potential* tangible and intangible, necessary resources for preparing the future of the enterprise and its participants (Savall & Zardet, 2005b).

In addition, the socioeconomic approach to management helps in measuring **human well-being** investment profitability. This method demonstrates that the **intangible investment** in *human potential qualitative development* turns out to be much more profitable than any technological investment, hence the slogan: "*Take care of your collaborators, they will take care of your equipment and your customers*". It is worthwhile to take time, both in public and private organizations, to ensure a real *integrated training* of actors, unrelentingly renewed with *innovation focus groups* and a participative, structured and exigent management in order to lead persons and teams. The cost of this intangible investment does not damage corporate funds because it is composed by the elimination of hidden costs entailed by a disinterest of employees concerning the ongoing actions that aim at renewing equipment and technical capital in order to remain in the running competitively (Savall, H., Individual, enterprise and nation; how GDP is created? in Association François Perroux *Acting in a new world: Man development and costs*, 2013).

Professional life satisfaction sources for organizations' and companies' actors, producers, suppliers and customers exhibit multiple natures and reveal themselves to belong to physiology, psychology and sociology. A simple observation presents that individuals are not, by nature, inclined to obey, be subject to control or rather be subordinated as it is disposed in a legal contract of employment. In workplaces, in companies, they are agents driven by contradictory pulses and impulses: conflict/cooperation, individualism/team spirit and autonomy/dependence. Human and social performances are the results of eminently dialectic, instable and dynamic behaviors. It is necessary to ensure the cohesion of individual, team and collective behavior, that existing standards are not sufficient in harmonizing or reconciling. This is the object of the negotiated commitment to quote the opposite paradigm that considers that some men are subordinated to others in the company, and must obey, *ipso facto*, the orders and instructions of those who run them, which lead to a certain depersonalization in relationships with superiors. The contractual commitment acknowledges, conversely, the existence of the natural phenomenon of spontaneous organizational disobedience and seeks to manage in a more effective way, in a deliberate effort of personalization of the relationship at work. The competitive advantage of a company lies in its ability to work actors (naturally and legitimately disobedient) as a team. In other words, it is a question of aligning people strategies with team or company collective strategy, even if it means that people are willing to give up some of their personal strategy, whether it is not compatible with that of the company or team (Savall & Zardet, 2005a, p. 167).

In addition, socioeconomic theory shows that a basic worker or employee gets considerable power for destroying economic value, which he could not exert alone as an individual. The study of individual behaviors within a workshop allows us to understand better how the actors' games during a classical working day create or destroy value. When one says that the worker who is in interaction with others, the supervisor and other companies' actors generates, most often without any intention, the destruction of €20,000 to €70,000 per person and per year of value added or economic value, that comes to recognize the existence of a **considerable power** in workers, managers and CEOs, while the huge majority of the literature considers, implicitly or not, that the simple worker does not get economic power because when he/she is at work, he/she is at the lowest level of the hierarchy and also because his/her contract of employment consecrates the subordination link fully. Terri Ludwig, CEO of *Enterprise Community Partners* in an article from *New York Times* (August 21, 2001), notes that it is important for all workers to know that they "can influence change and outcomes".

The social performance of the company requires the sustainable cooperation between all its members, that is to say productive and efficient relations, regularly dismantled such that it is unceasingly necessary to rebuild. This economic capacity is exerted neither in autonomy nor in dependence but within the framework of the **interdependence** between all company actors. This is a key element in the socioeconomic approach, for which an organization constitutes a social space made up of complex relations. One can compare it to a theater insofar as it is about a forum, a meeting place where actors are exposed contentious points of view, which entail open discussions in order to lead the organizations' activities in the most effective way possible and to optimize their overall performance.

In this context, the word *conflict* could be interpreted differently. According to SEAM, in the framework of a socially and sustainably responsible capitalism, this word recovers divergences, dissensions, controversies, antagonisms and more largely emotional tensions, and their origin. The *interaction* concept is essential: it is present in SEAM through three fundamental principles, which are the **generic contingency, cognitive interactivity** and **contradictory intersubjectivity**. The *inter*-prefix indicates a scenario that tends toward synergy. Its transparency leans on an interactive and contradictory dialog between stakeholders in order to better understand and reduce the dysfunctions. In physics, the concept of **interaction** implies the energy **transfer** between elementary particles, between a particle and a particle's field or between particles' fields. In the socioeconomic method, it expresses a dynamic process elaborated through an iterative approach besides reciprocal influences exerted by actors that led to the dynamization of all company or organization' members. Synergies' creation between individuals allows them to reach a high level of interpersonal effectiveness in order to edify together a brand-new representation of the company. John Mackey and Raj Sisodia (*Harvard Business Review Press*, 2013) also notice that "if the free-enterprise works as it has to be, it leads to societies that maximize prosperity and establish conditions fostering happiness and human well-being, not only for rich people but for the entire society including poor".

The progressive transformation of professional behaviors is often the cause of social performance improvement but also economic performance because it aims to reinforce the trust part of the dialectic dyad of *trust/mistrust*, which *determines stakeholders' relationships at all organization levels, including shareholders* that need to be made loyal. Alain Peyrefitte in his book "*La Société de confiance*" (Trust society) (Odile Jacob, 1995) already noticed the lack of trust from individuals regarding states and states' mistrust regarding private initiatives, while trust is an essential engine, for instance to encourage companies' productive investment or employees' creativity by establishing a socioeconomic climate which is favorable to innovative enterprises. Kenneth Arrow, Nobel Prize laureate in economics in 1972, found in the trust on economic stake the origin of the wealth of nations, and he observed how trust acts as a social lubricant in this context. The definition of the trust society given by Peyrefitte perfectly suits our conception of a trust company: the trust society is an expanding society, win-win oriented, a society with solidarity, common projects, opening, exchanges and communication.

The responsibility compact that has just been presented to French companies by French executive power refers to the trust agreement for growth and employment proposed by the French businesses federation, MEDEF and four other employers' associations. What we are waiting for now are decisions and concrete actions. The socioeconomic management approach (SEAM) goes in this direction because the tools that have been implemented in companies are priority action plans (PAP) or periodically negotiable activity contracts (PNAC). This trust notion as a source of motivation and as a condition of **sustainable and efficient commitment** of persons is also an essential factor in our enterprise approach and our conception of a *humanely and sustainably responsible* capitalism. The notion of trust is at the same time a value, a doctrinal component and an operational lever to increase performance. Indeed, in our view, it is impossible to obtain a sustainable performance if the company does not integrate simultaneously economic and social considerations. Both lack of performance and trust drive inexorably to the extinction of the organization, caused by its collapse, its liquidation or its merger and in the best cases, to its artificial survival under temporary external resources drip (Anthony Buono et Henri Savall, 2007, p. 7). Did one benefit from the economic and social crisis that we cross to reconsider the relationships between employers and employees according to their reorchestration and the restoration of a reciprocal trust between the stakeholders, these days when the companies' problems are used as food for political conflicts that play as pleasure of misinformation, with perhaps even the intention to harm? One thinks, for example, about the declaration of PSA-Peugeot-Citroën deputy chair when he insists on the fact that the redeployment of workers from Aulnay-sous-Bois factory is almost done while the first trade union of the site affirms that several hundreds of jobs are currently without solution. From the external point of view, the approach arises rather from a political and permanent contestation than the participation to economic dynamics. Might the competitiveness contract that an important trade-union confederation does not sign be considered as part of a socially and sustainably responsible capitalism or still a decoy? The threats that influence our economy had constrained the government to gather the social partners around the same table to count on a necessary revision of the labor market and working conditions. For employers, this contract should not represent an impediment to improving profitability. This implies, besides, the diminution of costs whose wages constitute an important part of them. This way to think has been accepted lately by trade unions' representatives.

The concepts of **flexibility, plasticity and agility** which otherwise earn their rights to citizenship should lessen restructuration plans by avoiding raw dismissals or anticipated retirements. That is to say, giving more suppleness to companies by guaranteeing more security to employees maintained in their jobs, in exchange for a working time reduction accompanied by a reduction of their wages. The daily press handles this new approach in working relationships, mainly under a political scope, nay ideological. This amounts to turning the social partners against each other by evoking a series of calamities of social bounds. Those had been described as much as massive restructuration plans (the using of the word *downsizing* does not change anything) instead of insisting on the existence of a real and concrete dialog on the local field, and not simple leeway to establish an authentic redeployment plan. Each future job creation opportunity appears to be hypothetical because it is linked to a regrowth considered to be an illusion. This form of

social demagogy is opposite to the expectations of a socially and sustainably responsible capitalism that refuses to accept struggle as a necessity and favors dialog and negotiation.

Are job retention agreements that allow companies to modulate working hours and wages in order to address order forecasting variations constituting an advance for trade unions? The answer lays in another question: are such decisions able to restore trust between social partners, or are they hiding a fool's bargain? We will answer by recalling that in Germany, that kind of contractual approach has existed for a long time. Employer and trade union **dialog** is established at the board level. This joint management imposes responsibilities on workers' representatives who have to accept sacrifices like the competitiveness agreement, in which we find the four-day weekly working time and the loss of wages related. A "full frame" of *Le Monde* (May 2015, 13th) dedicated to Volkswagen reminds us that Germany is the land of consensus and that the Wolfsburg factory "embodies all the specificities of made *in* Germany model". A reference is made to the former Volkswagen human resources manager (from 1993 to 2005) who had significantly decreased the labor cost thanks to this working time and wages reduction and "without calling social assets' displeasure into question". The influential metalworking industry trade union, IG Metall (where among its adherents there are workers from the textile, automobile and computing industries), sees in that a method to save employees while fostering activity. Nevertheless, when the beneficiary situation becomes the norm, does it get an automatic compensation? It seems not because IG Metall has to manage an election if it wants to enroll its workers in a major strike, an effective process in order to obtain wages that are generally increasing in the metalworking industry.

Something that remains certain is that the trust dose required could not be injected from the outside; it does not impose itself by contract following public injunctions. It has to be devised only by the interaction and interdependence of all organizations actors through continuous practices of social relationships. The dialog is still the best method to solve a conflictual situation. It is significant, for example, to notice in PSA the decision to step from two persons to a team on a production line had been taken at the end of a local discussion opened inside the establishment committee without any supplementary job deleting, like those planned in the social contract from October 2013. In France, the new labor market and relationships in the enterprise approaches (Employment securing law, 2013) could not avoid systematic or unjustified blocking in negotiations about such essential questions as wages or work organization. It does not depend on dialog-trained interlocutors who are realizing a trade union mandate, whether they are members of enterprise assembly or workers' representatives. The rise of their responsibilities brings them closer to their German colleagues because it entails a better commitment with the company direction and strategy, and also to the evolution of employees, and so on for restructuration's (social bounds) that may be considered. This is the essential condition to succeed in effective and fast adjustments and not an abstract analysis of a reform project.

In the SRC framework, the *social dialog* can only be understood as a series of conflicting relationships between employers and salaries within the class struggle background. Let us recall the definition made by ILO for social dialog. Social dialogue is defined "to include all types of negotiation, consultation or simply exchange of information between, or among, representatives of governments, employers and workers, on issues of common interest relating to economic and social policy" in order to "promote better living and working conditions as well as social justice". A recent panel discussion between the new secretary-general of the French trade-union CGT and the vice president of the French employer's trade union MEDEF plants seeds of doubt on the favorable evolution in this domain. Each participant was standing his anachronic ground, politely, of course, when it is a question of working hours, wage levels and austerity. However, what happens at the top could lose its influence on field decisions, during unofficial meetings and negotiations that are driven at the highest level. As proof of that, we would point out the inescapable divergences on a formal plan which forbids each possibility of agreement. But those could be signed by field-grounded unionists close to enterprise' realities that should not be just the spokespersons of protesting confederations but belonging to reformist organizations. One could finish with postures and overbids that torpedo each chance to succeed. For example, the brand new "social pact" of the French Post Office had been put into a closet for six months, for lack of finding a sufficient number of signatures from the staff representatives. Six months later, following new elections, the negotiations' participants had become more accommodating and validated all the text clauses, excepting one that concerned mobility.

Otherwise, the state should attempt to tackle it with a law to solve the essential question of social dialogue in companies and establish a "social threshold" while an excess of formalism harms the quality of dialogue. However, in our conception of **daily democracy in proximity**, the meetings between employers and staff representatives should unfold according our principle of **contradictory intersubjectivity** that allows understanding the psychological reluctances which cause a systematic rejection of the "technical" solutions considered. This same principle should lead to a collective feeling of effort that reduces split risks among all the categories of persons. An on-demand system should satisfy the stakeholders and lead to solutions that would fit the realities in the field. We notice by the way that VSEs (very small enterprises) do not want one to modify the direct social dialogue, which rules in companies where the functioning is often characterized by a lack of conflicts. Regional external committees should of course be useful, as mediation tools, when the companies reach a certain dimension, but they would bring nothing to VSEs according to the results of a sounding carried out by Opinion Way (French poll institute) on behalf of the General Confederation of Small and Medium Enterprises (CGPME), a French employer's association.

Labor Value and Employment Crisis

The classical definition of **labor value** as we find exposed in William Petty's, Adam Smith's, David Ricardo's and Karl Marx's books is too restrictive. The quantity of work realized does not constitute a standard of measure fully satisfying This classical definition has the *raison d'être* of determining goods' value and lacks any symbolic signification while the socioeconomic approach to management endeavors to demonstrate that the richness of this notion is left in the shadows by a purely economic approach and excludes rather its social or societal implications.

It is true that if we consider for example, on one hand according to Smith's definition, "*Labour . . . is the real measure of the exchangeable value of all commodities*" (Smith, 1776, p. 86) and on the other hand, Ricardo's definition is more focused on goods production when he advocated "*the value of commodity . . . depends on the relative quantity of labour which is necessary for its production*". Those extrinsic and intrinsic formulations put into the shadows the value that could eventually impart external circumstances. The labor value theory developed since the nineteenth century is judged incomplete when it affirms that the product value is composed of the quantity and the cost of the incorporate work. It ignores that an unsold product does not get any value since it has not been desired or bought and paid for by anyone. First, let us observe that in early seventeenth century, some authors such William Petty have been completing the quantitative evaluation criteria by the value of the technical means used, the training mobilized and the cleverness deployed. We could also notice that if the goods' value derived their origin from their **utility**, this value could not be immediate as in the case of registered patents. The labor value is not the result of the market: it is a potential value.

The attentive reading of *The Wealth of Nations* highlights that Smith did not dissimulate his aversion for foolhardy exploitation of labor. However, by differentiating it from the slave case, as is the case for Locke, they give their labor up by losing their *freedom* and their *property*. Locke justifies the right for individual property by labor. Xavier Lagarde in his article from *Le Figaro* (February 23, 2012) declares, "*Marxist's thought vulgarization has been built on the conviction that capitalism perverted the labor value*". He adds in a questionable manner about the labor "*one could see in it an emancipation and freedom source*". If that could be held to be true in the puritan conception of labor in the sixteenth century, it seems that to the contrary, that the Industrial Revolution played a primordial role in developing criticism regarding manufactured work as a factor of less and less bearable worker alienation, without forgetting to underline that the workers' exploitation did not start from this era. The strained relations between employers and employees had seen the day since the formalization of the relationships between masters, fellows and apprentices whose profitability needs a rational work organization. Labor was central to English humanists' reflections in the seventeenth century when the matter at hand was to fight idleness. Its most effective treatment laid on a repressive legislation that put labor an obligation as *Workers Status* in 1350 and *Artisan Status* in 1563, including an essential clause that each available job position had to be filled.

We notice that contentious situations already existed between workers (*working poor* that need to be distinguished from *poor*, those requiring public assistance) who occupy jobs without any qualification (*laboring employment*) and a minority who knew reading and writing and so could pretend to employment that includes a semblance of professional training. The question was not to consider them as artisans but as workers with a certain expertise, the "expert workmen" (Pollexfen, J., A *discourse of Trade, Coyn and Paper Credit*, 1697, p. 47). In this period, one did not distinguish economic, social and political domains. The worker was considered a simple production factor without recognition of who would accept any proposed employment. If not, by being unconvinced of laboring virtues as put forward by the church, the worker might be delivered as a slave to anybody who would be disposed to hold him/her without any wage, of course; we do not talk about punishments and penalties that the law exposed (Hull, 1889, p. 67). An organized social struggle context ended up developing before the early Industrial era. The increasingly tight relationships between the sped-up growth of economic activity and the evolution of social life are entailed by technical development and worldwide opening to modernization. The consequence for the *laboring poor* was often to end in a brazen exploitation that leads no more than a virtuous indignation from authorities.

William Petty and his contemporaries would appear to attack the exclusion phenomenon even in the seventeenth century according to Marx, who quoted them. Despite their similar will to resocialize the workers, as we could qualify nowadays, and to foster integration, it results in an angelic lecture of employment-related parts. However, we notice that Petty observed the necessity to ensure best wages because there could not be encouragement in labor without the absolute certainty of expected remuneration "*there can be no encouragement to industry where there is no assurance of what shall be gotten by*" (Hull, 1889, p. 964). This is precisely what allows our hidden costs and performances method. Indeed, according to popular spirit that predominates among mercantilist period, the quote from Jean Bodin **"the only genuine form of wealth is people"** ("il n'est de richesse ni de force que d'hommes") (1530–1596, La République [*The Republic*] 1576, Les six livres de la République, Lyon, Gabriel Cartier, 1593, livre 5, chapitre II p ; 705) remains the key dogma. However, it aims mainly at demonstrating that the most important thing is the workforce's degree of use in an economy, whose vigor does not lay on soft insertion and the commitment of the worker in the social structure but in its upholding to be above the survival threshold. Jean Bodin's quote clearly suggests that the *human material* gets a certain value of productivity and has to be maintained as the wheels of a machine. Consequently, workers (or laborers) are designed in Anglo-Saxon literature under the term *hands* that sums up their situation. Workers' intellectual faculties are not solicited, contrary to qualified craftsmen. The first use of the word *hand* pointed out by *Oxford English Dictionary* reaches this point.

We have to notice that the importance of labor (*employ*) in the market, begotten by the start of industrialization, has been considered as an important social peace factor, and Bodin, keeping to this perspective, takes an interest in the development of the middle class. The chapter title is revealing this point; "means for resolving Republics' changes, which result from excessive wealth of the ones and extreme poverty of the others". William Petty advocated in the following century the same speech by declaring that real poverty consisted in a scarcity of population (*fewness of people is real poverty*, Hull p. 34). He insisted on the richness and the strength that represented numerous inhabitants, but he noticed several times that one has to distinguish between technical work and simple work (*Art and Simple Labor*, Hull p. 182).

Those issues in their whole dimension are perfectly analyzed in the collective book published by Paris Sorbonne Nouvelle editions under the supervision of Martine Azuelos entitled *Travail et Emploi, l'expérience anglo-saxonne, aspects historiques* [Labor and Employment, the Anglo-Saxon Experience, Historical Aspects] (2001). Otherwise, they are the often-referred-to phenomena that we still observe nowadays. It is also worth mentioning some particular issues from "drudgery ethics" broached by Weber and his affinities with the spirit of capitalism (*The Protestant Ethic and the Spirit of Capitalism*, 1904). The analysis is not only on the labor value but more specifically the labor value for Protestants. This ethics implies a continuous bodily and mental labor, which is at the same time the objective of the [puritans'] existence and a preventive cure against all the temptations called by Puritanism under the term "unclean life. It implies a labor division that entails qualitatively and quantitatively production and serves the general interest. It presents as an offensive against entertainment, pleasure and consumption, the life of each individual should be reached to self-accomplishment by laboring".

Financial Sphere and Real Economy

Socially and sustainably responsible capitalism should go in the direction of what the Spanish economist Bernácer (1883–1965) proposed, yet nonetheless be confronted by speculations tied to excesses of financial capitalism, that is to say stock exchange suppression. However, it would be a utopic approach because the financial areas are vital to the good walk of economy. Their *raison d'être* was to ensure financing of the economy, while being careful not to forget that globalization changed our scale. However, we notice that insisting on "the senseless gap dug over the course of thirty years between the financial sphere and the real economy". François Morin (2011, p. 29) for whom we did not call his competencies and his expertise on financial systems into question, proposes the same cure to the current crisis in an essay "*A World without Wall Street*" [Un Monde sans Wall Street]. He does not consider it as utopia. He underlines that this is a concrete utopia, which would need to recourse to the overall reconstruction of the international financial system whose instability is increasing.

One solution might be to forbid long-term transactions on the Stock Exchange because those are not socially responsible in the sense that they could lead people to sell securities that the seller does not owe. The objective of speculators is not to take shares in a company in order to participate to its development but to gamble on fluctuations of its stock price, moving up or down in a *casino's logic*. This represents a perversion of the pure speculative origin of capitalist system, which only could be put to an end by bringing short-term investment policy to a complete halt. Profits from financial speculation constitute diversions from savings, inasmuch as the profit of speculative bubbles leads to a drying out of real economy financing actions. In their introduction to the new edition (2014a) of *Reconstructing the enterprise* (*Reconstruire l'entreprise*), Henri Savall and Véronique Zardet notice "*resort to financial cash market leads to the macroeconomic development stripped from excesses of inflation and toxic speculations*" ["le recours au marché financier au comptant contribuerait à un développement macro-économique dépouillé des excès d'inflation et des spéculations toxiques"]. Nevertheless, is it possible to forbid trading in the raw materials markets or stocks and to allow only cash operations or long-term transactions in order to avoid certain extremes in exchange rates' fluctuations just as crisis waterfall effects?

Generally speaking, corporate strategies under the influence of shareholders who are obsessed with financial profitability tend to foster more and more return on investment (ROI) maximization and short-term economic performance while SRC aims at guiding companies over time. Moreover, the development of *hedge funds* is the cause of several bubbles because they are short-term funds, the objective of which is not to foster growth and even less create value added because they are speculative funds. By the way, markets' authorities still monitor them for possible misdemeanor manipulation of price rates.

Socially and sustainably responsible capitalism, on the contrary, has to attribute to investment funds the role of growth catalyst. It sees they have a guiding function that does not aim at seeking the highest level of ROI but the optimization of economic performance (growth, value added) and social (hiring policy and training) from firms in which they made the decision to invest. However, in considering these ways to consider investment, it is prudent to ask, "Does it apply to traditional techno-economic company, from the Industrial Revolution?" Alternatively, "Does it expect challenging the structures and changing actors' behaviors?" In the framework of SRC, it is essential to avoid the destructing dichotomy between shareholder sovereignty and stakeholders' governance.

Investment and Real Economy

In seventeenth-century England, the notion of investment was expressed by the term *venture* that also included the amount of far-away escapades on the stage of international business as the risk factor related to these expeditions. The investment represents an important part in carrying out entrepreneurial responsibilities and constitutes a privileged domain for CEOs who, unlike speculators on exchange markets, invest in **real economy**. At the heart of capitalism rises the entrepreneur who holds capital earned by savings and which has to be invested in order to create activities and value. Before Industrial Revolution, the accumulation of capital was the primordial condition for the flourishing of the national economic power. The former entrepreneurs, the *merchant-adventurers* who play both the role of investors and backers, accumulated the capitals that are necessary for the good walk of business. They rose against hoarding and fostered *productive savings*, which they used in their *adventures*—that is to say, inside companies they already drove under the form of *joint-stock companies*. Each entrepreneur is in that sense some investor who has to complete his business's own resources by using capital markets in the straight line of a responsible capitalism, instead of using "financialization" that constitutes a deviance.

Not much new activity shall be developed or simply be created without the support of capitalists. Littré Dictionnary defines them as "*the ones who lend their capital to an industrial entrepreneur*". This definition is accompanied by Mirabeau's clarifying quote "*Reproving capitalists as useless for society is like losing its temper against the labor tools*". Capitalists were settled in real economy. As Adam Smith (1776, p. 301) wrote, "*whenever capital predominates, industry prevails*". The association between entrepreneurs and financers has always been vital for putting inventions and innovations from the blueprint phase to work. This is particularly relevant for the Industrial Revolution's pioneers in England and unavoidable for the development and the creation of Silicon Valley *start-ups*. Indeed, the trust notion is not unbeknownst to investors who elect to finance projects whose immediate profitability is not ensured.

Money is not an end *per se* but a means, a tool and an instrument for growth. Only **active factors** of value creation that constitute the **human potential** will make it happen. In a *Le Figaro* opinion piece dated 23 August 2012, Luc Ferry stated the rejection of capital accumulation by the official Catholic Church's catechism (§2424), which supports "a theory that made profit the exclusive rule and the ultimate end of economic activity is not morally acceptable". However, we notice that this is the criticism of a skimpy conception of capitalist system that finds its real roots in entrepreneurs that create wealth and individuals who revalue their potential by accepting globalization risks in Mercantilist epoch. That is how each development of **democracy** belongs to a rise of capitalism.

Nevertheless, the situations that entrepreneurs have to face today are very different. The money crunchers are disconnected from the real economy, which was not the case of *Money Lords* well described by Matthew Josephson in its eponymous book (*The Money Lords: the Great Finance Capitalists 1925–1950*, 1972). There are often no links between investing and undertaking. Investing is becoming a pure short-term speculation endeavor that implies debt-supported financing outside of entrepreneurial and concrete activities and for the real circulation of economy, which requires long-term investments.

Tim Parks, in a book entitled *Medici, Money, Banking, Metaphysics and Art in Fifteenth Century Florence* (2006), already notices that in the fifteenth century, the financial sphere aimed to claim its independence vis-à-vis the economic activity by the appearance of the bill of exchange that "separates business and finance each other" and "banking industry is getting autonomy". We would rather say that financial innovation is at the heart of capitalism and that globalization has been largely contributing to its expansion. **Creative innovation** in matters of financial instruments has largely contributed to economic development, but perverse innovations, as the *hedge funds'* and *subprimes'* crisis demonstrated, are producing a predatory value. The financial economy is siphoning resources from real economy needs and is locking itself into a sphere that Petty and his contemporaries would judge as more and more unattainable.

Putting money in a company is not the only act that will make it more dynamic and effective. The survival and the development of businesses rests essentially on a better accounting of "*change strategy and intangible investment on qualitative development of human potential*". The latter does not figure into accounting documents but should appear in a visible position on the balance sheet. It is "strategies founded on competencies development, but also on professional behavior" evolution, delegation's development, processes of empowerment and the company's commitment. The qualitative investments may be made complete by investments in qualitative development that encourage creation. Those investments engender not only economic advantages but also **psychological and physiological advantages**. The economic advantages lie in the incorporation of hidden costs into value-added recycling and allowing for evolving and financing wage levels inside the company. The psychological and physiological advantages are a reduction of harsh working conditions, the improvement of professional relationships and of the working atmosphere. (Véronique Zardet, *Human potential and economic value creation in* enterprise [Développement du potentiel humain et création de valeur économique dans l'entreprise], in [Acting in a new world: development and Human costs] *Agir dans un nouveau monde: le développement et les coûts de l'homme*, 2010, p. 88). One should, in one part, be helping individuals to develop all their potential by involving oneself in a continuous improvement that is supposed to put the company's actors in a position to create and to commit themselves in all domains. This is the definition of intrapreneurial. We subscribe without any reservation to what Charles Beigbeder, Gravitation Holding's president, proposes as a cure for employment market volatility when he advocates that one should "reason in terms of 'employability capital' of employees who would increase their 'professional value added' at each occupied position by the acquired experience and practiced responsibilities" (*Le Figaro*, November, 2013 12th).

The internal training actions we propose go in that direction. The **integrated training,** that is to say training efforts in ensuring a better matching of skills and real positions to fill, given their accelerated evolution, is often insufficient and leads to *"relative illiteracy gaps"* (Savall & Zardet, 2005a, p. 123). Integrated training as we conceive of it, does not only have the goal to develop new skills for employees. It rather aims at ensuring a certain flexibility of employment that guarantees workers the adaptability that is necessary to survive in a constantly evolving employment market. Training represents a key element of sustainable performance because it confers to the company a certain degree of **plasticity** and an anticipating power. It remains less expensive than part-time unemployment. Socially and sustainably responsible capitalism has to rectify the incompatibility between labor supply and demand and also to the waste of competencies that entail its cortège of dysfunctions and hidden costs.

We define **intangible investment** as the cost entailed by a creation of potential with an intangible nature (for example integrated training sessions or the setup of strategic or operational focus groups, communication development, working conditions, better taking into account of both internal and external environment, the manager's role development by fostering local and closer **management**) should be considered as profitable investments and **not** as *recurrent expenses* which could be attributed to the result, in the opposite of the accounting norms. Companies' employees are directly concerned. Addressing employment concerns in crisis mode is a temporary solution that we reject on principle. Focusing its effort on intangible investment is, on the contrary, investing in human capital, the essential lever of sustainable improvement and recovery of social and economic performance. That is why we named **human potential** as the prime factor of economic value creation in socioeconomic theory (SEAM), in order to distinguish it from the traditional concept of labor used in classical approaches of management theories and their substitutes whether they be Keynesian or Marxist criticisms.

Financial Capitalism

Social responsibility is incumbent upon the Schumpeterian entrepreneur and those espousing all other forms of governance with the essential finality of stopping the exclusive primacy given to financial domain. It is suitable to reject the idea of tipping over a pretended new economic system: financial capitalism. Fernand Braudel and François Perroux notice, not without reasons, that the finance has always been part of economic development. The foremost mercantilist's theoreticians, like Munn, Misselden and Child, were almost business practitioners contrary to for Locke and Petty. In a certain way, they saw in financial instruments the essential factors of production. Capitalism is in essence a financial, *sine qua non* condition to be linked to the real economy. This condition is rejected by its opponents even if the expansions of trading and industrial activities development do not cease to depend on it. From the Renaissance, pamphlets' authors who gravitated toward the economic sphere have arisen, and continue to do so, against sterile hoarding in states' vaults or in individuals' hands. They wished a rational and productive distribution of wealth between persons who desire to invest, helping the economic machine to work by supporting a circulatory movement in the external exchange rhythm. The Spanish economy went into collapse because they did understand this circulation idea and this movement idea, which was spread by Harvey, Copernicus and Galilee. The latter insufflated their dynamism into trading and manufacturing activities and "*it was not a empty in movement but a circulation into reality*" (Jean-Michel Servet, [*The masked prince, economic policy formation and politic occultation: the money example*] *Le Prince Masqué, formation de l'économie politique et occultation du politique: l'exemple de l'argent*, 1979). For Misselden, capital represents "*the vital spirit of trade*" (Free Trade, or the Means to make Trade Flourish, 1622, p. 28). According to Locke, it constitutes the essential element "*to move the Several Wheels of Trade, and keep up Commerce in that life and thriving Posture it should be*" (*Treatise on Interest*, London, 1740, p. 36). According to Petty, the specific characteristic of *stock* used, instead of capital, lies in its affectation of a productivity objective, as an engine which could allow for national and international trade functioning. Smith gave the classical definition when he noticed "*As soon as capital has accumulated in the hands of particular persons, some of them will naturally employ it in setting to work industrious people, whom they will supply with materials and subsistence, in order to make a profit by the side of their works, or by what their labor adds to the value of their materials*" (Smith, 1776, p. 42).

According to Petty, capital's constitution process shall only come from the exploitation of gold and silver mines, whose only origin is human labor that determines the growth of national wealth. Financial capitalism does not constitute a brand new economic system, even if public and private actors are increasingly under the influence of finance. The states could not afford the means of their policy. Crisis deprives the business world of its resources and hurts the monetary system. Asking who will get the final word on this conflict between financial and entrepreneurial capitalism does not make any sense. It is curious that three types of capitalism are always mentioned, *trading, industrial* and *financial* capitalism, while history makes us think of it as a continuum. Perroux in his remarkable book dedicated to the evolution of capitalism (Perroux François, [The capitalism] *Le capitalisme*, 1963) observes, "*Trading capitalism has launched industrial capitalism and industrial capitalism is, sometimes, under the influence of financial capitalism*" (Perroux, 1963, p. 28). There are simply different industries on "*the road to important relationships*" (Perroux, 1963, p. 28) and which participate in the holistic approach to entrepreneurial capitalism.

The **discarnate financial**, *disterritorialized, uncontrolled* and *speculative* type of **capitalism** is not assimilated to any system, but it can be considered as an obstacle to an intelligent growth and to the establishment of a responsible and democratic development model. In his 1905 book entitled *Frenzied Finance*, Thomas W. Lawson, a finance-man from Boston, denounced the dangers of an unencumbered capitalism and the irresponsible attitudes of companies, in the manner of *Muckrakers'* writers whose social preoccupations and violent criticism about financial cartels would actually be realized nowadays. Those are the speculative spin-offs of a perverted capitalism and the disasters that contribute to this representation of a financial metastasis consistent with that presented by Braudel.

The necessary financial dimension has always been ever-present. In order to set up a far-away exploration, to create a company or to experiment new techniques, one always needs the support of *moneyed-men*, the sixteenth and seventeenth centuries' *joint-venturers*, the *venture-capitalist*s from today, the "*Money Masters*" according to Gilbert Blardone or "*Money handlers*" from François Perroux who uses also the expression "*pennies handlers*" in order to designate the market's predators. It is useless to emphasize that the type of crisis we just experienced is similar to past occurrences in economic history. The *Oxford English Dictionary* teaches us that early in 1636, Jonathan Swith's "useful projectors" also became speculators. They aimed at stealing from rich men and tricking poor people without being concerned with public wellbeing. At the end of the seventeenth century, hazardous speculations on big trading and manufacturing companies' stocks that coincided with the creation of the bank of England in 1694 entailed lots of bankruptcies, which had been described by Karl Marx as "*the sudden apparition of bankcards, financials, annuitants, brokers, stockbrokers, tycoons and Canadian lynx*" (Karl Marx, *Œuvres*, La Pléiade, 1963, p. 1218).

It is therefore not surprising that Joseph Stiglitz emphasizes that "bankruptcy is a crucial characteristic of capitalism" (Stiglitz, 2012a, p. 200) or that Reinhart and Rogoff hold in their book an expectation that "This time, it would be different" (2010) than "eight centuries of financial madness". In a volume of *Financial Time* entitled "Capitalism in Crisis: The Code that Forms a Bar to Harmony", there is an article titled "Financial Amnesia: A Factor Behind Crisis". This article tells us that "the Chartered Financial Analysis Society of the UK says investment professionals should study financial history to reduce the likelihood of future crashes". Indeed, on par with contemporary scandals such as Enron, the South Sea Bubble in England or those from the Oriental company in France in 1720, entrepreneurs' long-term projects are distinctive from illusory projects which not only lead to the bankruptcy of investors but also to the inability of first banks and gold-smiths to recover loans given for doubtful titles on stock companies that sometimes do not have a physical existence apart from on paper.

The *London Gazette* (N°3280/2) mentioned early in 1697 a law aiming to limit the number of lenders and regulate their illegal practices. The 1719 law is well known under the moniker, *Bubbles' law*. According to Stiglitz "*bubbles and their consequences are as ancient as banks and capitalism*" (Stiglitz, 2012a, p. 73). Michel Beaud, in his *History of Capitalism: 1500–2010* (2010) is interesting for his discussion of the *Great Depression Crisis (1873–1895)* and observation that in each of these crises "*the most spectacular sign is from the nature of the Stock Exchange (collapsing prices and panic) or from the nature of banks (Great institution's bankruptcy or bankruptcies)*". This is how "*bubbles*" entail a speculative bolting which not only creates inherent risks but also deprives the real economy from liquidities in the profit of stock exchange games. The "*victorious capitalism, not regulated, who takes uncontrolled risks on a global scale*", described by the former French economy and finance minister Francis Mer (*Le Figaro, April, 2013, 12th*), goes against the socially and sustainably responsible capitalism that we advocate, because predatory capitalism has not been conceived in order to sustain businesses in the long term.

Speculative Dissoluteness

In the nineteenth century, Smith previously mentioned, in opposition to "a long life of labor, frugality and attention" (Vol 1, p. 102), the trade of gambling exerted by speculative merchants in no one regular, established or well-known branch of business. Nowadays, it is speculation, which is denounced by the Occupy movement, whose watchword is "Occupy Wall Street", which disrupts the capitalist system. One could define speculation as the realization of profitable activities without efforts and risks contrary to the Schumpeterian entrepreneur. This is a way to get revenue without consideration of real activities. Bernácer already underlined in 1922 that there exist goods that produce unearned income, in other words an income without entrepreneur's risk, without labor or creative activity. This is just the opposite of what is happening in real goods and services markets. The investors, who do not deserve that name, are redirecting the liquidities to us. This situation leads to the drying up of the whole economy. Keynes takes over this theme in 1936 in his General Theory of Employment, Interest and Money, where he denounces the purely speculative behaviors of capital holders who redirect them from more productive investment. He came to announce in his famous quote "the euthanasia of annuitants" defined by Littré Dictionary as "middle-class persons who live on private income without trade nor industrious activities". This became prosaically persons who receive nonprofessional incomes doomed by the decrease of the rate of interest.

We notice that the seeds of this idea have long been present because John Law went after the **sterile annuity** of savers in 1718. The lack of tangible and sustainable capital invested in productive systems is caused by a too great an attractiveness of speculative markets. This condemns the companies to under-development or mutilation by the lack of financing for really productive activities (Savall & Zardet, 2005b, p. 139). The art marketplace is often listed as an example, although the artists themselves often rise against speculative drift caused by merchants and trade in this industry. Martial Reysse was declaiming during a retrospective on the Pompidou Center "*I have been selling things for the past 40 years, yete the last five years my pictures are experiencing an extraordinary appreciation without my doing anything*". The speculation (without forgetting corruption and the generalized muddle denounced by the Dakarian movement "*Y'en a marre*" [That is enough] in all African countries) feature in the top enemies of the socially and sustainably responsible capitalism. That is to say "*a capitalist system is likely able to cross over generations with its high degree of democracy and a fair degree of equity and sustainable effectiveness*". That should not be the case for a system whose only concern could be summed as self-fattening by trades and money.

The French Financial Market Authority (AMF) and the American *Security and Exchange Commission* have been forced to react. In an article published in *Les Échos* (July, 2011, 22/23th), the vice general secretary of AMF underlined that the reaction of the institution did not concern investors who are considering the trade marketplaces with the objective of creating financing opportunities for new and innovative activities, in other words as allowing real investments by avoiding speculative movements. He took care by specifying that "*those we target are a bunch of very active investors and very well listened to in the Stock exchange's forums and who have power to influence markets for certain speculative values*". Against the criticism of his own monetary policy, Ben Bernanke, the former chief of *Federal Reserve System* (FED), reacts to the new financial bubbles by stating that it could entail a new rush on *junk bonds*. He declares in front of bankers and analysts in Chicago, "*We will follow closely the examples of profitability research and other forms of excessive risk-taking which could affect active prices and their relationships with the fundamentals*". He insists on the close monitoring of financial instruments which are financing this taking of risks which could provoke again, on one hand, a liquidities crisis in real economy stocks and on the other hand, the failure of investments funds and whatever negative consequences that includes for the whole society.

A socially and sustainably responsible capitalism, *in contrast with unbridled capitalism*, should not be embroiled in the perverted practices of financial markets, which ask for more and more regulation without being sure that they would be palatable. There is no need to argue for a *new capitalism for a new world* as suggests an international symposium held in Paris in 2009. This is not the capitalist system but rather the orientation of the economy toward short-term issues, which is the origin of the crisis that we have not yet passed. In financial and raw materials markets, the day-to-day quotation favors the privation of value added. This short-term-only orientation just reaches its apogee with the *high-frequency trading* that plays on the micro-gaps between exchange rates that could appear suddenly within a second and influence exchanges in a way that is not very favorable toward the moralization of market. It follows the multiplication of speculative operations that are perfectly abstruse and disconnected from the real economy (see Albert, 1991, *Capitalism against Capitalism*).

The future of socially and sustainably responsible capitalism should not lie in the accumulation of capital policy, nor in responses to the injunction *"take the dollar and run"*. In the seventeenth century, Petty, as Bacon before him, asserted that money, like manure, was not useful if it was not allocated. He emphasized the inert characteristic of capital in its current form in labor/capital coupling. Similarly, Benoît XVI, in the third encyclical of his pontificate, wrote (July 2009): *"the economic sphere is not by nature ethically neutral, neither inhuman nor antisocial. It belongs to the Man activity and, as human, it has to be structured and institutionalized with an ethical manner"*. His successor Pope François denounces *"money fetishism"* and the invisible tyranny of a financial sphere that gets out of hand, in order to ask for a financial reform, which could be made ethical by emphasizing that *"money has to serve and not to rule"*. Nevertheless, our relationships to money make man undeniably *"a good that one can use and after throw away"* (*Le Figaro*, May 2013, 17th).

Capital Yield: The Rate of Interest

No one would deny that the most acute problem is aroused by the financing of trade exchanges, industrial investments or informatics systems development remains the yield of the capital. Muhammad Yunus asserts with conviction that *"social objectives chased by employers will be put aside as soon as they will conflict with the objective of profit maximization"* (*Vers un nouveau capitalisme [A World Without Poverty]*, 2007, p. 74). At first sight, in order to produce more, build new products or modernize, classical companies have to find other sources of financing than their equity. That is why Jacques Bichot (2004) notices that already St Thomas Aquinas, who refused the legitimacy of interest loans that *"legitimates the remuneration of the money handed to a merchant or a craftsman by association modal [. . .] in order to make the loaner participating at his own risk to artisan's or merchant's business"*. The interest paid constitutes a fair retribution of the lent capital of an investor or capital-risker that could pay the entrepreneur as would yet Richard Cantillon (1680–1734) in his *Essay on the Nature of Trade in General* published in 1755. He forestalled Schumpeter by adding the entrepreneur (word that he used) to the three other production factors: earth, labor and capital. We notice also that Smith (1776, p. 46) emphasized the necessity to give to the entrepreneur a retribution for his taking risks: "*Something must be given for the profits of the undertaker of the work who hazards his stock in his adventure*".

However, the profit could also have been considered as "*wages of a particular sort of labour, the labour of inspection and direction*" (Smith, 1776, p. 43). In the same section, Smith also mentioned capital management supervision as a task relevant to the entrepreneur. For the *merchant-adventurers* who make the capital yield a profit in companies, the money ceases to be *that thing* which Nicolas Oresme, in the fourteenth century, qualified as "*sterile and dry*" like Jean-Michel Servet (1979, p. 182) remarked. The unearned-income recipient has to be transformed into a productive investor. The *no-dividend business* wished by Yunus should admittedly work for organizations that aim at improving the quality of life of poor populations. The Spanish economist Bernácer tackled interest and should have appreciated the creation of a new type of company implemented by Yunus under the designation of *social business* because "*investors who support it get no profit from its activity: they only get back their initial stake after a certain time*" (2007, p. 52). The model put forward by Yunus is that of the company Danone communities in Bangladesh. On the *Trait & portrait* [Trait and portrait] page of *Le Figaro* (February, 4/5th 2012), Danone's vice-President commented "*instead of taking the investors like only interested in financial yield for granted, we propose to them a financial tool which give to their investment a low profitability but a lot of sense*".

Does it represent a challenge for the new capitalism or a normal situation for the risk-averse and low attractivity saving, safe investments that traditionally lead to the lowest rates of interest?

Recent developments seem to indicate that in periods of financial upheaval as we are experiencing, it is commonly accepted to pass an additional step with no longer a zero-based rate of interest but a negative interest in the matter of sovereign debt. Germany has raised a two-year loan for four billion Euros with 0.6 percent, which represents a loss of six cents per year and per security for the investor (but a profit for the same amount for German Treasury). This example reinforces the analysis made by Bernácer because it demonstrates that some investors are able to risk losing profit without any other compensation than securing their capital. Bernácer explains that a moneylender should be satisfied to get back the entire value of his/her capital, of course at the end of the refunding with no depreciation due to the inflation rate. Consequently, the borrower provides a service to the lender by sheltering his/her capital during a certain length of time. According to this reasoning, the lender does not consent to any sacrifice. The loan and the mortgage appear to be a balanced quid pro quo. But we are passing a step in line with Bernácer's theory: to lose money but gain a measure of safety. Would this be the inevitable consequence of what Nicolas Schimmel CEO,

Union Financière de France, private banking, qualifies (*Le Figaro*, August 2012, 7th) as "*swaying in a world where safety saving becomes no-yield saving and in this world, without inflation it guarantees. . . . The impoverishment of patrimony*"? Reading from some information letters sent by banks to their customers, inviting them to invest without any stress on financial markets, seems undoubtedly to demonstrate that their product is now simply insurance to get back the completeness of their capital at maturity. At this time banks, in statements of account, do not fail to indicate the debtor rate of interest associated to this account and the wear index for overdrafts! Does the Islamic finance present a more responsible and ethical characteristic when it enacts that losses have to be shared between debtors and lenders? France favors this approach in judicial liquidations procedures, for example.

In the seventeenth century, William Petty and John Locke, who had given consideration to the *mystery of money*, agreed that in order to see in interest the *income* of capital, the annuity and wages as incomes from Earth and Labor. Francis Bacon in his *Essays* (1597) declared that the interest loan should be authorized and that it introduced a semblance of moralization by proposing a consumption loan with a majored rate for individuals and a speculative loan for merchants, which took into account the risk factor (Bacon, Francis, *Essays*, 1597, French translation 1948). However, Bacon was not a mistrustful partisan of interest because he laid as a principle that "*interest loan is the most safe means to earn, albeit one of the worst; . . . where one earns its bread by the sweat of others'avants*" (Bacon, 1597, p. 187). For Petty, and this remark remains valid today, there exists a minimal threshold of lender capital profitability if we want to avoid the run of capital. This is favored by the existence of tax shelters. He affirms also that "*to lower too strongly the rates of interest comes back to forbid this latter*" (Hull, 1899, p. 247). Here Petty places himself in favor of the loaner. He writes that a part of renouncement and another of risk (Hull, 1899, p. 246) compose interest. Nevertheless, he insists on the time factor linked to the interest. He transcends the simple idea of temporary renouncement to a certain amount of money in order to give way to a concept of transmitted value.

This stance (the one from Protestant ideology) shows the breach with Catholic church dogma, which affirms, according to Jacques Le Goff, that "*time only belongs to God, by selling the time which flows by the moment of the loan and the refunding, the loaner is God's patrimony stealer*" (*La bourse ou la vie* [Your money or your life], 1986, p. 42). Petty bypasses the time issue by insisting on the permanence of long-term invested capital as different from a speculative placement. Not far from us, in his theory of interest, Bernácer deletes the "*time preference*". For him, the interest is not the price of time; it is in the end only the appropriation of an income without labor. From his side, Petty indicates that different temporary conditions should match different rates of interest. Ricardo in the nineteenth century considered the benefits that the borrower could get from the rational use of the entrusted capital. As the English historian R. H. Tawney formulated, to demonize interest is a superstition from the Middle Ages (*Religion and the Rise of Capitalism*, 1922, p. 194).

The dissoluteness of financial markets and banking institutions had led states to be in so disastrous a situation of over-indebtedness that they could not pay it off. This does not constitute a new fact in history development. King Edward III of England caused a ministerial crisis in 1340 by being dissatisfied with his subordinates' efforts to reach his financial expectations. The wars he carried out and his sumptuous expenses drove him to bankruptcy in 1345, the year when he refused to honor his debts and caused by the way the ruin of several great Italian banks. The Flemish lenders were also strongly affected by the king's loan collapse and his poor reputation. More recently, during the summer of 1982, Mexico, Argentina, Poland and Brazil all declared themselves unable to meet their liabilities. A secondary tremor seems always possible nowadays.

2 Forerunners of the Socially Responsible Capitalism Concept

Given the large number of references or quotes related to more or less remarkable authors in economic literature who are present in this book, we considered it necessary to dedicate some pages to those who, in our sense, demonstrate a derivation or, on the contrary, an opposition regarding the main principles broached in our work.

We consider it relevant to envisage them as significant milestones, landmarks or obstacles to better understand the genesis of our *SRC*. Indeed, it is enlightening to place in their historic context all of the changes in social structures as well as mind-sets, following the successive scientific revolution owed to Harvey, Copernicus, Newton and Einstein. This approach is embodied in the application of our *SEAM* model that we will expose in its main lines, in order to succeed in uniting split factors into a whole and coherent system. For in so doing, we highlight all the underlying elements that could not only help to *avoid the sclerosis of capitalism*, but also help to revive the economy by switching from a society of exploitation to a *well-being sharing society*.

William Petty in the seventeenth century, Germán Bernácer, John Maynard Keynes, Joseph Schumpeter, François Perroux and Maurice Allais have offered *constructive* theories, which are likely to support our concept of *socially responsible capitalism*. On the other hand, Karl Marx advocated the class struggle as a solution to social and economic issues.

William Petty (England, 1623–1687): From Mercantilism to Liberalism

The historical approach put forth by François Perroux forces us not to neglect the first thoughts of mercantilist and neo-mercantilist writers to whom we owe more than a hint of gratitude for an economic science whose paternity is often attributed, rightly or wrongly, to Adam Smith. Our readers will find in this book several references to a certain number of them with a preponderant place granted to William Petty, economist, physician, "*speculative*" philosopher, inventor, businessman and founding member of the Royal Society and Parliament member. In his whole work, he offers the keys for an effective understanding of issues that underlie more and more complex socioeconomic relations, more and more imposed by a divergent opposition of strengths in the developing globalization context. He deals with currency, interest, capital and its accumulation, tax systems, international relationships, state-controlled economic systems or *laissez-faire*, national accounting, division of labor and full employment. Those topics are still accurate nowadays.

Certainly, this author is reckoned for his quantitative approach to economic phenomena. This fact led him to be known as a founder of statistics, demography and econometrics in the framework of his new concept of political arithmetic, which does not constitute such a dehumanized technique as statistics. In another part, his political anatomy comes from a certain way that a profusion of numerical data should not hide the recourse to *"political observation"*. This method allows him to ascertain the condition of economic growth by an *in situ* analysis of economic and social relations that are considered the most able to ensure the happiness of citizens and national prosperity by taking Ireland as investigation field. The cold scientific curiosity is not here deprived of human warmth.

In SEAM, the arithmetic approach as well as empirical approaches that accumulate only raw data are rejected: both have to be integrated in a single instrument of analysis. The preliminary observation method remains indispensable for a further mathematic modeling. Furthermore, it exists in those different approaches the cult of which could be considered progressive (this is symbolized by the research on blood circulation from Harvey or also the one on movement from Newton). This belief shows the importance given to change process in order to comprehend the economic and social issues.

William Petty's main books are: Traité des taxes et contributions, 1662; Quantulumcunque concerning Money, 1682; Observations upon the Dublin-Bills of mortality and the State of that City, 1683a; Another essay in Political Arithmetick. Concerning the growth of the City of London, 1683b; Two essays in Political Arithmetick, Concerning the People, housing, Hospitals & of London and Paris, 1687; The Political Anatomy of Ireland, 1691; Petty & Graunt, 1899).

Michel Péron has carried out an in-depth study on Petty's works (Péron Michel, *Sir William Petty, sa pensée économique et sociale* [Sir William Petty, his economic and social thought], Thèse d'État soutenue à l'Université Lyon II [Doctoral dissertation defended in Lyon 2 University], 1982, 3 volumes). A biography had been published by Strauss (Strauss, E., *Sir William Petty, Portrait of a Genius*, London, 1954).

Germán Bernácer (1883–1965), Spanish Visionary Economist: From the Roots of Crisis, Before and Beyond Keynes

The economic crisis, emanating from an acuity and unexpected scale that has been hitherto unseen, is asking for reflection and major actions in order to avoid a global catastrophe or the creation of a social and economic rut in most countries that are experiencing globalization effects. Bernácer, the great but little-known Spanish economist, has delivered a clear, basic and original explanation that had been supported by several years of research and observation on the roots of crisis and the way to reduce their effects, at the head of Bank of Spain Department of Studies.

At this time, no one dares to advocate the recourse to a scheduled and centralized economy because it has failed since the collapse of the Berlin wall in 1989. At this time, everyone feels the ferocity of aberrant and destructive attacks on employment, economic prosperity and social well-being, which are dangerous for political democracy. Those have been caused by an uncontrolled excess of financial hurricanes, which periodically overrun the political sphere of real economy and show the cynical arrogance of chaotic excess from speculative markets. At this time, the major parts of states are bankrupted, and sometimes one is tempted to trust the illusionary promise of welfare state from Keynes, that is rescuing the bereft and lost citizen. It matters in this context to bring the light of the robust theory, proposed by Germán Bernácer, on the structural and chronic explanation of crisis. He calls for more actions that are radical on economic and financial policies more sustainable than the vain handling on currencies or the ineffective gesticulations aiming at regulating the polemic and outrageous speculative games of financial markets. Those actions belong to SRC ahead of its time. They also call for more courageous and less demagogical policies in a short-term view from public authorities.

Bernácer was a visionary supported by a rigorous scientific method, which he had inherited from his training as a physicist (he also taught physics all his life). In early 1916 he published a book entitled *Happiness and Society. Essay on social mechanics*. A few years later in 1922, he published his seminal article on the theory of disposable funds as an explanation for economic crisis and social problems, i.e., unemployment. This article inspired some famous scholars, in particular Anglo-Saxons and German economists. Before the *General Theory* of Keynes (1936), Bernácer set forth the very fundamentals of modern macroeconomic theory by grounding it on three pillars: functional theory of currency, synthetic and functional theory of rate of interest and structural theory of economic crisis. These pillars are related to the existence of speculative markets for goods that yield unearned income, i.e., goods that provide income without labor, neither entrepreneur's risk or real and shareable value added between stakeholders, which are the actors of the social and economic game.

Germán Bernácer was born in Alicante (Spain) in 1883. He attended a business school and earned the first rank to the competitive recruitment exam of industrial physics. He was the cofounder of a cultural club in Alicante, which got a certain reputation by the fact that some of his friends, writer Gabriel Miró and composer Oscar Esplá were also attending. Bernácer soon interested himself in economics. He had discovered it alone with his books and thoughts. He was deemed noteworthy by the famous Spanish sociologist José Ortega y Gasset in the last days of Alphonse XIII's monarchy. Bernácer founded and managed the department of studies of the Bank of Spain, dating from the early advent of the Second Spanish Republic in 1931. In Madrid, Bernácer jointly carried out his physics lessons at the High Business School and the supervision of studies at the Bank of Spain until his retirement in 1955. He died in San Juan de Alicante in 1965.

A "Keynesian" Before Keynes?

Since the publication of his first book in 1916 "*Happiness and Society. Essay on social mechanics*", Bernácer presented the first economic analysis whose content would be qualified a few years later as Keynesian, in that period where Keynes, himself, was just a loyal disciple of the Cambridge School. It was in his 1922 article "*the theory of disposable funds as interpretation of crises and social problems*" that Bernácer set forth the fundamentals of his macroeconomic theory and insisted on temporal analysis. Aware of the scientific importance of his contribution, he sent his article to some 150 famous economists worldwide. Among them, spontaneously, Robertson was the first to recognize the importance of Bernácer's theory (see Robertson (1940). *A Spanish contribution to the Theory of Fluctuations*, Economica, p. 50). Scrupulously, he asserted that he should have been subconsciously impressed by the *successive periods analysis* method employed by Bernácer in 1922 and those he made famous in Robertson's book published four years later "*Banking policy and the price level*".

Bernácer published several articles in Spanish journals and after 1940, especially in international ones in Germany, Italy, Switzerland and France. During the same period, he maintained relationships with several foreign economists: François Perroux, Jacques Rueff, Henri Guitton, André Piatier, Louis Baudin, Andreas Predöhl, Joseph Ackermann, Dennis Holme Robertson, Erich Schneider; Fritz Machlup; Henry Christopher Wallich, Gottfried Haberler and Giovanni Demaria. Thus, Bernácer was well known by his contemporaries but only within a specialized circle of peers who appreciated him a lot. We hold as proof his private correspondence that we got access to in 1971 and that is now on display in Alicante University.

Yet, Bernácer's works were victim to a double combination of factors. In the first part of his works, before 1930, the language in which he expressed himself constituted a serious obstacle to the diffusion of his thought. He was so conscious of this problem that he included a French abstract to his Spanish article on disposable funds when he sent it to his foreign colleagues. In the second part, in those areas where he appeared as a most complete theoretician, more clear-sighted than Keynes, he fell victim to the dominant ideology in economics: Keynesianism, whose historic opportunity (Villey & Nême, 1973, p. 297) was fitted into the political, economic and social events that preceded, accompanied and followed World War II. If it is right that

Bernácer announced the Keynesian theory beginning in 1916, it remains important to understand that in 1922 he overtook it to lead to a real general theory we choose to call a *General Theory of Employment, Unearned Income and Hoarding.*

We are in some ways held to situate Bernácer's contribution in reference to Keynes' contribution because each researcher likes to recognize himself according to a reference system that is well established. However, since the publication of the Keynes' *General Theory*, Bernácer criticized the gaps earlier than his contemporaries from all over the world. He also took care to show to what extent this new dogmatism, proposed by Keynesian followers more than Keynes himself, was dangerous for the achievement of the ultimate objective shared by the two authors: *full employment* and *development of demand.*

Doctrinal Options

Bernácer's doctrinal options are clearly defined. They offer an example of a melodious combination of tendencies whose *origins* are contradictory but also coherent. At the normative scale, Bernácer is a liberal in the sense that he situates the fundaments of responsibility, conscience, knowledge, improvement and transcendence of the material fact at the individual level. However, at the descriptive scale, his analysis is founded essentially on sociological data, far from adopting the individual parameters of psychology abusively annexed by marginal economists and Keynesians themselves.

Among the non-Marxist authors from the first quarter of the nineteenth century, Bernácer is without any doubt the one who gives the greatest importance to social facts in economic analysis. At the normative scale, the social fact position is equally important because in the reform he recommended that we qualified as the *New Economic Regime* (Savall, 1973); production and distribution of the structure is collective. The pivot point is the self-managed micro unit of production, inside a macroeconomic decentralized organization, apart from monetary authority, which should remain centralized.

What is this liberalism that advises in its reform the abolition of unearned income, i.e., goods exposed to speculation in general, such as pieces of art, at least by forbidding their alienation against payment? It is to answer this question that we place Bernácer's economic teachings in a certain Christian humanist trend, both liberal with the respect of the individual and *deeply* reformist by its awareness of man's double status: as an individual entity enjoying a certain autonomy and as one subject into a moving society.

The Methodological Contribution

Bernácer's methodological options are in essence innovative. At the time of his first works (1905–1930), economics saw the triumph of psychological analysis, and the confusion seems to be totally between the different levels of analysis (micro/macro). At this time, economists' worry was to analyze the balance and optimum in a static point of view that Keynes, 20 years later, did not succeed in overcoming in spite of his intuitions on the necessity to integrate **time**. As for Bernácer, he *intentionally built all of his analysis* at the macroeconomic level. Quesnay and Marx outstripped him. The most discriminating point of Bernácer is that his approach is elaborated from a dynamic perspective where time is not a vain, fuzzy concept that is not well integrated, but rather plays a key and *determining* role (Cf. the econometrics model of currency value for Bernácer in *La teoría funcional del dinero*, Consejo Superior de Investigaciones Científicas, Madrid, 1945a; 2nd edition 1956, and *Una economía libre sin crisis y sin paro—A free economy without crisis and without unemployment*, 1945b, 1955).

All Bernácer's works are tinged with the methodological tools he chose: macroeconomy, core concepts' functionality (labor, value, capital, money, etc.), time, structure, history and sociology, positivism, experimental and moderate use of mathematics. This prompted Jacques Rueff to say: *"Bernácer's approach is from econometrics while he affirmed as this other physicist Maurice Allais a few years later"* (*Prix Nobel d'Économie [Economy Nobel Prize Award Discourse]*, *Annales des Mines*, Mars 1989) that each important truth may be expressed in an accessible language, using mathematics to be just present at one moment of the analysis or as an exposition process in its own right.

The General Theory of Employment, Unearned Income and Hoarding

Keynes' forerunner, Bernácer, puts aside every other *objective-constraint* at the high level of employment by introducing an ethical condition: that each human being lives only thanks to the labor supplied by the community, which results from the sum total of individual efforts (Savall, 1974a). This labor is applied to natural and corporeal endowment (land, natural resources in general) and intangible resources (natural human skills) in order to provide products. The only activity that legitimates the appropriation of the product is human labor in all its forms: manual work, administrative work, supervision, management, coordination, etc. Anyway, each individual form of necessary work is useful to the accomplishment of the social object *par excellence*: to produce goods and services in order to satisfy human needs. The division of work implies solidarity and so the abolition of any individual income that should not be engendered by a current or former labor.

Consequently, political and social organization has to allow each person to assume his productive role in society, without any form of restriction. Unemployment constitutes, in a way, the *entropy* of the system. Unemployment is not ineluctable. It is just the natural deterioration process of energy due to time that has to be overcome.

According to Bernácer, the monetary economy is a superior and histori-cal form of social development. However, he notices that one has not set up the institutions that are suitable for the good functioning of this kind of economy. Quite the reverse, this organization has been tainted on the grounds that unearned income created new forms of income by means of individual appropriation of some goods, such as (but not limited to) land. Furthermore, the existence of a market for these unearned-income-yielding assets keep alive the trend toward an unbalanced economic system. This market has engendered a harmful phenomenon of an income that is not based on labor: the interest of capital.

The **rate of interest** is the kind of plague, which seizes up the economic apparatus. Bernácer delivers an original theory, which Robertson underlined in his article by getting closer to Keynes' one, but really, Robertson did not really understand Bernácer's theory. This latter is one of the most synthetic theories: it presents positivist, physiocratic, monetary, real, sociological and functional aspects (and deserves a privileged rank, next to "*dynamic synthe-sis of interest*" from Perroux in 1950; the generalization of Keynes' theory of interest in *Banque* [Banking review]) and Llau (1961) (*The rate of inter-est determination*, Paris: Cujas). It excludes on the other hand one element, which underlies many controversies: the time preference. According to Ber-nácer, interest is not the price of time. His conclusion is logical and coherent: interest is *ultimately* only the appropriation of an income without labor. One has to eliminate it for this reason but also because interest is a struc-ture which fundamentally destabilizes the system, and forces it to choose between *full employment* and monetary stability while those are, according to Bernácer, not only linked but really *inseparable* in this both cybernetic and humanist approach of economic and social organization.

We say that Bernácer's is a cybernetic approach because the physicist he was, until the end, seems to teach the economist that the dynamic process of economic activity has to get back its balance, which implies some con-straints. One of them is the control of currency issuance, not from a point of view we qualify today as monetary, because Bernácer is fiercely against quantitative theory of money and had formulated before Nogaro and Aftalion the *income-theory of money*. All this illustrates another fundamen-tal quality of this author: his approach toward national accounting, which has been demonstrated in his work ever since his first papers, a quarter of century before the first works of specialists in this subject.

Such is Bernácer's superiority on Keynes. He not only preceded the latter by 20 years but also had overcome him before that *General Theory* was published in 1936! Indeed, Bernácer in his dialectic approach of phenom-enon, i.e., from a both dynamic and causal point of view, highlights the interactions of phenomena. He also sees clearly that monetary stability is a condition for sustainably maintaining a high level of employment and that the conjunction of those situations, added to the perfectionist genius of humans, leads naturally to growth and economic and social development.

The unprecedented worldwide crisis of 2007–2008 has revealed the astonishing topicality of Bernácer's theory.

In all his works, Bernácer vigorously criticizes the *noxiousness of inflation*. It is a misleading mirage and a mask, and very dangerous because it tends to cancel the detrimental effects of the real rate of interest, namely the nominal interest rate reduced by inflation. Nevertheless, this advantage is illusory because the prices' and interest rates' instability provoked by these permanent adjustments are obscuring the path, determined by traditional economic decision-making tools. Since the publication of Keynes' general theory in 1936, Bernácer has denounced the chronic inflationist characteristic induced by the *imprudent* and systematic recourse of the state's intervention. This latter cannot ensure on its equity the financing of the needs of economic actors in order to assure growth and qualitative development of their economic and social shared prosperity. Indeed, when the state weighs down taxes, it also sterilizes companies, employment and the creation of decentralized development projects. It also dissuades the entrepreneur from taking risks. Anyway, the state generates a phenomenon of "*economic and entrepreneurial abstentionism*" that is even more toxic than political abstentionism.

In the panic that grasped the whole world between the two world wars in the twentieth century, provoked by the Great Depression of 1929 and the simultaneous rise of fascism and Nazism in certain European countries, Keynes' propositions logically found a very favorable echo and a strong reception from political persons whose premier role had been revaluated accordingly. Indeed, strong doubts, legitimated and proven by the citizen and the complaisant ear, less courageous, have favored *the emergency call* for the interventionist state from certain governments. This was the start of the belief, naturally becoming popular, in the unlimited capacity of a state to address financial, investment and economic impulsion needs, in order to ensure national prosperity.

The reconstruction of destroyed economies during World War II played an important role for the prosperity of the well-known period referred to as "*les 30 glorieuses*" (The Thirty Glorious Years) especially in France, Germany, England and other European countries that had been blighted by the war. The conjunction of this reconstruction and the policies of facilitating financing inspired by Keynes were probably the major cause of those three decades of prosperity without major crisis and constant economic growth. Unfortunately, it went along with an addiction to permanent inflation, which reached high levels during some periods after war and engendered a severe vulnerability regarding *natural* fluctuations of economic activity. That is why the consequences of the Oil Shock from 1973 caused an increase in the level of unemployed persons in France from 500,000 to more than 3 million, the new "standard" for the past 30 years.

Bernácer's influence on our works in economics and management science has been considerable and constant. It is located in the macroeconomic roots of our socioeconomic theory of enterprises and organizations and for the SEAM model (see Part 2: Socioeconomic Management and Theory). All our research works in economics and management science are inspired by Bernácer's legacy—in particular in our natural reflex, which consists of reasoning systematically in terms of *temporal dynamics* by dating each data and analysis variable of economic and organizational phenomena in order to study them by splitting them into successive periods. This allows one to take into account through a *learning process* the knowledge rules acquired during previous periods and to integrate them into the stimulation of the next. This logic of a *heuristic process* helps in improving the quality of forecasts during the decision-making process. We recall that this approach incorporating the learning from successive periods is constant throughout the works of Bernácer. Since 1922, it had inspired the English economist Sir Dennis Robertson when he recognized this influence in his published books from 1926, and explicitly in an article published in February 1940 in the English journal *Economica* "*A Spanish contribution to the Theory of Fluctuations*".

Bernácer's complete works demonstrate his independence of mind, pertaining to the established ideologies that inevitably inspire the trends of economic thought, namely the classical school and its three antagonist relatives: the Marxist criticism and the neo-classic liberal school and its variation, neo-classic Keynesian. This independence has printed his mark on each of our works and fostered us to deliberately adopt a *heterodox* posture. As in natural sciences, it consists of always giving priority to rigorous observation and integrating a strong epistemological reflex in the scientific working process, in order to ensure a suitable level of intrinsic quality, with societal utility and academic credibility.

Our work is in a deadlock with the vain quarrels between old ideologies of outrageous liberalism, failed Marxism or imprudent Keynesianism. Those consist of extending Bernácer's theory, going deeper and making it operational. Therefore, our concept of *socially responsible capitalism* constitutes our proposition to move past the international crisis and to get back on the road toward sustainable and equitable prosperity. Socioeconomic theory tries hard to serve humanist morality and the highest level of possible freedom, a condition of individual and collective sustainable *dignity*. The **hyperfinancial** and speculative brands of capitalism arouse the state's intervention, which is becoming less and less effective in the framework of globalization and by supposing that it will not lead to the return of a "liberty killer communism".

John Maynard Keynes (England, 1883–1946): The 20th Century's Most Popular Economist?

After World War I, Great Britain adopted a deflationist policy that has incurred, since 1924, the unemployment of one million workers. Lloyd George proposed a policy of public construction, an idea advocated by the economist John Maynard Keynes. Those, instead of really anticipating on events by prospective analyses, knows at least how to hold in all what is expressed, written or made in this period in terms of clear-sighted concepts which he arranges in a new theory. However, conservatives continued to carry out a traditional policy up until the great crisis of 1929. Keynes proposed, besides, the devaluation of the pound, which was realized in 1931. As a result, the crisis became less intense in Great Britain than elsewhere: but it is reported of its main competitor, Germany, that unemployment rose in 1932 to afflict half of that nation's industrial population. From his accession, Hitler, advised by astute financiers such as the famous Dr. Schacht, carried out a policy of major works, which responded to industry's demands, with state financing, and picked up the German economy. This is the consolidation of this regrowth by seeking external outlets that gave the Third Reich the pretext for a territorial expansion.

This economic situation observed by Keynes inspired in him a new conception of the theory of economic equilibrium. He noticed that this is not granted by classical mechanisms (which determines his opposition to classical mainstream thesis) and that it establishes itself under psychological influences into an *underemployment* level, which calls for state intervention according to him. He exposed a new theory in support of a new economic policy.

J. M. Keynes was the son of a logic and political economy professor from the famous University of Cambridge. He studied in Eton College and worked in the *Civil Service* the high English functionaries' profession where he realized an intermittent career before he became professor of political economy in Cambridge University. More than an academic, Keynes was a man of action who closely followed business and public lives. He enriched himself through favorable Stock Exchange speculations; he managed an insurance company and was several times a Government advisor. He was appointed the director of the National England Bank and led the British delegation to the Bretton Woods Conference, in 1944, where the after-war international monetary system was organized, according to the American delegate's plan and not according Keynes' plan. On the eve of his death, Keynes tried to negotiate an important loan from the USA in favor of England, but he did not succeed.

He was one of the few economists to taste celebrity in his lifetime. Linked to the liberal party, he was ennobled in 1942 and became Lord Keynes, first baron of Tilton. The man was a philanthropist, an artist and a curious mind in all domains with a taste for eccentricities in his life and in some aspects, in his works. He married a dancer of the Diaghilev ballet.

The range of his works has not always been coherent. He abandoned in his *General Theory* his analysis of equality between saving and investment, which is central in his, *The General Theory of Employment, Interest and Money*. He also renounced his severe judgment on saving in *How to pay for the war* that is in his previous works. The general attitude of Keynes is one of an enlightened bourgeois, attentive to economic issues of his time, keen to save the private enterprise regime by leaving the integral *laissez-faire* in place. He vigorously criticized the conservative government of his country and was clearly opposed to socialism.

Classical and Neoclassical Theories Criticism

Keynes rejects the automaticity of the full employment equilibrium founded on the outlet law, the price mechanism and money neutrality. He particularly remains attentive on the interest and on money, the price for renouncing to consumption transferred to the saver. According to Keynes, the rate of interest is not a reward; the reward for renouncing to liquidities does not depend on capital supply and demand but on two factors that he analyzes.

The first factor is qualitative, from psychological order: it depends on the degree of savers' preference for liquidity. Here, Keynes is close to the "float desire" of Walras, but he is inspired by disposable funds analysis from Bernácer. Keynes distinguishes three motifs: the float of *transactions* in order to face the usual exchanges, of *precaution* (hoard money) and of *speculation* (wiggle room in order to take advantage of a gap in securities prices). The second factor is a quantitative element, the varying quantity of money in circulation. Money supply acts on the level of the rate of interest and guides the decision to invest. Money plays an active role that could lead (the increasing of money supply makes the interest rate low, which stimulates the investment) or brake (the preference for liquidity improves the interest rate level).

The Keynesian theory of equilibrium has been elaborated in two steps. The publication of *a treatise on money*, in late 1930 at the start of the Great Depression, is the first step. By taking back the distinction of the two production sectors from Marx and Wicksell, the one from equipment goods and the other from consumption goods, Keynes obscures the issue of global balance in the first one by affirming that production is made according to demand. The issue of global equilibrium is reduced to the production of consumption goods. Prices are getting high and exceptional profits are appearing and engender the expansion of activity, but the economy as a whole is tending to naturally slow down. The excess of investment is explained by innovation (new products or outlets) or by a psychological factor of trust in business. As for stopping expansion, it is generated by the excess of equipment, whose accumulation entails, at a certain time, the stroke of expansion. The hypothesis of expansion is not very strong in Keynes' analysis, because the latter is influenced by the economic context, which is at this moment depressive. He does not exploit the mechanism of cumulative processes highlighted by Wickseil (who he admitted be inspired by) and by Bernácer (who he does not speak about, despite having met him in Madrid before World War II in 1930). The Spanish economist would recognize the mark of his article from 1922 in the general approach in *A treatise on money*, Keynes' book, and would find incoherent the abandonment of hypothesis of inequalities between savings and investment in the *General Theory of Employment, Interest and Money*. More recently, other commentators have informed this fact (Daniel Villey & Colette Nême, *Petite Histoire des grandes doctrines économiques* [Little History of great economic doctrines], 1973).

Less than six years after *A treatise on money*, Keynes publishes his *General Theory of Employment, Interest and Money* (1936), a book that has a considerable impact, more for economy theoreticians than practitioners: a general theory of balance in which he explains the relationships between the level of employment, interest and money. He does not hesitate to renounce the notion of balance between savings and investment, which he introduces in *A treatise on money*. By taking up the objective of explaining permanent unemployment, he elaborated a doubtful notion of underemployment equilibrium, which would seduce generations of economists. Bernácer, as you have seen before, had the same objective, but with his dynamic reasoning, he did not need to give concessions to mainstream analysis, forcing him to permit the economic movements to enter the baking pan of equilibrium. Keynes, whatever he said, was regressing regarding to his *treatise* and immured again his analysis into the static framework of a supposed equilibrium; we will go back to this criticism.

Keynes would seek to escape from the mainstream analysis within his theory. In fact, he keeps away from it, especially with his doctrine and with his propositions of economic policy. His theory is not compatible with his intentions, and it is with several dodgings that he believes himself to reach the necessary demonstration for the consolidated economic policy he advocates. He subordinates his analysis to his political objective, without reaching that coherence, which demands a scientific analysis. Keynes' theory fits into the short period defined by Marshall; this option allows Keynes (at least he believes so) to affirm that some variables of activities remain constant during the analysis. At the same time, he endeavors, following Swedish School, to take time into account by considering entrepreneurs' anticipations. The levels of production and employment depend only on the future demand, given their production costs. The *effective demand* (in French the forecasted demand), a notion inspired by Malthus, is the global income that employers hope to get from the employment volume they decide to implement.

The general and spontaneous balance results from three categories of decisions: one from entrepreneurs, one from consumers and one from savers. In order to elaborate his model, Keynes needs free variables: he assures that these three types of decision are independent. From the supply side, the incitation of entrepreneurs to invest depends on the gap between expected profit (marginal effectiveness of capital) and the interest of capital. This variable masters the supply level. The marginal effectiveness reasoning is partly borrowed from Walras (there is decision to invest when the marginal effectiveness of capital is higher than the rate of interest) and partly innovative (the rate of interest is mainly a monetary phenomenon. He depends on supply money and not only from the fraction of saved funds but also from the preference for liquidity). If the investment rate is low, that means the marginal effectiveness of capital is too low compared to investment rate.

The difference between Keynes and mainstream economists lies in the fact that he explains the equilibrium based on income (reminding us that Bernácer, the first, put the light on income by elaborating his income-theory of money) and that classical economists explain it through prices. The adjustment to the equilibrium is made through income, created and multiplied by the decision to invest taken by the producer. As Bernácer, Keynes insists on the effect that creates investment incomes. Investment plays a main role compared to savings: the classical sequence is tilted. We find here the influence of Schumpeter on Keynes who, as his English contemporaries (especially Hawtrey) did, gives a good rank for credit. Banking assistance could foster investment, which would produce its counterpart in savings and should realize the equilibrium. The successful experience of Dr. Schacht in Germany in 1933–1936 is founded on this chaining. In an underemployment situation, the rising of investment from companies (starting from former savings, loan or inflation) provokes the rising of entrepreneurs and workers employed in production incomes of investment goods who, formerly, were unemployed. It follows the rise of national income.

The Keynesian Doctrine and Keynes' Influence on Development of Economic Thought in the Twentieth Century

Keynes observes the harmful effects of deflation policy carried out since the pound revaluation in 1925. This is the entire policy of Great Britain in the nineteenth century that Keynes questions. In place of the savings supportive policy, he substitutes expenses' policy; the one of gold standard and the budgetary balance has to be loosened at least, and he recommends a neo-protectionism in order to face uncontrolled freedom.

The unearned-income recipient, as non-entrepreneur capitalist, should disappear progressively because he has no socially useful function. "The euthanasia of the unearned-incomer" will be obtained by the high decrease of the rate of interest, thereby causing a relative scarcity of capital. Therefore, Keynes shares the opinions of Proudhon and Bernácer, who fight against unearned income. As did the Spanish economist, the English one proposes a policy that discourages hoarding: Bernácer recommends a radical action, suppressing the sales of unearned-income-yielding goods; Keynes advocates a tax policy of income reallocation, thinking that both reduction of fortunes and increasing of small incomes should reduce the influence of incomes that tend toward saving and would increase the incomes of those who have a high propensity for consumption.

Unlike several great economists, Keynes had the luck to see his ideas implemented in many countries and extended by other economic theorists.

The adoption of Keynes' ideas has been facilitated by the simplicity of his propositions: full employment, public investment, low rates of interest. Even the principle of state interventionism on that economy was in that sense an historic evolution of the twentieth century. The way to present some analyses, some proposals, associated with Keynes' public life had a considerable impact. The publishing of *General Theory of Employment, Interest and Money* in 1936 has been prepared and elaborated through state-of-the-art marketing. The theory core was held constant from 1930 to 1940 by changing waves of conjuncture and influenced by the contributions of other theoreticians less than opportunists, in the proper sense or less clear-sighted.

In spite of his past successes and his influence, the end of Keynes' career is obscured by two failings. He took part in the 1944 Bretton Woods Conference, where the new global monetary system should have been released. Keynes had prepared a reconstruction plan for an international exchange system aiming at replacing gold with banking operations and instituted a supranational currency: the "bancor". However, it was the American White plan, which was approved: it marked beginning of the dollar's supremacy and allowed its development, while Keynes' plan depended on the deposit of U.S. gold into an international bank. For the same reasons, his second failure, in all likelihood, consisted of Keynes' negotiation failure for an important credit from USA and GB. He was luckier within national policies of full employment that followed the major part of industrialized or barely, exception for Germany, which, after war, followed quite the reverse, a neoliberal policy under the guidance of Dr. Erhard.

Critical Assessment of Keynes' Contribution to Economics

Keynes was a happy master: he got several disciples, especially in Anglo-Saxon countries but not only there. His continuators had précised, extended and detailed his analysis and had contributed to develop its operational prolongations. A neo-Marxist stream, born in one of the post-Keynesian families, has been developed (Mrs. Joan Robinson, Nicholas Kaldor, Piero Sraffa) by synthesis efforts, which could be seductive for a part of the younger generations of economists and are situated between Marxist theory and Keynesian theory. Some commentators affirm that Keynesianism completes the insufficiencies of Marxist economic theory and that Marxism completes the insufficiency of Keynesianism social theory. Some orthodox Marxists think, *on the contrary*, that Keynesianism is the last resort for a decadent capitalism. At least, neo-liberals think that Keynes left a bastard to the economic science that does not innovate in terms of materialism while subjecting economic activity to more and more of the ponderousness of state intervention.

Too often, Keynes has been presented as an innovative theoretician in order to not be tempted to appreciate his real theoretical contribution by dissociating what is from him and what he borrowed from trailblazers.

However, the confusion must be avoided between the historical interest of certain analysis that has incontestably guided the economic policy of this second tierce from the nineteenth century and the solidity of a so-called revolutionary theory whose limits and ambiguities could be demonstrated. A deeper examination shows that conceptual innovations from Keynes are not so numerous as they seem to be. The study of Spanish Bernácer works shows his historical anteriority and his superiority on key points when compared to Keynesian analysis. Keynes had discreetly recognized some quotations and some influences (Malthus. Wicksell and economists from Stockholm School and Robertson). By reversing the outlet law from Say, which had been done before, Keynes goes back to Malthius by retaining the principle that demand is that which arouses production. With that difference, being influenced by Swedish school of anticipations, Keynes takes into account the future demand and not the current one. The income-revenue, which is, in all likelihood, the less controversial contribution of Keynesian works, *had been elaborated before him by Bernácer*; Aftalion and Nogaro also stressed it.

Keynes did not build a theory of cycles. He does not understand (while Bernácer made an admirable analysis on this point) how full employment and inflation could provoke underemployment and start over a cumulative process of deflation. The famous *multiplier*, which the majority of contemporary economists are celebrating or have celebrated, is accountable for the same criticism. Started from a right intuition (the propagation of effects on income from an autonomous investment), Keynes deduced an automatism of multiplication from income based on a constant propensity for consuming, on the implicit confusion, which he makes between saving and hoarding, and also on the constancy of propagations' effect in time.

Keynes induces a caricature of saving. Keynesian theory of the rate of interest is only monetary, which economists no longer believe. The interest is not an independent variable, unlike Keynes affirms, because it is itself a function of credit which depends on investment, another variable of the model. Keynes, Bernácer and Wicksell should be subject to the same criticism; despite the importance of the rate of interest, the observation of facts shows that innovation weights more in the decision to invest. On this point, Schumpeter is overcoming the other heterodoxies, and Perroux will generalize the notion of innovation.

As to investment, Keynes obscures the issue of its quality. Bernácer vigorously criticizes (as did several commentators that followed him) the idea in which one makes people to work without being worried about the social utility for such an investment, just for its effect of supplying them an income. The English author loses vigor in his argumentation by recommending, if the worst comes to the worst, to dig unnecessary holes! Investments and human labor are endless. Keynes gets merits, as does Bernácer, to define a social horizon to economic policy: that of full employment. Nevertheless, he is at the same time focused by this objective, tending not to see that the instability of prices and money could jeopardize the realization or the maintenance of this objective (criticism from Bernácer and Rueff), and he neglects to readdress the social issue in its globalism. Bernácer, even more liberal than Keynes, is recommending the most far-reaching reforms in terms of economic and production system structures.

Bernácer, while a liberal, and also retaining the profit motive, discusses the materialism of capitalist systems and proposes deep reforms, by conserving the structure of market economy. Keynes' objective of full employment for all remains quantitative because it does not include the issues of quality of working life and does not take into account the intensity phenomenon to which Bernácer's analysis is sensitive: the elasticity of employment level, wages and yields.

The social and economic facts themselves have contradicted the *General Theory of Employment, Interest and Money* and almost its universal ambition. The nominal interest rate has not progressed, unlike what Keynes forecasted, in nations where functional financial policy has been applied. This type of policy has not always proved the efficacy of the act of direct tax deduction, because it ignores the principle of agents' reactions to state intervention. Keynes is here caught on the field he chose: psychology. Indeed, maybe his theory failed more by its lack of psychology than by excess. The economic history, since the publication of the *General Theory of Employment, Interest and Money*, 80 years ago, has not validated the assumption about stagnancy, founded on a decrease in marginal effectiveness of capital and the decline of investment opportunities, assumptions that flourished in the Anglo-Saxon world of 1930 (Keynes, Hansen, Robertson and even Schumpeter). Without falling into euphoria, we may consider that the human genius has demonstrated its capacity of adaptation, creation and technical progress. Social and economic progress, more dependent upon political structures, has not reached its expected level of real quality. Some have not followed the budgetary deficit policy (Germany and Great Britain). On the other hand, the worries expressed by neo-liberals (Hahn: *"l'engrenage de l'intervention"* [the gears of intervention]) have been realized by the increasing dominance of states on economic activity. However, should this evolution owe anything to Keynesian theory?

In many ways, on doctrinal and theoretical stakes, Keynes' ideas have become obsolete. They have suffered from the lack of a true prospective long-term vision (while Schumpeter has one) and from the position of Keynes himself, a theoretician, regarding the external environment. The British economist, excessively pragmatic, let his theory wander at the whim of waves of economic conjuncture, and his theoretical contribution seems late compared to issues that express the economic universe to economics. Keynes, despite his errors and gaps, helped us, according to Schumpeter's expression, to become better economists. The seductive attempt to synthesize justice and prosperity that he presented has stimulated economic action and research: Keynes is more admirable for the progress he stimulated than for the qualities of his own theory.

Joseph Schumpeter (Austria, 1883–1950), Entrepreneur, Politician, Economist: The General Mobility of Innovation

Joseph Schumpeter was an Austrian economist (1883–1950). With a law background, he was a lawyer for Cairo Mixed Court before serving as the Austrian finance minister in 1919–1920. Starting in 1927, he taught at Harvard University, having also been a professor at Columbia University from 1913 to 1914. The major books that marked his works are "*The theory of economic development: an inquiry into profits, capital credit, interest and the business cycle*" (1935), "*History of Economic analysis*" (this book published posthumously in 1954), "*Business cycles*" (1939) and "*Capitalism, socialism and democracy*" (1942). Joseph Schumpeter was a heterodox economist, neither Keynesian nor neoclassical, that has often been presented as consistent regarding to the Austrian school of economics.

Major Schumpeterian ideas can be summed up in five themes: economic and technological rhythms, innovation and creative destruction, the role of the entrepreneur, technical progress and social change, and the end of capitalism.

Economic and Technological Rhythms

According to Schumpeter, the economy is characterized by the regular alternating of prosperity and depression cycles. His analysis for these cycles could be summarized as well: expansion phases are characterized by high profits that engender both investments and an increase of demand. The credits granted generate inflation of production and consumption goods. Deflation phases are emphasized by the recovering of credits; profit opportunities are decreasing, and bankruptcies appear. The *imitation* entails the nature of markets, the saturation and subsequent descent of monopolistic unearned income markets and therefore investment, which in its turn entails a decrease in the level of activity. Deflation phases may be overcome only if there are waves of innovation.

Innovation and Creative Destruction

Indeed, Schumpeter explains economic cycles with the innovation phenomenon, especially with innovative clusters: technical progress appears as clusters or swarms. A major innovation is often a disruptive innovation for technical or scientific progress, which spurs in its turn other innovations. After this major innovation, industrial cycles are first characterized by a growth phase, job creation and after, a depression phase because the next cycle of innovations chases out old-fashioned companies, which provokes job destruction, thence the term of creative destruction proposed by Schumpeter in 1942. Creative destruction, according to Schumpeter, is the characteristic of capitalist systems, and his analysis gets closer to that of the cycles identified by Kondratiev or Juglar.

Innovation is an ambivalent phenomenon, both a source of growth and a crisis factor. The succession of expansion and deflation phases is explained by the arrival of innovations in clusters, at the trough of the depression wave. Indeed, the crisis shakes up established positions, by inciting people to explore new ideas and open opportunities. *A contrario* in stable periods, the initiatives are stuck, the innovations are limited . . . this is how a new recession phase is prepared, then a crisis. Innovation plays a key role in the impulse of economic systems. The starting point is stationary economy, characterized by general equilibrium, free competition, private property and the division of work between actors whose predictable behaviors and adapting mechanisms lead to this stable state. *Routine* is broken down thanks to innovations, which are boosted by the **entrepreneur**—which is to say the qualitative transformation of production system whose determinant is innovation. It might be the product or process of innovation, in terms of manufacturing processes. According to Schumpeter (1911), in this second type, the central actor is the entrepreneur. This author identified five types of innovation focused on: consumption goods (products, services, new raw material sources); new production methods; new transportation methods; new markets; at least new industrial organizational methods.

Innovation leads to a favorable position into its business sector, its diffusion comes down to trade rights that are similar to a monopoly. According to Schumpeter, monopolies born from innovation are necessary for good functioning of an economy. From a competitive point of view, the entrepreneur has to lower his production costs by achieving economies of scale in order to restore his margin. A monopolistic or oligopolistic economy is not obviously negative because leading companies are earning an "excess-profit", which allows them to innovate. Then innovation produces positive externalities in terms of a driving force on economic sectors. This monopoly or oligopoly situation does not last because the existence of "excess-profits" forces other entrepreneurs to ceaselessly differentiate or lower their prices. Imitating strategies bring innovations in clusters: the aggregation of innovations generated by the success of an innovative entrepreneur, whose position is temporarily leading, spurs imitative strategic behaviors. The degree and the scale of innovation depend on the entrepreneur's predisposition to take risks and seek exploitable inventions.

The Entrepreneur's Role

Schumpeter established a clear *distinction* between entrepreneurs, managers and owners. According to him, being an entrepreneur is generally a temporary function. The entrepreneur is not the inventor of a discovery; he or she is the one who knows how to introduce it into industry, by realizing a new combination within introduced innovations. Four forms of entrepreneurs have succeeded historically according to Schumpeter (Perroux, 1935): the manufacturer-merchant, when property and entrepreneur's position were linked and even transmitted through heredity, the industrial captain, the non-capitalist director and the founder.

According to Perroux (Introduction to Joseph Schumpeter's book (1911) "*Théorie de l'évolution économique. Recherches sur le profit, le crédit, l'intérêt et le cycle de la conjuncture*" [The theory of economic development: an inquiry into profits, capital credit, interest and the business cycle] French translation, 1935), "*He [the entrepreneur] realizes earnings resulting from the running of new combinations or profits on which the capitalist deducts a kind of tax: the interest. The crises are explained by the distress that results from the execution of the new combination and by the mode of appearance from entrepreneurs on the economic scenery*". The entrepreneur is of course motivated in realizing benefits, but his conception of profit is unique. Indeed, he is motivated by a whole of irrational motive, among which the power will, the taste for victory and adventure, or the simple joy to give life to uncommon ideas. The profit is the creative sanction for the risks undertaken. This conception is the opposite for classical economists and Marxists for whom profit corresponds to the confiscation of capital gain from the workers by unearned-income perceivers.

Schumpeter does not confuse the chief executive officer, simple administrator, or the unearned-income receiving capitalist, owner of the means of production, with the entrepreneur, who is an adventurer who gets off the beaten track, pulling other persons along, and beats change resistance in order to question the ambient conformism. For Schumpeter, Henry Ford, for example, was not an entrepreneur in 1906. He became so in 1909 when he started to produce the T1 model for a very low price. The entrepreneur's specific function is to beat both objective and subjective orders of resistance, and in particular, the social and psychological ones, in order to make the innovations accepted by the workforce as well as consumers.

Technical Progress and Social Change

The **innovative entrepreneur** inspires many imitators, which engender important changes in matters of work organization and the production function. The brand-new work organization constitutes for Schumpeter a radical innovation. However, from the consumer point of view, innovation entails also a changed mode of consumption and answers non-satisfied needs, even creates new ones. The combination of capital and labor production factors is thus modified and entails the mobility of production means, a change in the nature of employment qualifications, a new spatial distribution for jobs or a change in ratios of power between countries. Notwithstanding, one could

emphasize that Schumpeter, unlike Galbraith, did not anticipate the reorganization of direction and governance instances of companies, with the apparition of boards, supervisory boards, general assembly, techno-structure, etc.

The End of Capitalism

In "Capitalism, socialism and democracy" (1942), Joseph Schumpeter is
convinced of the benefits of capitalism, but he also considers its collapse
unavoidable. Indeed, the success of capitalism leads to the concentration of
capital into big companies managed by CEOs, simple administrators, and
owned by capitalists who are the real owners of these companies. Quite
the opposite of Marx, he does not think it is the proletariat who will put
an end to capitalism, but rather the support of the major part of intellectuals. Indeed, capitalism generates development of the educational system
and overproduction of intellectuals. The latter, considering themselves as
discredited and rather not much paid, have every interest in fighting against
capitalism and deluge the public opinion with discourses facing money and
enterprise's spirit. According to Schumpeter, they are focusing the general
hostility against capitalism, which is progressively immobilizing from the
inside.

The intellectual and social climate necessary to the entrepreneurial spirit
and innovation leads the replacement of capitalism with socialism to be
paralyzing. To be popular, governments develop a tax state and transfer producers' incomes to non-producers, and then demoralize investment saving
in favor of consumption. Democratically elected governments are tending to
foster a short-term focus. According to Schumpeter, capitalism can only last
if the entrepreneurial mind-set, which makes its strength, carries on. Indeed,
the big company struggles with any weak will of imagination because of
the multiplication of managing executive, experts and bureaucrats who are
reasoning in terms of career, regular incomes and social position, and are
not tending to take risks. For these reasons, Schumpeter forecasts the end of
capitalism. According to some authors, if he dressed up like a socialist partisan, it was in order to encourage Marx's disciples to read his works, hoping
that they would recognize from themselves socialism's idiosyncrasies.

The contemporary works on entrepreneurship may be gathered according to Fayolle and Verstraete (Paradigmes et entrepreneuriat [*Paradigms and
entrepreneurship*], in *Revue de l'Entrepreneuriat*, 2005, pp. 35–52) into
four paradigms: one of them analyzes the tight links between entrepreneurship and innovation, finding its source in Schumpeter's fecund works. The
second one is based on Austrian school of economics and is interested in
entrepreneurship based on the detection of business opportunities. The third
one studies entrepreneurship as a phenomenon of both value and wealth
creation, according Ronstadt's and Bruyat's works. At least the fourth one
concentrates itself on the creation of the organization by the entrepreneur
(Gardner & Verstraete).

According to François Perroux (1965) in his imposing introduction to the 1911 book of Joseph Schumpeter, translated into French in 1935 *"Schumpeter has tempted the synthesis of Austrian school and Lausanne's school systems in one part, and in the other hand, the synthesis of both historical and sociological system of Werner Sombart and the one's from Max Weber"*(Schumpeter & Anstett, 1935, pp. 16–17). Even if not expressed, the notion of essential economy opposed to concrete economy impregnates the whole works of Schumpeter and puts the stress on the opposition between static and dynamic. Schumpeter's theory is essentially a qualitative theory because it lies on the idea of a new combination between static and dynamic. Notwithstanding, according to Perroux, Schumpeter neglected to solve the issue of the non-insurable risks of production.

François Perroux (France, 1903–1987): To the Transcendence of Two Main Streams in Economic Thought

The two paradigms of modern economic thought are, on one hand, mainstream neoclassicism with its classic roots and its Keynesian prolongations, and on the other hand, Marxism to which one could add some aspects from institutionalism. Perroux, an authentic heterodox (as Bernácer), refuses to choose and to lock his thinking system in such alternative. His works, first inspired by neo-marginals, are oriented to Keynesianism and later gain real autonomy by taking into account phenomena that are most often excluded from the consideration of an economy, especially power (domination effect, which he identifies in his famous 1948 article). Through the reciprocal integration of paradigms, in all of the ways they are compatible, Perroux transcends the dichotomy of the twentieth-century economic thought. His disciples sometimes claim to be from the neoclassic school, sometimes the Marxist school or even from a very particular branch of liberal heterodoxy, occasionally called the radical school.

His works realize a fortunate synthesis between great disciplines, which stimulate economics: social sciences (sociology, history, etc.) and some hard sciences (mathematics, physics and their applications: econometrics, quantitative). The authentic interdisciplinary approach which inspires the economic analysis of Perroux is not only the cause of the richness and relevance of his personal works, but it also explains the attraction of his work for several generations of young economists and their impulsion to carry forward his influence via their own scientific creations. The renewal of his works' "impact on the actual young generation is revealing the influence of Perroux's thought, despite the minimal inclusion of his works in academic training programs".

Perroux refutes dominant mainstream theories, whether it be Walraso-Paretian equilibrium, neoclassical approach fundamentals, or Marxist dialectics (Marcuse, 1970). He creates new concepts and rebuilds a "General Theory of General EquilibriumTheory".

The Refutation of Dominant Theories: Walraso-Paretian Equilibrium and Marxism

A former and fervent adept of neo-marginals, which he knew through Schumpeter, von Mises and von Hayek, for whom he hoped getting a fundamental economy, Perroux took an interest in Keynesian theory, on which he gave one of the first presentations in 1947. However, from 1950 on, he was among the first and most vigorous critics of its deficiencies and after that he conceived the project for a "generalization of General Theory". This is the title he gave to a book he published that year. In this, he reproaches Keynes for obscuring a certain number of difficulties such as aggregate analysis and global scales, the rudimentary characteristic of conceptual categories, and the transition to a real generalized theory of harmonized growth.

Perroux does not satisfy himself with a neoclassical analysis founded implicitly on egalitarian individualism and built on the assumption of balanced and equal strength relationships between agents (individuals, firms and nations). The implicit rejection from classical and neoclassical analyses of strengths, pressure, constraints and domination phenomena that the pure economy confines in the lumber-room of extra-economic data, embarrass him. The economy becomes once again a science of Man and distances itself from physical sciences, which are often badly assimilated by the economists.

The starting point of Perroux's refutation is noticing a whole host of very influential phenomena in this second part of the twentieth century and which mainstream classical and neoclassical theories do not take into consideration: the oligopolistic structures of strategic production industries; multinational companies whose power challenges modern states; the relationships between economic units and their environment; the external economies realized in profit of some agents and to the detriment of others; the multiplication of social costs; the asymmetric relationships in economic activity, etc. Nevertheless, most of those phenomena are located outside the market, in such a way that the basic hypothesis of pure and perfect competition ignores.

The ambitious project he formed to generalize the general theory of competition equilibrium, aimed at integrating economic phenomena really observed in a scientifically controlled test, inspires an imminent criticism of Walraso-Paretian equilibrium. There are four essential features in this theory:

> *Agents' independence* from one another: the system is frozen by indifference; the only means of communication between them is reduced to the price of products and services;

> The *limitation* of each unit by the others' actions: agents are so to speak inert, without life; they are enduring the maximization, without being able to act on it; prices and the level of equilibrium are mathematically co-determined: no agent is master of its decisions.

The *coincidence* of individual and social optimums: the social optimum is obtained through the addition of individual optimums, founded on marginal utilities of different agents.

The *equivalence in exchange*: agents are supposed to be equal and with no differentiated negotiation power.

One could not blame the model in that it simplifies the reality, for which it proposes to give a pedagogic and operating representations. But what one could ask him to do (François Perroux as well as Joan Robinson, the Marxist and heterodox disciple of Keynes) is not to destroy the scientific object. This is, however, what the Walraso-Paretian model did, by reducing economic analysis to a market study of pure and perfect competition, by annihilating the economic agent who is a decision-maker. The characteristics of the Walraso-Paretian equilibrium are explained by philosophical, moral and scientific assumptions which dominate in this bourgeois period where it seizes the day: individualism from Kant's inspiration (continental), or pragmatic (Anglo-Saxon); egalitarianism and its political expressions (parliamentarian democracy) and mathematical (excerpted from Lagrange's mechanism, 1788, which inspired, more than a century later, Pareto and his current disciples).

Perroux blames even the essence of such theory, based on the hypothesis of the sanitized homogeneity of human agents, goods, and services that they employ. Keynesian theory deserves the same critique.

François Perroux (Lyon, 1903—Paris, 1987) is the French economist of the twentieth century who contributed the most to economic science's progress. His influence abroad is considerable, and some of his books are translated into seven languages. He belongs to more than 15 academies, in France and abroad. Notably, he was the member of British Academy and American Academic Association. He taught in more than 30 countries of America, Europe, Africa and Asia, especially at Harvard University. He was an honorary doctor of more than 20 universities, in America and Europe.

He dedicated 27 books to economic analysis, covering a half-century of contributions to contemporary economic thought, and nine books to social issues. He supervised the writing of the *Encyclopédie française* volume, dedicated to the economic and social universe, published in 1960 and unanimously greeted (see *References*). He was also member of the Conseil économique and social [*French Economic and Social Council*] and of Commission des comptes de la nation [*National Audit Board*]. His disciples and researchers such as François Divisia, René Roy, Maurice Allais from the *Institut de Science Économique Appliquée* [Applied Economic Science Institute] are numerous in Academy and in French economic administration.

Perroux's criticism of the automaticity of equilibrium through prices is based on the idea that *agents have a certain capacity to modify their environment*, according more various information than the only pricing system, and that they are gifted *a priori* from an unequaled energy which makes the automatic balancing toward general equilibrium of economy impossible.

His methodology presents some points of contact with Marxist theory. This explains its influence on some domains of contemporary Marxist thought; he always situates the economic phenomenon in a social and historical context. However, Perroux is quite toppled from the essential categories of Marxist's theory. He especially criticizes historical materialism, even the dialectic negativism of some neo-Marxists. He rejects determinism and advocates for an economic voluntarism, which takes its roots in his philosophy from Christian inspiration.

Perroux's economic analysis is fundamentally **dialectic**, but his dialectics are generalized and synthetic, in Hegel's sense. It admits tightest categories; it rejects the simplest dichotomy on which the class struggle is founded and the fatalist end of this one: communism. The ineluctable characteristic of the dialectic movement toward this issue results, according to him, in the arbitral sorting of contradictions, which have really been observed. The economic dialectic of Perroux is closer to the general sociological analysis of power; it admits workers' diversification, conflicts of interests and ideologies between workers subsections, a discrepancy between the favored classes from industry and the rest of workers, the generalized claim in the "multiclass mass". It includes its own overtaking: all groups, *a priori* unequal, evolves in a universe of struggle-competition, conflicts and dialogs, in order to own and employ rare goods. The development of society intended by Perroux is one from a focus on growth to a participative society where objectives would be defined by social dialog, based on objective information and under the attentive supervision of public authority.

Perroux rejects the strength-ideas of Marxist analysis: capital gain, the organic composition of capital, the so-called trend laws for equalizing profit rates and their decrease, laws contradicted by strategies of profit implemented by transnational units. He does not admit the *exclusive* characteristics of class and class struggle, neither the fact that the worker's class be the *sole* agent of social revolution because it still not homogenized. It is, in reality, in minority (less than a tierce of the active population) and forced to seek for alliances.

Perroux is distinguishing the advent of mass and masses (then joining the Spanish philosopher José Ortega y Gasset) and classes. This rising results in a certain measure of frame dynamics. He considers that the concept of class struggle must be revamped to accommodate a larger scale of struggle than the more to the real dialectic masses minority. Therefore, he does not reject the idea of struggle; quite the opposite, he *extends* it to relationships that are endlessly more complex and numerous than those which result from the summary fragmentation between classes established by Marx. So he enlarges the concept and affirms notably the dialectics between masses and small groups that try to manage them (for example, trade unions).

Poverty, analyzed by Perroux, is not only present in some nations. It is multidimensional and exists in advanced nations as well. It is characterized by under-development and social exclusion; "poor" groups do not communicate among themselves or with other social groups; they depend on dominant groups because they do not have negotiating power; in these groups, man's costs are not covered. The formal democracy practices unavowed and unofficial ways of excluding certain social groups, this multitude of "citizens of partial exercising".

François Perroux's Conceptual Innovations

Creativity is the capacity of creation, which is in its essence collective, for example, England from the eighteenth and nineteenth centuries, and the United States since the middle of the twentieth century. It is not the prerogative of the innovative entrepreneur, privileged by Schumpeter the inspirer of Perroux. The "collective creation", concept borrowed from Saint-Simon, is organized in different scales up to global level. It is the origin of growth and economic progress, and takes an active part on both. While the neoclassical analysis of growth by production factors tends to consider economic progress as an inert time factor, as a residue, collective innovation plays a considerable role in all economic regimes.

The economic movement and *development* lie on a dynamic of inequality and a dynamic of progress. In 1948, Perroux lays the first stone to the inequality of dynamic construction by creating the domination effect. The **domination effect** is defined as *a dissymmetric or irreversible [. . .] intentional or not, that an individual, a firm or a nation rub off on other units less powerful*. It includes three factors: the dimension of the economic unit (e.g., its market position), its negotiating power (capacity in order to influence the terms of trade) and its strategic position into the whole economy.

Perroux establishes a distinction between domination and independence, between domination and imperialism. In the nineteenth century, Great Britain was economically dominant but dependent (supplies); the domination is a wider concept, more general than imperialism because it includes unintentional and quite mechanical effects. Starting from economic domination, Perroux succeeds in generalizing the asymmetries in relationships between economic agents and in structural and spatial analysis, such as development cluster; driving force effects by the flow of material goods, investment and information; propagation effects in structured spaces: *the propagation of price changes and flows could never be usefully analyzed by supposing that the environment is homogeneous.*

Beginning in 1937, Perroux introduces the concept of *economic structure*, and he gives it an important position in his analysis until the elaboration, in 1969, of the concept *of structural influence*. There is the asymmetric action of a strong structure, which changes for its own advantage a weak structure at the expense of its development. Starting from the generalized concept of *asymmetries*, Perroux establishes a theory of *"growth clusters"* (1955) starting from the concrete analysis of Ruhr field. Those clusters are driving units that have multiple effects: technical-economic (driving effects, sectorial polarization), geographical (agglomeration effects, regional polarization), psychological (born of development climate) and institutional (structural transformation, centralization, decentralization).

The Generalized Theory of General Equilibrium and Active Units

Perroux proposes to establish a comprehensive theory that is able to overcome the incomplete studies of his predecessors. The theory that he presents in his last published book (1975) integrates, generalizes and galvanizes the monopolistic regimes of imperfect competition. It tends to substitute the equilibrium of *things* by the balance and regulation of *human* activities evolving in a universe characterized by inequalities and differences. It realizes a synthesis encompassing former concepts created by Perroux or privileged in his analysis: structure, asymmetry, leadership's effects, polarized spaces, structural and dynamical frame influences. The model is based on the fundamental concept of *active unity*: *an energy holder agent able to locally change its environment, the economic space.* The topologic representation resorts to normalized, vectorized spaces: applied or not in a territorial space. The agent is changing itself by experience (*learning*) and changes other agents by influencing its closest environment. The transformation energy is unequal between agents. Their relationships are a mix of free exchanges and ratios of power.

This generalized equilibrium does not depend on a mechanical game with regular rules of global quantities belonging to artificial categories of classical, Keynesian or Marxist classifications through a mechanical or predetermined evolution. In Perroux's model, the dynamic analysis is always sectorial. Sector A acts on sector B, that is inducing investments, supply and demand, an information. The effects of these asymmetric relationships are differentiated. The model lays on the basic principle of economic efficiency (cost to income relation): however, incomes and costs are calculated by other means than they are today. By applying economic spaces on territorial spaces concept, the analysis embraces the whole of exchanges between multinational firms creating their expansion spaces and the structural influences between organized groups: nations, regions and social groups acting one on another. The generalized theory presents itself as a linked optimization, in accordance with the economic norm on the one hand, and on the other hand, with the maximization of energies from human resources (consumption, production and freedom).

Epistemology and Method in Economic Analysis

Perroux's ambitious conception of economics, as a human and social science, is based on open-mindedness. He proposed *the theory confronting the reality.* He has the modesty not to believe that economics has achieved what other sciences did not succeed in (physics and biology, despite their achievements), that is to say reaching a formal rigor by a correct translation of real, economic, human science and the science of all humans into mathematics. Unlike the intentions of common and implicit reasoning, François Perroux considers that the scientific intention of a theoretical analysis is first measured by its level of realism.

Perroux denounces that in analyses, supposed to be presented under the criteria of neutrality or scientific prowess, there are *implicitly normative conceptualizations*. The economist with *scientific intentions* has to explicitly separate from him/herself the **implicitly normative assumptions** that underpin his/her analyses, as a required loyalty sign.

Economic rationality is not only defined by the way the economic activity is established, but first and foremost by the analysis of its objectives. *Perroux's conception of science is a finalized science.* The economic analysis is from scientific intentions in that it forces itself to answer to issues such as "What is the object which is maximized by the economic activity? What is the scarcity overcome? By whom and for whom?" According to him, the economic problem is never posed in a social and historical vacuum. The economic rationality is validated only if the proposition explicitly states its values, political and social structures and philosophical preferences.

The object and the perspective of economic science is human resources. "The complete development of human resources, affirms the author, of each human being without exception, is the postulate of a scientific economy and, without it, maximizations are always questionable". It is to this quest for total man that Perroux invites us, with the refusal of the dichotomy between social and economic. Such is the sense of the deep message from Bernácer; such is the signification of the research we personally carried out on socioeconomic approach to management (Savall Henri, [Work and People: an Economic evaluation of Job-Enrichment] *Enrichir le travail humain*, 1973, 1981).

In Perroux's approach, the economic system is a dual social system, which includes self-guided sub-systems, and sub-systems led by a pilot, at different levels of public authorities. It remains that Perroux's economic system grants a considerable place to actors and not to inert objects, wherever they are public or private macro-units or micro-units. "*The actor is a person (or a group) which takes an active part in an activity and inflicts the incidents of a drama not imposed by fate. It is not a plot, moved by invisible hands— neither the human flesh which disposes, after having been priced, the symbolic usurer which smiles to universal destruction*".

Perroux's Method Includes a Dynamic Synthesis and a Structural Analysis

The Perrouxien synthesis, of Hegelian nature, proceeds from the notion introduced by the philosopher Merleau-Ponty (Les aventures de la dialectique

[The adventures of Dialectic], 1955) "generalized economy from which capitalism and communism are particular cases". Perroux's approach does not tend to prophesy an inevitable convergence of systems as Schumpeter did; it tends to lay the alternative: will it be a war of powerful nations' blocs or the advent of a generalized economy liable to establish a "synchronized growth on a world scale"?

Perroux's analysis replaces the traditional mechanisms, or even flow dynamics, by a dynamic of power. At the beginning, he undergoes the influence of Joseph Alois Schumpeter and Edward Chamberlin, who highlighted the decisive importance of unilateral actions of creation and power in the economic process. Pure and perfect competition is rejected not only as an unreal hypothesis but also as an ideal structure for market, because it does not allow a sufficient development and propagation of progress. Perroux deduces from his analysis of the French economy from 1815 to 1914 that it had experienced some progress, but it was not a *progressive* economy: the innovation did not spread out well, social costs remained high, scientific discoveries did not realize the economic applications they deserve (Bernácer made the same analysis since 1916); for the dominant groups, they were protectionist and conservatives.

Time in the Perrouxian approach gets an historical, spatial and sociocultural (men evolving in a geographical space) thickness and a signification that guides movements: progress. Economic time is shaped by the dialectics, which combine human projects, individual and collective actions to functional structures and structured spaces.

Perroux's *economic space* (defined geographically and by industries) is not isomorphic. It includes growth clusters, which result in dialectics of spaces; the economic space of an agent results from an expansion of conflict. The economic space is different from geographical and political space: "*the national economic space is not the territory of the nation, but the field which the economic plans of States and individuals espouse*".

Greatness and Servitudes of Perrouxian Research

At its *doctrinal stage*, his work demystifies the idea of scientific neutrality, which dons an unrealistic formalism or a naturalism, which does not suit social sciences. *He inscribes his thought in an explicit social commitment*, which he includes in the object and in the signification of economic science. He has, according to the traditional expression, a vision that is that of a great economist. This commitment gives to his thought the criticism bound in his Universalist orientation (the generalized economy).

All agents, individuals or groups have a role to play in the Perrouxian economic system. The individual is not privileged as he is in neoclassical theory; and he/she is not fixed and predetermined as in Marxist theory. Groups have an important place, and their dynamic is redeemed (some macro decisions are beneficial and contribute to development).

The *political economy* of synchronized growth that he advocates is strongly supported. It is based on the choice of motor imbalances: it aims at maximizing the global real product in the frame of a change process to meet some expectations. It is also based on the intervention of public authorities on real factors, by fostering two prior propensities: for working and for social innovation. The intervention aims at mastering the imbalances, not to annihilate them but to transform the *imbalances* which our socioeconomic theory (SEAM) qualifies as *dysfunctions* into effective and efficient balances that are socially *sustainably bearable* by fostering social dialog that allows projects and plans from social groups to emerge and make possible the additive allocation of resources necessary to the realization of those plans.

Perroux contributed to the launch of the national accounting system in France. He had helped the quantitative technique of scheduling to progress, especially by a model of sectorial polarization. He inspired directly in France and abroad applied research, concrete studies and econometrics' prolongation of some of his conceptual innovations: especially on development clusters, the motor effect and structural inequalities. Several operational applications have been aroused by the development cluster theory (France, USA, Canada, Latin America) and by structural influence (World Bank and technological transfer), such as the notion of dominant and driving force firms.

Maurice Allais, First French Economy Nobel Prize Awarded (1911–2010): Steered Social Liberalism

Until 2014, when Jean Tirole was nominated, Maurice Allais was the lone French recipient of the Economic Nobel Prize. Until this recognition of his scientific works, Maurice Allais was ignored by the majority of French academic economists. He was the victim, as were some other theoreticians, of a sort of civil war, which occurs in France between higher engineering and business schools and universities. Maurice Allais, born in 1911, was a ward of the state and lost his father during First World War. He was from a modest family, which probably explains his tenacity and his determination to improve his status in the social hierarchy. His orientation to economics resulted from a trip in the USA, after the Great Depression in 1929, during which the future economist observed very many jobless persons, victims of the crisis. First attracted to public reforms from Front Populaire government, Allais kept his distance by refuting the effectiveness of assistance to the poor and by showing that competition, *via* the labor market, is a more effective principle of optimal resource allocation.

According to Arnaud Diemer and Philippe Laurier (2013), four masters inspired Allais' theory: Irving Fischer, Léon Walras, Vilfredo Pareto and François Perroux. The discovery of Fischer's works convinced Allais to become an economist and to write a book on economy. His *Pure Economy Treaty* (1943), with more than 1,000 pages, was written during World War II. He drew inspiration from Léon Walras, concerning the purchase of lands by states to eliminate unearned income—a source of value creation without any work and no entrepreneurial risk. In this period, Allais still did not know the works of the Spaniard Bernácer, who had made analogous recommendations since 1916 and in his seminal 1922 article. As Walras, Allais is in favor of **organized competition** and calls for a "competitive planning" as an alternative solution for the two extremes; he criticizes the *authoritarian planning* and the *laissez-faire*. The *Pure Economy Course* of Pareto inspires the structure of the book that earned Allais the Nobel Prize, the *Pure Economy Treaty*. The *Sociology Treaty* and the *Theory of Elites* of Pareto were also notable influences for Allais. In a great article entitled "*Social Classes and Civilization*", Allais "*defends the theses of heredity (importance of genes) and socialization (importance for education and teaching)*" (Diemer & Laurier, 2013, p. 63). Perroux noticed Allais' works, received him into his Institute for Applied Economic Science (ISEA) and published his works into the journals he ran.

Like Perroux's, Allais' thought is of a social liberal and heterodox nature and refutes gladly the theories considered as established and without validation, by confronting them with scientific observation economic and social facts. Tempted by the neoliberal movement following the observation of liberalism, which furthers the crisis of 1929, Allais kept his distance regarding Hayek (who preceded him to the Nobel Prize record). Indeed, according to Allais, the state has an essential role to play in economy in order to define the framework necessary for exchange and for the good functioning of market. In his last years, Allais would stigmatize the cult of *laissez-faire* by qualifying it is from "*laissez-fairisme*" (Allais, 1943). At last reputed for his works in economics, Maurice Allais would like to be also recognized by French Sciences Academy for his works in the physics field that we liked to evoke and not to dissociate from his scientific investment into economy. By the way, one could notice the proximity as physicists, between Bernácer's path, born in 1883, Jacques Rueff, born in 1896 and Maurice Allais born in 1911.

In our thinking's about the evolution of economic thought since the nineteenth century, the first third of the twentieth century appears as a transition period in which emerges the macroeconomic approach, under the influence of physics (Savall, 1973, 2010). The success and the progress of macro economy in this period would relegate during several decades the works on the microeconomic level and foster the birth of a new science: *management science*. Unfortunately, the liberal return to micro economy has been faded by new microeconomic approach, which is financially and highly mathematically oriented, and which gets the entrepreneurship and hyper financial capitalism mixed up and moreover stimulated by the geopolitical movement of unleashed globalization.

Allais contributed to the renewal of liberalism in the 1940s. Nevertheless, his positions came later from those of Hayek. He considers that unlike the thesis of "**laissez-fairisme**", where freedom has to be organized because each part has to respect the identity and the interests of each other in an exchange-based relationship. The state's role in economy consists in defining the legal framework necessary for exchange and for the fair functioning of the market. According to him, the question is not to know if the means of production shall come under public or private property; it is convenient to observe the effects of those two modalities before adopting an ideological position. Allais highlighted the misdeeds of globalization (*Comment vivre ensemble: conditions économiques et sociales de la démocratie* [Living Together: economic and social conditions for democracy], 2008). According to him, there is indeed a big confusion between liberalism and *laissez-fairisme* because a liberal and humanistic society is not a lax society. Yet, without accurate rules of the game, the mastering of economic activity is not possible. It entails economic, social, monetary dumping and institutes practices belonging to the law of the jungle. Only *one criterion* dominates: money—and every ethical consideration disappears.

Both the dysfunctions of the European Union and the global economy contribute to the current situation. Indeed, since 1973 (the entry of England, Denmark and Ireland into the European Union), the community preference has been abandoned. Europe has become a free-trade area within the rest of the world. The politicians have progressively abandoned their power in favor of the EU Commission: the technocracy substitutes itself for democracy, through political disengagement, in favor of European civil servants. Today, the European Union suffers from a deep deficit of democracy in its management. The progressive abandonment of the community preference breeds severe economic difficulties. Allais proposes the political organization of all the European countries, which rests upon a confederation of sovereign states. The latter were adopting a confederation charter and an institutional framework in which the democratic and fundamental rights of member states would be preserved. The definition of common objectives for member states would make the collective action more effective. The progressive abandonment of the community preference entailed the development of foreign and wild competition. The global liberalization of exchange has been doubled within the liberalization of capital movements and in particular, with the massive relocation of enterprises. These entailed the destruction of jobs, industries and agricultures and the European Union growth.

According to Allais, without this policy that had been carried out since 1974, the real gross domestic product (GDP) *per* inhabitant in France should be 30 percent higher than today and equal to the USA's GDP. Maurice Allais, as François Perroux, with his concept of organized exchange areas, proposed the organization of regional ensembles economically and politically associated, by gathering countries with a comparable economic development. The recovery of a community preference may work under the form of market economy, with for example 80 percent of the purchases into European Union and 20 percent abroad, *via* treaties and requests for proposals based on the quality-price relation.

Thus, at the global scale, the ideology of *laissez-fairisme* and the shortcomings of each form of regulation that the World Trade Organization (WTO) conveys have multiple consequences. Free trade is more and more radical and becomes the rule as well for goods and services, intellectual property and investments. The promoters of this ideology are personally and directly responsible for an important *social misery* and the existence of millions of unemployed persons. Allais advocated a more **humanistic** economy, giving more importance to psychology and to actors' behaviors and considering that such disciplines as history, sociology and psychology are as important as economy in order to better understand the world. Consistent with Perroux, Allais gave priority to the observation of phenomena or facts. He forced himself to do so, by applying the scientific methodology of physics (Poincaré) in order to raise awareness of regularities, which appear via the **rigorous observation** of economic and social facts.

Karl Marx (Germany, 1818–1883): From Capitalism Criticism to Class Struggle

Several authors stressed the limits of Marx's theory, most notably by pointing out that the actual world is no longer the same as it was in England during the nineteenth century and that social laws and norms imposed by the International Labor Organizations (ILO) on working conditions have limited the excesses of capitalism since the first industrial revolution. Nevertheless, one could not deny the importance of the economic debate provoked by this theory, which put the lid on alienation induced by a badly regulated economic system and the predation of value creation by a minority. We now revisit the seminal principles of Marx and the relevant criticism thereof.

Reminder of Marxism's Main Basis

In the theory developed by Karl Marx in *Das Kapital* (1867), labor is considered like a type of merchandise, and capitalists sell workers' production by taking advantage of higher exchange value than their remuneration of workers' cost. Capitalists seize what Marx calls the *overwork, which* was not paid to the workers, that constitutes alienation. In order to increase the value added, a pressure is practiced on workers to maximize the duration of work and its intensity, while limiting the wages at their lowest level for reproducing the strength of work. Regarding the competition of the great industry, capitalists have again raised productivity by setting up the division of work, mechanism, and automation. These reduce the cost of work and make the wage workers unemployed, while capitalists accumulate capital. This activity has the ultimate effect of decreasing profitability. Capitalism is self-destroying, a victim of its own contradictions. Then Marx proposes as a solution the advent of **communism**, a social system that releases the workers and ensures that the work contributes to the common well-being while transforming labor into pleasure.

Marx's Theory Criticism by Perroux

In the forewords to Marx's works published by *La Pleiade* in 1963, Perroux offered a drastic criticism of Marx's theory, while recognizing the existence of conflicts between workers and capitalists. At the epistemological scale, Perroux noticed that Marx chose to neglect the potential existence of an alternative to class struggle, proposing the struggle as only solution: "*if we want a death struggle, we opt for concepts that impose the antagonism and eventually, we rely on a praxis which misrepresents the views on reality and transforms ratios of power in order to give us reason*" (Perroux, 1963, p. XXVIII). By favoring the **antagonism between capital and labor,** the contradiction could be overcome only through destruction of one or other of them. The underlying value system of Marx tends to propose a communist system, which is derived more from a prophetic posture than a scientific analysis. By paraphrasing Perroux, we could say for the Marxists that they have demonized the enterprise and proclaimed that only state services are virtuous. Perroux showed that the contradictions of the capitalist system have not been eliminated by communism, but on the contrary they have been reinforced: "*in the communist system, there is a top, where we command, and a bottom, where we obey and it subsists by dominating wage-workers, exploiting groups and exploited groups . . . where domination phenomena persists*" (Perroux, 1963, p. XXVIII).

Then, Perroux proposed to replace the social struggle concept with the *dialectics of social struggle/dialog*. He noticed that each human is original and has the possibility to contest or to escape from the projects that are imposed on him. He also affirms the fact that "*before productive strengths, there is the creation power of persons*" *(Perroux, p. LI)* that is what Marx's theory had obscured. It is convenient consequently to organize the compatibility between each one's project by means of social dialog, where a voice is given in a structured manner, in order to allow a real economic development to the benefit of all and for giving back to each man his/her **dignity** through social recognition and action, different from the conceptualization of man in Marxist dialectics (Perroux, p. XXXVI). The *social dialog* supposes at the same time mediation devices, and the "*development of generalized education, the free-trade union, the right to strike, the fundamental freedom of thinking and expression . . . and the adjustment of social dialogues in a democracy that does not cheat*" (Perroux, 1963, p. XXXI). He also noticed that some difficulties need to be overcome on the scale of economic value-creation measurement: "*the economic relationship became humanly significant overflows the sphere of calculable things . . . their senses are translated, quantified and drained in no-account. The account is a kind of social convention which is suitable for human exchanges that overflow*" (Perroux, 1963, p. XXII).

Socioeconomic Theory Position Regarding Marx

The *socioeconomic theory* developed by Henri Savall and ISEOR contains a prolongation of Perroux's approach, by showing that social dialog needs to reconstruct the instruments of measure for economic value creation (Savall, 1974b) by taking into account hidden costs and performances. These cost-performances are largely ignored by classical, Marxist, neoclassical and Keynesian analyses. The works of ISEOR reconsider the pertinence of traditional economic and accounting methods by opening the black box of value creation, which exists as much in Marx's theory as in traditional economic and accounting theories, which reduce the value of labor to simple merchandise. First, the calculation of hidden costs relative to *absenteeism, turnover, work accidents and professional diseases*, to the *non-quality*, and *productivity gaps* show that all actors get a *huge informal economic power* of value destruction when their projects are not taken into account neither negotiated (see Part 2, the high level of hidden costs measured into several organization: €20,000 to €70,000 per person and per year).

Second, it is necessary to better take into account the double dimension of value creation by *clearly defined human labor*: the immediate results (short-term economic results) and the creation of potential (middle- and long-term economic results). The measure of hidden performances from creation of potential is particularly underestimated, quite forgotten in economic and accounting models. These oversights often lead to neglect, and quite mutilate the creative and innovative dimensions of human labor, because the stress is placed on cost reduction, in particular with regard to wages, by destroying the hidden potential of innovative projects that social dialog could help to increase. ISEOR researchers (Bonnet, 1988, 1996) have measured the considerable hidden costs of illiteracy. The socioeconomic projects experienced by ISEOR show the necessity of a **structured social dialog** based on measuring tools that takes into consideration a more complex reality than the reducing approach of value added emphasized by Marx.

This renovation of tools is based on **qualimetrics approach** (Savall & Zardet, 2004), which consists of a negotiated measure of complex reality through an interaction among all the concerned actors (cognitive inter-activity principle) and from an agreement, even temporary or partial, on the qualitative, quantitative and financial measures of phenomena acting on value-creation processes (contradictory intersubjectivity principle). For example, the socioeconomic balance of an insertion project for youth in disadvantaged districts (Savall & Bonnet, 1996, in a communication presented to Conseil Économique et Social [*social and economic council*] in Paris) or the hidden costs of musculoskeletal injuries (Savall, Zardet & Bonnet, 2002), in a report for the French Agence Nationale pour l'Amélioration des Conditions du Travail [*National Agency for Improvement of Working Conditions*] shows that the coordination of actions from different actors in the district is a project that costs mere pennies while the simple superposition of partial actions without this dialog engenders very high short- and long-term hidden costs: costs relating to violence, delinquency, addiction and the sacrifice of youth that could have potentially been productive. ISEOR's database also includes hundreds of socioeconomic balances, which demonstrate **the compatibility between social development and sustainable economic development.** For example, the enrichment of employees and workers work in case of Brioche Pasquier company, which has practiced socioeconomic management since 1984 (Pasquier, 1995; Savall & Zardet, 1995, 2005a) has allowed improvements in working conditions, wages, trajectories of career development for staff while increasing workforce and allocating a more important part to innovation investments while fairly remunerating shareholders. Those experimentations show that one cannot skip the scientific analysis of visible and hidden costs-performances if one wants to set up a real dialog.

Some Actual Criticism of Financial Capitalism

Several economists, including Nobel Prize winners Joseph Stiglitz and Paul Krugman, are criticizing the excesses of financial capitalism in the context of economic globalization and deregulation. They notice an excessive trend toward the accumulation of financial capital and casualization of employment, relocation development and dismantling of social protections. Some CEOs, who also benefit from capital holders' generosity according to the *theory of agency*, are by the way more and more inclined to express themselves about this topic wherever they are not susceptible to joining the Marxist theories. They consider the actual system to be unbalanced. We could quote, for example, the testimony of John Bogle, Vanguard Group CEO for whom *"our governance system of enterprise is deeply flawed and has led to outrageous remunerations for CEOs"* (Fried & Tosi, 2005). Two major criticisms of the actual economic system are addressed: the misdeed of speculation and a loss of both sense and legitimacy for the economic system.

The excesses of speculation are made to the detriment of the **common good**. Joining Bernácer, for whom he does not quote nor appear to know his works, Krugman warns that financial people who had made their investors prosper did not make it by creating value for other actors (Krugman, p. 103). As Krugman, Stiglitz shows that speculation is destroying value in such important proportions that speculators seem to have won.

The loss of sense and the legitimacy crisis of *financial capitalism* under his *hypertrophied and actual* form, which results from the accumulation of capital and speculation are mentioned notably by Stiglitz and could threaten democracy itself: *"if markets did not take their promises to improve the quality of life of most citizens, all the sins of companies- flagrant social injustices, insulting our environment and exploiting poor's should have been forgiven"* (Stiglitz, 2012a, p. 18). This author considers that this kind of financial capitalism is losing its legitimacy in citizens' view because it did not respect its promises. In developed countries, young, indignant demonstrators are rejecting capitalism, in which they do not believe and consider to be the cause of injustice, pollution and unemployment. According to him, citizens are also observing the irresponsible behaviors of *elites* and the degradation of values. They want to reject capitalism as a whole. In several developing countries, the impoverishment of masses and corruption also entail a political instability. It is not, for Stiglitz, regulating capitalism by replacing a functional system of regulation with yet another. This latter recalls to this topic what Adam Smith was aware of, the existence of situations where private and social yields are diverging, and that he did not completely believe in his theory of *"invisible hand"*, which is, by the way, not very mobilized in his works.

Socioeconomic Theory Position Regarding Critical Approaches to Capitalism

The socioeconomic theory of **tetranormalization** (see Part 2) also takes into account the dysfunctions and the hidden costs engendered by speculation, unearned income, and the outrageous accumulation of capital. However, not unlike Marxist economists and the partisans of this stream of thought, the observed phenomena of value-added predation should not be analyzed only at banking and financial market levels, because *"since the beginning of the time there have been some people whose aim was to live off the others"* (Savall, 1973, 1975, in his book on Bernácer, p. 51) because it is in man's nature to prefer the highest ratio of *income/cost*, quite seeking sources of income without working. The quest for unearned income, hoarding and speculation is not to be assigned to capitalism, but rather to the fact that one condones **unethical** behaviors without institutionalizing wholesome rules of economic management and especially without educating decision-makers and citizens as to the stimulating effect of contributing to prosperity and common good by means of a labor force which is also a source and a holder of dignity. Socioeconomic theory shows that the behaviors of predation have some impacts at different scales of economy, enterprises and organizations, but also that they remain obscured in economic indicators. The hidden costs affect those different levels (Savall, Zardet & Bonnet, 2006: *Isomorphisme dysfonctionnel de la petite à la grande entreprise* [Dysfunctional isomorphism from the small to the big company]).

At a global scale, the **conflicts of norms** denounced by our theory of *tetranormalization* reflect hidden interests and business goodwill, which stop the sustainable and balanced creation of wealth (Savall & Zardet, 2004). The speculation on financial markets entails deep dysfunctions and hidden costs, in particular the fact that creation of potential destruction ensues when one maximizes only immediate visible performances. At national scales of economies from different countries, one can also take an inventory of very numerous hidden costs related to situations of unearned income: appropriation of decision organs by elites that stop the necessary changes, production of wealth supported by less than half the population, estate speculation entailing territorial unbalances and transportation difficulties.

At the territorial scale, the research for the preservation of *domains* by actors entails the desynchronizing of actors, which is paid into hidden costs at short- and long-term intervals. One could see this, for example with the poor level of young people insertion in businesses, because economic actors and those from education actors do not work enough in cooperation. Each of them forgets to calculate what one youth's lifetime of illiteracy will cost society. At the enterprise scale, the absenteeism or the unanticipated departure of a colleague *have enduring effects* for people working around the person who left and for all the value-creation chain, due to an overcharge of work and a risk of the enterprise losing customers (Savall & Zardet, 1987). At the human group scale or even for a family, tensions exist for the day-to-day life operations and for children's education; sometimes children are victims during a great part of their life, when one neglects to train them. Those examples show that the so-called class struggle is just one *very particular case* of conflicts, small or big, trivial or severe, that permeate daily social life.

However, socioeconomic theory shows that the participation in a collective project, the enrichment of human work and the balanced exchange are judged to be favorable for all concerned, unlike the perverse games of **value predation**, the very basis of class struggle proposed by Marx. In the book *Reconstruire l'Entreprise* [Rebuild the enterprise] written by Henri Savall (1979), the reference to Herzberg's concept of the two dimensions of human nature and on the work sense (labor-punishment *versus* labor-creation) indicates that one could set up management tools for economy which foster the individual contribution to economic prosperity instead of the low trends of illegitimate unearned incomes. Then, Marx and Marxian's approaches have to be considered as partial theories: they are denouncing an unsteady system only by situating themselves at the macroeconomic level, while root causes are situated at the scale of the lack of management of "living together" rules of the game by taking into account the globalization context (see Allais, in Perroux Conference proceedings, 2008: *Comment vivre ensemble: conditions économiques et sociales pour la démocratie* [Living together: economic and social requirements for democracy]). The assumption of socioeconomic theory is that those rules do not emerge spontaneously from the "*laisser-faire*" but they have to be **built** through a socioeconomic process: inventory of dysfunctions and hidden costs calculation, elaboration of the project in a collaborative manner, steered and synchronized; creation of economic balances for expected performances of the project; periodical negotiation on expected performance in the short and long term (principle of the periodically negotiable activity contract).

Socioeconomic theory does not object to some assessments of Marxian approaches on the refusal to treat the social issues of contemporary society.

However, it differentiates radically from these approaches, as for the underlying philosophy and the proposed method for treating those problems. The solutions it advocates are breeding and stimulating communication, consultation and cooperation practices inside teams, enterprises, private, public and associative organizations at each level of the society (local, regional and national). There exists a generalized need for education to the entrepreneurial spirit, the organization of a type of work and a society that *creates sustainable wealth* and that make possible the individual and collective development of human potential. These are the assessments that reinforce solutions.

Part II

Socially Responsible Enterprises and Organizations

3 Socioeconomic Approach to Management
A Socially Responsible Organizational Approach

Management as a Tool for Change

It is necessary to underline that what is characterizing the economic world nowadays is fast-changing and perpetual innovation, which the sole application of new rules on the labor market, whatever they be, loosened could only hinder. What enterprises would be entitled to expect from a socially and sustainably responsible capitalism might be freedom to adapt the contractual framework of labor law to their specific and respective contexts in order to study with the full spectrum of employees the solutions to consider and the decisions to make depending on the problems posed by the reality in the field. It is on this principle of *norms acclimatization* that the socioeconomic approach to management was founded.

We mentioned above that the ideological climate, which underlies, from an external point of view, the relationship between employers and trade unions in the company PSA (Peugeot Corporation), does not necessarily reflect the real situation. It is undeniable that the opposition to change dooms the enterprises. The *cost of doing nothing* offers a superior alternative to those acting, according to Unilever's CEO in an interview of *Figaro* (March 2015, 20th). Jean-Dominique Sénard, head of Michelin, declares with reason "we cannot wait for the company to be in a perilous situation to make industrial decisions. The ones who do that are creating more severe situations. *On the contrary*, I consider that we have the duty of **anticipating**". Patrick Kron, Alstom's CEO, echoes in his comments reported by *Le Figaro* about this "fighting CEO": "One could not accuse employers of missing to their duty of anticipation when their companies are flagging and blame those who saw it coming".

Our insistence on the implementation of the **strategic vigilance** principle gives genuine body to this word, **anticipation**: "only an organized anticipation, based on an effective vigilance from internal and external environment is likely to ensure a level of activity which allows one to maintain and increase the survival-development capacity of the enterprise, its level of employment and the professional quality of life in its core" (Savall & Zardet, *Ingénierie stratégique du roseau* [Strategic engineering of the reed], 2005a). In opposition to a reactive management style, it has to foster a *proactive strategy*, which only could allow each type of organization to stay in the running for performance and creative innovation. Proactive enterprises are transforming each new threat into **an opportunity for change**. We have frequently observed that some draconian restructuring said to be *"surgical"* comes after years, even decades, during which genuine reorganization had not been effected in a salutary and gentle manner. In this case, we notice that lack of mobility and *status quo* created either by companies' myopia and social actors, or by seeking a shortsighted social peace, succeed brutally at restructuring, which touches considerable proportions of the workforce (Savall & Zardet, *Ingénierie stratégique du roseau* [Strategic engineering of the reed], 2005a, p. 39).

Socially responsible capitalism has to create an environment that can be receptive to the *socioeconomic management tools* that allow one to regularly question the evolving organization of enterprises, on setting "gentle micro-restructuring", gradually evolving employment specifications, and preparing the individual to pursue technical progress for the enrichment of human potential and increasing their capacity to communicate. The socioeconomic model works in that direction because it does not count on a massive reduction of costs (excluding hidden costs) in order to ensure the recovery of enterprises because their impact is discouraging actors' initiatives whose only preoccupation remains often to subtract from incoming plans. Such an attitude could only worsen the social climate. The typical statement we hear during each decision that is part of a reorganization is "this situation is a vital necessity in order to insure the durability of the company and to protect is **competitiveness**". We also hear that all will be done in favor of minimizing the impact on employment with the promise of an "exemplary social accompaniment".

In the framework of socially and sustainably responsible capitalism, the key factor is found in the definition of management as a tool for change. Our principle of **3C** (**communication, coordination, cooperation**) aims at making internal communication more fluid and preparing in his globalism the implementation of an effective cooperation in the whole company by avoiding the creation of an opposition front thanks to more social dialog. The negotiation of "employment safety", which aims at modifying the essence of the labor market's functioning, comes to introduce more norms, which will only constitute new barriers to discussions on the field. Their negotiations, if this is in case, are taking place outside of the workplace and do not escape the dysfunctions provoked by the centralization of the norm's negotiation process.

By the way, we notice that this latter is the cause of several dysfunctions, but our concept of **synchronized decentralization** supports eliminating them. Our interventions within enterprises have led us to record that moving the decision-making process closer to the place where the decision applies does facilitate its implementation and avoid absurd and costly consequences as the French Court of Auditors report constantly. We have opted for a synchronized decentralization process. We define it as "*moving the initiative of the decisive act to the level of responsibility at which its implementation will be triggered, while establishing the game rules of communication, coordination, cooperation to ensure its compatibility with the action of other areas responsibilities and the strategic management of the entire organization*" (Savall & Zardet, 2005a, p. 482). This principle is thus a key element of our socioeconomic approach to management (SEAM) in the framework of a socially, economically and sustainably responsible capitalism, in accordance with our conception of *proximity management* as we conceive it for each territorial organization or, at the national scale, as within enterprises.

Our interventions in these last years have led us to show that centralization was the cause of many dysfunctions and that this observation applied at the stage of the state management. Decentralization makes it possible to develop the **initiatives** of the greatest number, therefore of human energy, creativity, commitment for responsibility on individual, team, establishment and company scales. It would involve a turning in the social relationships within the large groups. The **Periodically Negotiated Activity Contract (PNAC)** is a key element and tool in our design of socially and sustainably responsible capitalism (Perroux, 1979). It constitutes an effective way to avoid the kind of disillusionment that centralization generates. It is an improvement contract of socioeconomic performance signed between each employee of the company and his or her direct manager. The manager speaks for the company by delegation of authority from the CEO. She/he "*commits his/herself to bring better structures of activity, specific means best adapted and also an additional compensation to the employee. All these are self-financed by reducing hidden costs, that is to say recycling into value added. The worker commits him/herself to develop more effective and productive behavior, improve immediate results and get a better involvement into creation of potential*". The PNAC has been conceived of in order to allow a certain degree of safety for employees while preserving the competitiveness of the enterprise. It is also an essential tool for developing a feeling of personal self-achievement and satisfaction, which rises from the recognition by the hierarchy of the performance achieved by the person, quite as important as the study of his/her personal assessment, his/her personal contribution, his/her objectives or his/her wishes of professional evolution.

Internal procedures of an employee's transfer between departments or promotion should benefit from facilitation using a **competency grid**. Those constitute a genuine tool for explaining these procedures, answering to the issue of evolution and change and make the changes more acceptable to the workers. That avoids incantational resolutions whose implementation would depend upon a large collection of norms, running counter to flexibility and sustainable efficiency. They highlight, in the form of a synopsis, the unemployed knowhow at each stage of the company and allow the development of the **multiskills** of members from different teams. They also could lead to the increasing of each worker's responsibility. As Savall and Zardet also note, "the *competencies* and *human potential* constitute the *first strategic lever* for a *sustainable* improvement of economic performance. One of the fertile ways consists of developing the *implementation* of human competencies, instead of simply accumulating more or less virtual and volatile skills" (Savall & Zardet, 2005b).

This policy which aims at better *integrating* the actors of the company and at improving competitiveness must be accompanied by a qualifying training program, which promotes personal development and better educates the unskilled. Our concept of **integrated training corresponds to an internal and external training on adaptation** because it aims at concretely answering to the evolution of a company's professions and addressing new market needs, which is not always the takeaway from supposed professional training to support the promotion of individuals. Concerned to **capitalize** on the expertise acquired by the experiment, we define training as the structured, reusable assimilation of knowledge obtained in the real execution of the occupation. Our integrated-training concept is not limited to the acquisition of technical knowledge. However, it rests on a transformative approach, which involves the employee in the evolution of the field itself. There is certainly, in France, an individual right for training (DIF), which should be replaced by a personal account for training (CPF) following the agreement on securing employment. Nevertheless, it is up to the employee to make his training program financed as in the case of individual vacation. The tool proposed by the SEAM makes the integrated training a genuine factor of development for the individual as well as for the organization, by inducing a more participative management style with **an integrated-training manual**, which capitalizes on the acquired knowledge and skills. This process belongs to the field of strategic human resource management, which requires a high level of intangible investment on and from the workforce. This is authorized by the savings obtained by eliminating hidden costs entailed by dysfunctions, which are related to the insufficient matching between employment and training in the context of volatile demand.

An Obstacle to CSR: The Pernicious TFW Virus (Taylorism-Fayolism-Weberism)

Henri Savall and Véronique Zardet (Savall & Zardet, 2006b) have created the concept of the TFW virus (Taylorism-Fayolism-Weberism). It appeared under this denomination in 2006 in French, American and Mexican conferences and has been used by different authors. The metaphor of TFW virus (Savall & Zardet, 2005b) refers to the anachronistic survival of Classical Organizational School principles, which were proposed by Taylor (1911), Fayol (1916) and Weber (1924). Those authors had contributed, in their time, to social and economic progress. Nevertheless, it is regrettable that one century later, theoreticians, experts and practitioners keep propagating three principles which became obsolete: (a) the maximal division of work; (b) the dichotomy between conception, decision making and realization of activities; and (c) the depersonalization of workstations, organization charts, processes, competencies, social environment and national or international policies (Savall, 1974b, 1981, 2010). A wise criticism should not be addressed to Taylor, Fayol or Weber themselves but to their successors, theoreticians, experts and practitioners as imprudent users of outdated theories. Indeed, the economic, social and geopolitical context and the education levels have changed in one century. The combined model of these three authors has aroused an abundant literature on work analysis, hiring and organizational theory.

A *virus* is defined as a little infection agent, constituted from sub-microscopic entity group that is reproducing inside animal, human or vegetal cells. The majority of viruses are pathogenic. The infection degree of TFW virus in dominant organizational models and managerial practices refers to the greater or lesser degree of **cooperation deficiency** between the participants of activities, the individuals in a team, or the establishments from a same organization, the subsidiaries from an industrial group or services company.

The main criticisms of the traditional work organization, evoked by the metaphor of TFW virus (Taylorism—Fayolism—Weberism) are based on the fact that the tradition has only focused on the internal organization of the function or **individual** workstation and also that standard times for realizing tasks do not take into account *working conditions*. However, the latter interfere in *productivity and quality*. Indeed, the dispositive cooperation between individuals and between teams is not structured: the necessary times for communication, negotiation, coordination, consultation, cooperation; permanent integrated training, methods improvement and innovation are not taken into consideration.

Let us now, as an illustration of the TFW virus' demonstrations and impacts, examine the case of a hospital where the care of a patient requires the contribution of several trades: physicians, nursing (nurses, assistants), administrative and management people (management controllers, HR personal, registration, accountability), technical and paramedical staff (biology, radiology, psychology, physical therapy, pharmacy, cooking, laundry, maintenance and security). Some of these trades are working in high geographical proximity, e.g., medical units, and some are more distant. Nevertheless, this geographical criterion does not explain, often, the quality defects of inter-professional cooperation. The organizational change actions, which aim at developing cohesion and reducing the effects of the TFW *virus-infected organization*, demonstrated in 1854 enterprises and organizations, in 72 industries and 40 countries, are reducing simultaneously the dissatisfaction generated by dysfunctions and the losses of economic resources (hidden costs).

Both organizational and management principles proposed by the classical school, Taylor, Fayol, Weber, (Lussato 1972; Montmollin, 1981) in a certain economic, technologic, demographic and geopolitics context, at the end of the nineteenth century, have been largely spread out in enterprises and organizations during the twentieth and twenty-first centuries. Their anachronistic application constitutes a deviancy regarding the objective of social performance—satisfaction—and economic performance—development of value creation and retribution—of **stakeholders**. Indeed, this "virus" provokes a deficiency of cohesion in different categories of actors, from top management to staff-line, and the destruction of value added that results from hidden costs, which remains unidentified—neither in accounting systems nor in performance metrics. Those represent in average €29,000 per person and per year.

Links Between SRC and Socioeconomic Management

The concept of **SRC** has been patiently built by means of numerous experimentations in private and public enterprises and organizations. The **socioeconomic theory**, sketched in 1973–1974, after the elapse of one decade of macroeconomic research, was built upon the refutation of two factors of production theory and the classical theory of work organization.

The germ of an **implicit concept of SRC** had grown up in the course of experimentations realized within 1854 enterprises and organizations that constituted the application of a SRC thumbnail (miniature). Those intervention-research cases have shown that this concept would *simultaneously improve* their *economic* performance and the quality of work conditions (*social* performance).

Therefore, a return to the macroeconomic level should be possible and relevant. It had been initiated around 2002 with the discovery of the **tetranormalization** in order to design today the outline of a recommendable economic regime: socially responsible capitalism, skinned from its speculative coating.

Socioeconomic Management and Theory of Enterprises and Organizations (SEAM)

In 1979, François Perroux prefaced Henri Savall's book *Reconstruire l'entreprise* [Rebuild the enterprise] by proposing his lecture on socioeconomic theory: "*Beyond the formal powers of organization, the broad scope is opening, so often unexplored formal powers of the individual [. . .] The hidden costs might be summarily [. . .] those imposed to the entrepreneur the resistance of agents [. . .] The reader will know with . . . surprise that the hidden costs . . . come to 25% of the production budget (of the enterprise). The employees are not robots and they know that. [. . .] The employee self understands [. . .] that his/her activity gives to him/her, also a purchasing power, but the occasion to progress [. . .] and to improve his/her social status. [. . .] The complete development of human resource potentialies [. . .] is initiated*". Those few excerpts put into evidence the proximities that

François Perroux spotted between his own works and ours, emerging of the **socioeconomic theory (SEAM)**.

Some years before, Jacques Delors expressed in the preface of "Enrichir le travail humain" (Delors, 1975): "The originality of this book is to present an economic approach of working restructuration [. . .]. I express the wish that employers and unionists would use the tool prepared by Henri Savall and experiment with it. It would be, without any doubt, the best possible test". Closer to us, David Boje presented the special issue of the review *Journal of Organizational Change Management* dedicated to socio-economic theory: "[This approach] constitutes an innovative theory in the field of organizational change since it contributes in linking together the social dimension of change and the economic dimension" (Boje & Rosile, 2003; Boje, 2004).

Itinerary and Basics of the Socioeconomic Theory of Organizations

The work started in 1973 with the seminal book *Enrichir le travail humain* (Savall, 1974b, 1975). After highlighting its origins and the itinerary followed, we will expose succinctly the main characteristics and after we will present the main results obtained along these 40 years. Originally, Henri Savall established a notice from macroeconomic order after his in-depth study of Bernácer's works (1883–1965), the great Spanish economist, and precursor of Keynes (Savall, 1973, 1975). This observation rested on the important limits of macro economy, the drying of socioeconomic theory, related, for a large part, to models *without rigorous scientific observation* of real economic facts.

The socioeconomic theory of organizations lays on *a double refutation*. At the macroeconomic scale, the classical theory (liberal, Marxist, or Keynesian), and at the microeconomic scale, the accounting model do not explain the performance level of organizations, nor did it inspire more pertinent decisions. The *two founding assumptions* of socioeconomic theory are indeed (1973):

> The human potential constitutes the *only active factor of creation* of value added, the technical and/or financial capital being a precious but sterile tool, when it is not activated and guided by human potential;
>
> It is possible to reduce the imperfection of the classical accounting model and improve the pertinence of the decision-making process.

These two principles founded the concept of *hidden cost-performance* and those of *value added on variable costs* as an indicator of overall sustainable performance (1974b). Indeed, Malinvaud's team has demonstrated that the "residual" factor which remains **unexplained** by the production function

(Carré, Dubois & Malinvaud, *La croissance française. Un essai d'analyse économique causale de l'après-guerre* [French growth. Essay on causal economic analysis of after war], 1972) is only explaining 55 percent of the value. Thus, the level of measured hidden cost, since this moment, by the researchers of ISEOR within enterprises and organizations contributes to explain the consistency and the scope of this residual factor. In addition, the neoclassical paradigm includes a deficiency by the fact that it maximizes the creation of value (financial) *only for shareholders*, so that the "*cash-flow*" plays a usurped and primordial role in establishing appreciation criteria of performance. Yet, the *real system of governance* which bears on decisions and performance level of organization is constituted by the innumerable interactions between the main company stakeholders and not by the solely financial strategy of public and private shareholders.

Since 1974, the socioeconomic theory of organizations initiated the concept of overall and sustainable socioeconomic performance, founded on the idea of a *better-integrated social responsibility* by the enterprise. The *Académie des Sciences Morales et Politiques (Institut de France)* awarded Savall and Zardet, in 2001, the *Médaille du Prix Rossi* for "their works on the integration of social variables in corporate strategy". The *ILO* recognized the contribution of ISEOR's works by publishing a book in English, French and Spanish on the theory of hidden costs-performances (Savall, Zardet & Bonnet, *Releasing the untapped potential of enterprises through socioeconomic management*, 2000, 2008).

Another observation is that the managerial paradigm of subordination is based on rationalism, individualism, depersonalization of work, the static function definition, exclusive hierarchy and elitism. But our observation of the functioning of enterprises has shown the limits of that subordination of the individual to his or her superiors, that one could identify by the countless dysfunctions and their economic consequences measured by hidden costs.

The socioeconomic theory thus based itself, in contrast with other approaches, on the effectiveness and the efficiency of the *negotiated commitment*, the contractualization of the performances between stakeholders, the personalization of both activity and actors' mission, listening to them, in a framework that favors the animation of teams, the educational role of managers and the cooperation of individuals in professional activity.

A major epistemological and methodological option consisted of *going down* right into the heart of enterprises and organizations (Savall, 1979; Savall & Zardet, 1987, 2004) in order to **observe** the real functioning and **experiment** with more effective and efficient organizational models, and to discover inside them the preeminence of the steering quality and intensity of organization in explaining performance. For 40 years, an impressive database of thorough cases has been patiently built. Nowadays it represents 1854 enterprises and organizations from 40 countries over four continents. Since the 1990s, these *in vivo* works have also been applied to *the management of territories*. It gradually allowed the discovery of new phenomena and factors, exogenous to organizations, creation or destruction of value added, which characterize the increasing complexity of environment. We gathered them under the concept of *tetranormalization* (Savall & Zardet, 2005a).

Genesis of the Socioeconomic Performance of Organizations

The socioeconomic management of organizations considers (Savall & Zardet, Mastering hidden costs and performances, 1987, 2007, 2008a) that an organization is a complex set that includes *five types of structures* (physical, technological, organizational, demographical and mental) that *interact with five types of human behaviors* (individual, activity group, category, affinity groups and collective). These permanent and complex interactions are creating *activities' pulsations, which* constitute the functioning of enterprises. Nevertheless, if one discerns in that functioning anomalies, perturbations, gaps between the expected fair functioning (orthofunctioning) and the observed functioning: those are *dysfunctions*. The latter could be classified into six families: working conditions, work organization, communication-coordination-cooperation, time management, integrated training and strategic implementation. Those six families constitute at the same time explicative variables of real functioning and improvement domains of practices, related to the dysfunctions identified through organizational diagnosis.

The effects incurred by these dysfunctions generate *hidden costs* endured by the organization that tarnish the pertinence, the effectiveness and the efficiency of decisions. The socioeconomic model of hidden costs analysis includes five categories of indicators. Three are *social indicators*: absenteeism, work accidents and professional diseases, turnover; and two are *economic indicators:* quality of products (goods and services) and direct productivity (produced quantities). These hidden costs affect the economic performance of the company. They include six components. The first ones are *charges* which the company could partially avoid, if its level of dysfunctions were lower; they include over wages, overtimes and overconsumptions. The fourth and fifth components are not charges but *non-products*, i.e., a loss of value produced by dysfunctions, loss of income, an opportunity cost. They include non-productions, non-creation of potential and risks endured by the enterprise (Savall, *Reconstruire l'entreprise* [Rebuild the enterprise], 1979; Savall & Zardet, 2014a).

The socioeconomic analysis and management of organizations are a conceptualization, with a *postmodern essence* (Michel Péron & Monique Péron, *Journal of Change Management*, 2003) of the functioning of company, which is intended to increase its *capacity of survival-development* and define socioeconomic steering as the arbitration between on one hand ethics and deontology, and on the other hand, effectiveness and efficiency.

"In order to start the **metamorphosis** process of the organization, it is suitable to apply an engineering method of change actions and implementation of strategies" (Savall, 2003) (see hereinafter *socioeconomic intervention*).

This process of socioeconomic intervention proposes to improve the *integral quality*, both internal and external, of organizations as well as the *steering of socioeconomic performance* with two axes:

- A *problem-solving methodology* or *change management device* which allows the improvement of products' quality, the functioning of enterprises and team management thanks to the simultaneous development of structures and behaviors quality. The process is made up of four steps: diagnosis, project, implementation, and evaluation;
- The setting up of a steering structure and a management method with *stimulating tools* which mobilize the human potential and improve the management analysis and the quality of decision-making processes.

The course of a socioeconomic intervention in an organization includes two actions: one *horizontal*, which involves top-management and management teams, and the other *vertical* in at least two units (department, service or agency) which mobilize the management and the employees. This double action consists of the "*horivert*" process, which ensures a better articulation of socioeconomic intervention to the strategy of the organization and solves both strategic and operational dysfunctions.

Main Research Results Derived from Socioeconomic Theory

Many research results are contributing simultaneously to a scientific theory, which explains the creation-destruction of value added, and to the improvement of management practices *(praxis)*. Our scientific observations have demonstrated that each enterprise or organization spontaneously generates dysfunctions and the hidden costs that result from them. The improvement of its overall and sustainable performance will be done with a more *innovative* strategy and better negotiated with the efficiency of norms made compatible, multiple and various. The early development of hybrid partnerships between enterprises, organizations and public or private institutions proves to be effective and efficient. It creates value added for stakeholders and for the territories in which they practice their economic and social strategy, along with their complex competitive games. We have discovered and established an inventory of countless categories of dysfunctions (see Table 3.1), genuine organizational pathologies (metastasis) which explain the high level of value-added destruction (Savall, 1974b; Savall & Zardet, 1987, 2008a; Savall, Zardet & Bonnet, 2000, 2008). The 1854 intervention-research cases have allowed us to identify 4713 families of generic dysfunctions: 727 in working conditions, 929 in work organization, 920 in communication-coordination-cooperation (3C), 489 in time management, 355 in integrated training and 1312 in strategic implementation.

The unexploited deposits of economic potential, identifiable by the hidden costs measurement, is also contributing to the improvement of the

Table 3.1 Inventory of generic dysfunctions identified in 1854 organizations (Expert Software SEGESE® 1987–2009–2015© ISEOR)

Working conditions	727
Work organization	929
Communication-coordination-cooperation (3C)	920
Time management	489
Integrated training	355
Strategic implementation	1312
Total types of dysfunctions	4713

"loyal picture", for accountants. They report the capacity of an organization to prepare its development, when both sustainable prevention and correction of dysfunctions allow them to avoid new dysfunctions or, on the contrary, to mortgage the company's future by a heap of hidden costs that the enterprise carries all the time as if it were a millstone. The analysis of the *ratio prevention costs/absorption costs* of dysfunctions has both explicative and prescriptive dimensions. Its measurement and the monitoring of its evolution contribute to improving the decision-making process (Savall & Zardet, 1995, 2005a).

Three factors of socioeconomic performance improvement have been identified and are contributing to the intensity of steering organizational performance: the *synchronization* or orchestration of organizational activities and actors, the *cleaning up* (adaptation and periodical "cleaning up" of structures, activities, norms, strategies and human behaviors) and the *stimulation* of energies, competencies and human behaviors, through the quality management of persons.

The increasing of effectiveness-efficiency of an organization depends mainly on the increasing level of intangible investment in qualitative development of human potential

Only the *holistic approach of the enterprise*, in opposition to a functional or sectorial one, is likely to explain the level and the mechanisms of its economic performance and to arouse sustainable improvement of this performance. Furthermore, the spontaneous evolution of the enterprise does not allow for the "automatic" adaptation to its environment by preserving its capacity of survival-development and its competitiveness. A deliberate and anticipated evolution implies a structured process, which has been modeled through 1854 intervention-research cases (Savall & Zardet, 2004, 2014a).

The steering of this process *sustainably leverages the different categories of employees to implement innovative socioeconomic tools*. At the top of the company, it is essential that managers clearly define strategic orientations and validate the action plans proposed by their subordinates. At each level of the enterprise, the method appeals to the "*mirror-effect*" technique, which helps teams to become conscious of the importance of hidden costs and elaborate improvements solutions for dysfunctions. Likewise, the *metamorphosis* action needs clarification of the *rules of the game* of the enterprise's functioning (Zardet & Voyant, 2003). Indeed, the company needs *external energy contribution* in order to recycle its hidden costs into value added. It helps to identify the most important deposits and to apply *innovative* change management methods and development of human potential.

Table 3.2 presents the results of 40 enterprises where such processes have been implemented. The endogenous and exogenous *investment* in *human potential* earns a ROI from 200 percent to 4,000 percent depending on companies: 1 euro invested gets back from 2 to 40 Euros, which situates *the profitability of such a type of intangible investment* high above the ones from corporeal investments, traditionally proposed by economists and management scientists (Savall & Zardet, 2007, 2008b).

Therefore, we have discovered that the success of the external strategy of a company depends on its degree of internal *cohesion*. This one allows realizing strategic ambitions to varying degrees. Quite the contrary, strategic delays or failures are explained by breaks in internal cohesion. More than the pertinence of strategic choices, it is the internal *strategic strength of an organization* (competencies, proactive behaviors, internal cohesion between hierarchical levels and cooperation between sectors and individuals) that contributes to its strategic performance. This theory extracted from the meta-socioeconomic theory has been named *strategic bedrock* theory. It expresses the multiplication effect of performance obtained by the reinforcement of the company's bedrock, that is to say its **cohesion** (Savall & Zardet, 1995, 2005a, 2014b).

Very High Elasticity of the Collective Human Overall Productivity

The hidden costs measure the "hemorrhaging" of an organization. Their reduction, i.e., their conversion into value added, means that it is possible to improve the level of human productivity **without degrading** the working conditions (quite the reverse) by their improvement and preservation. Still more spectacular is the observation over a long period (more than 10 years) of continuous improvement of this overall human productivity. This is the proof of huge resources that humans achieve and that they are able, with

Table 3.2 Profitability of intangible investment on qualitative development of human potential (IIQDHP)

Profitability rate of IIQDHP	Enterprises and organizations from various industries and countries	
	Numbers	*% of the sample*
210% to 980%	15	37,5%
1000% to 1980%	16	40%
2000% to 3000%	6	15%
3000% to 4014%	3	7,5%
TOTAL	40	100%

higher commitment, to transform into real socioeconomic performances. Some of the most ancient cases are giving edifying testimonies as Brioche Pasquier and Trade and Industrial Chamber of Morbihan in France, Technord in Belgium, Aguacates Sánchez in Mexico, the hospitals of Ste Therese Congregation in Lebanon, La Lignière clinic in Switzerland . . . those cases have been confirmed by a lot of others in our database (Buono & Savall, 2007; Savall, Zardet & Bonnet, 2009a).

The Organizations Get the Capacity to Self-Finance Their Survival Development

The substantial deposits of hidden costs constitute recyclable **resources** for financing innovative actions, liberating resources and time in order to turns them into endogenous proactive strategies. Each enterprise could, however, without any additional external resources, self-finance its intangible investments in the qualitative development of human potential and so consolidate its internal cohesion, a source of sustainable performance.

Dysfunctions and Hidden Costs Isomorphism

Starting from the macro economy, socioeconomic theory has plunged itself into organizations all the way to the level of the work team in order to observe with rigor and proximity, how economic value is created or destroyed, in the organization and in the interface with its external environment. Then, the application field of our works, the size of companies (staffed from 3 to 30,000 persons) and the interorganizational issues have led us to pull up to the macroeconomic level of analysis. We have clearly identified isomorphic phenomena related to dysfunctions and hidden costs, which allows us to identify **macro-hidden costs** such as the waste of drugs bought but not used, which is estimated around 3 billion Euros per year in France. This direction led us to our new research program on *tetranormalization*.

Proximities with Perroux's Concepts

The main key concepts shared that result from the approximation between Perroux's theory and socioeconomic theory, converge around two mains ideas (the theory of active units and asymmetric relationships) and three theories of the enterprise highlighted by Perroux, Schumpeter, Coase and Marschak. The theory of active units (Perroux, 1975) is the synthesis of several decades of works carried out, starting with his famous article on dominant economy (Perroux, 1948). His analysis is macroeconomic scaled; however, it is remarkable that the fundamental phenomena are the same that we have observed within organizations: activity, change energy, creation, and asymmetric relationships.

Socioeconomic theory considers that man and work teams, production units (factories), enterprises and nonprofit organizations, groups of enterprises, territorial communities, i.e., social groups that are developing an economic activity, should be conceptualized as *relative autonomy agents*, so-called "active units", according to Perroux's concept. Indeed, they all have the main features of an *organization*: a social group gifted with an individuality, a formal and informal decision-making process, a physical capital, psychological and intangible resources. These actors possess an *essential attribute*: *the activity*. That is to say, the capacity to act on their environment, to restructure it by creating new economic and social values. The vision is systemic, and it is defined by an analogy with biology, which studies the relationships between a cell and its plastic environment. This capacity to structure the environment is called **change energy**. Our works have an a priori objective: to discover and measure the resource of change energy available at individual, team and organization's scales. The notion of *activity* is core in Perroux's theory as in socioeconomic theory (SEAM).

In his foreword to the book *Reconstruire l'entreprise [Rebuild the enterprise]* (Savall, 1979), Perroux underlines what we were proposing "this periodically negotiable activity contract which, being loyally practiced and in the best case scenario (a systematic and badly informed optimism is not in Henri Savall's mind) would raise the prescribed labor to the labor dignity freely granted" (Perroux, 1979). He leans therefore on his demonstration of the enterprise—active unit—for the equilibration of economic activities by resting on Schumpeter with whom he worked in Vienna before the World War II (Perroux, 1936, 1965), Coase (pioneer of transaction costs, 1937) and Marschak and Radner, promoters of the economic theory of teams. In the rest of his foreword, Perroux highlights the precursory contributions of Coase on the relationships between enterprise and market, while showing that Coase stayed in midstream in the evolution of his thought. We share with Perroux the criticism of transaction costs theory, which still serve the apology of the equalitarian market. "Coase, himself, questioned the theoretical *raison d'être* of enterprise. Why, in this market universe, does the enterprise be this 'organization islet'? [. . .] This singular organism which allows the individuals to save information costs, for it has a structure and a hierarchy [. . .] We are driven so close to the recognition of the organization, but the step would not be crossed [. . .] The fulfill confident economist in the market would grant to the firm chief the quality of coordinator . . . only as a last resort (peak coordinator)" (Perroux, 1979; see also Marschak & Radner, 1972).

Actors and organizations—active units—according to Perroux's concept, able to act and change their pertinent environments, are in that sense entrepreneurs or intrapreneurs of routine activities and socioeconomically innovative activities, when they are recycling hidden costs into value added, instead of enduring them. The high amount of hidden costs and their conversion helps to understand how the creation of value added can be generated or destroyed in organizations, in interaction with their environments.

Indeed, the dialectic of **conflict-cooperation** highlighted by Perroux in the economic universe is at the core of socioeconomic theory, in the interactions between individuals, groups and enterprises. The hidden costs are also the expression of conflicting relationships and the recycling of hidden costs shows that periodically renewed negotiating strategies allow, more than the imposition of top-down ones, the increase of economic performances shared with the different stakeholders.

Socioeconomic Intervention: A Structured Method for Carrying Out Change and Implementing Strategies

The socioeconomic intervention process proposes to improve the steering of both **social and economic performance integrated throughout two axes**. An engineering device of change management helps improve the integral quality of the organization, because of the simultaneous development of quality **structures** and **behaviors**. It also includes the setting up of a steering device and a management method with *stimulating* tools. Those engender the capacity to mobilize the human potential, to improve management analysis and the decision-making process' pertinence.

HORIVERT model (horizontal and vertical) has three components: a *"static"* model of actors' architecture such that it is suitable to implement a dynamic model of change impulsion and a sequencing model called the *chronobiological* of change (organizational development) and those of deep change (socio-technical approach). This method is so devised HORIVERT (Savall & Zardet, 1987) because it consists of articulating change management between top-management teams and middle management teams (*horizontal* process on the whole enterprise) with very concrete change actions carried out in many units of the enterprise (*vertical* process). This articulation generates the propagation of change dynamics in the whole enterprise. It allows middle management to steer the change management, because the horizontal actions are contributing to enhance its role while facilitating certain responsibilities' transfers to collaborators and employees under the form of *collaborative delegation* tools. Thus, this method leads to create both economic performance and develop the involvement and the empowerment of actors at each organizational level (social performance).

Horivert Architecture Facilitates the Integration of the Top Management and Teams in Change Process

This method articulates two synchronized and simultaneous actions: (1) a *horizontal* action that consists of organizing *"clusters"* (teams with their hierarchical superior) of training, each cluster being composed of its top-manager and its middle managers. The collaborative training in management tools is realized in each cluster. (2) A *vertical* action in at least two units (departments, services, agencies) that involve the management team of these units and their employees. The HORIVERT model allows, on one hand, one to ensure a better articulation of the socioeconomic intervention to the strategy of the organization, and on the other hand, to highlight and solve dysfunctions, of a strategic nature as well as those related to the day-to-day activity because of a lack of actors' *involvement* (Buono, 2001, 2003; Hayes, 2001; Boje & Rosile, 2003).

This intervention architecture ensures the *assimilation* of change within the enterprise, starting from the top-management team and extending to the shop-floor employees. This is also an architecture for *learning* and for actors and activities **integration**. The HORIVERT model is adaptable to a great variety of company cases: large companies or organizations, and very small ones composed by few persons. In this last case, the démarche called "*HORIVERT multi-SME*" is managed by gathering 4 to 5 companies. It consists in building a horizontal action inter-enterprise by gathering the CEOs from each company, accompanied by one of two collaborators. In addition, inside each enterprise, a vertical action is carried out.

The Change Is Carried Out With Three Impulsion Forces, Each of Them Being a Source of Energy for Change

The SEAM intervention process is designed according to a "Trihedron" model composed of three axes. The first one, called **improvement process**, represents the change dynamic in four successive steps, the second, called **management tools**, represents the bringing of management tools to the whole of management team in the horizontal action. Last, the third one represents the **strategic and politic decisions** and expresses the fact that change could not be realized without a decisional strength energy force, which results from the company's actors' game (CEOs, management, employees). This force shows the real will to change, far over the discourses of intention and is translated by decisions of transformation within the different sectors of the company. Thus, socioeconomic management, wherever it introduces strategic and innovative strategic choices, reinforces the *internal cohesion* of teams, the *external* coherence and their interactions.

A Participative Process of Dysfunctions Recycling in Four Steps

The first strength of the change impulsion called improvement process includes four main steps:

> First, a **diagnosis** of dysfunctions with a hidden costs calculation is carried out. The *horizontal diagnosis* aims at identifying the dysfunctions perceived by the top and middle management in order to establish a general and transversal diagnosis of dysfunctions. This is further deepened with vertical diagnoses which allow, in a second iteration, to involve the employees. Each member of the top-management and management

teams, part of a consultation-training cluster is individually interviewed. The diagnosis is composed of the expression of persons, under key-ideas illustrated by field-note quotes. It is presented to all the interviewed persons, in each cluster in order to provoke a *mirror-effect*.

At least two sectors are concerned by a *vertical diagnosis* more precise. This one consists of taking an inventory of dysfunctions inside the sector audited and calculating the *hidden costs, which* result from the latter. All the *competency grids* from the sector allow deepened analysis of the match between skills and activity. Interviews focused on sector dysfunctions will be further carried out with each manager and supervisor. Then, interviews are carried out with small groups (3 to 4 persons) of employees. This method allows facilitators to meet between 30 percent to 60 percent of the workforce, by ensuring the variety of the sample: in terms of profession, duration, age, sex. The *field-note quotes* (*specific* dysfunctions) from the whole of the interviewed persons are classified in themes and sub-themes, then synthesized under *key-ideas* (*generic* dysfunctions) with SEGESE® software (expert system in socioeconomic management) created by ISEOR for the analysis of qualitative data. The mirror effect of the vertical diagnosis is presented at first to the department management team, and then to the interviewed employees along with their management staff.

A Project for Elaborating Innovative Solutions

The *horizontal project* represents the whole of improvement actions aiming at reducing the dysfunctions inventoried in the horizontal diagnosis, and at deploying the strategy of the company. The diagnosis of dysfunctions and the strategic project are thus two sources, which supply the research of improvement actions. The horizontal project is elaborated under the leadership of the CEO with the support of a focus group. The four to six focus group meetings are spread over four months. In order to structure the search for solutions, the main ideas of the *expert opinion* are gathered in three to four "dysfunctions baskets". Each basket constitutes a *root cause* of dysfunctions and is the responsibility of a "working group". *The vertical projects* are elaborated by a focus group, whose project manager is the hierarchical supervisor of the sector. Those workgroups are steered by a member of the plenary group and other organizational persons, managers, experts and employees can participate.

The structured *implementation* of improvement actions is followed from the **qualimetric** *evaluation* of socioeconomic results, which are *qualitative, quantitative and financial*. They are steps 3 and 4 in the process. The concept of **qualimetrics** consists of recognizing that the pertinent representation of an object or a fact needs both words and numbers *at the same time* to be meaningful: an idea needs a number to be meaningful, and a number needs a word or an idea as well in order to be interpreted (Savall, 1974b; Savall & Zardet, 2004).

So, a comparative evaluation is realized almost one year after the very beginning of the intervention. It allows organizations to identify striking improvements and to evaluate the gains of value added. In-depth interviews are carried out with top managers and a sampling of other managers, supervisors and employees in order to make an inventory of the striking actions and performance, from actors' point of view. The gains in value added, which are really observed, are compared to the cost of action, which allows one to establish a *real economic balance* and to calculate the **change action** ROI realized by the company or the organization. This evaluation has a significant impact: it helps the company to be conscious of the realized improvements and generates a new cycle of *change energy* because it tends to decrease over the course of time.

4 The Core Concept of Human Potential

Human Potential Theory

The role of **human potential** is at the core of the genesis of sustainable economic performance. The macroeconomic and managerial decision-making process models ignore these considerable data. They inspire decisions, at macroeconomic and organizational levels, which are proving to be erroneous, irrational and anachronistic. They are dangerous for the survival-development of organizations but also for the human being. One of the fundamental assumptions of socioeconomic theory is that the *qualitative development* (quality of behaviors and development of competencies) of human potential constitutes an *intangible investment,* which generates a high level of value added, and a competitive advantage for the company, which is replicable only with a high degree of difficulty. The level and the intensity of organizational human potential are a function of three main components: *human energy, actors' behaviors in professional life and their competencies.*

Collective and Individual Energy

The individuals, members of an organization, are provided with an *endogenous* energy more or less mobilized in their professional sphere. They are *active units* according to François Perroux (1975). This level of energy depends on the *compatibility* level between each individual project and the collective strategy of the organization (Savall & Zardet, 1995, 2005a). The higher this level, the more the individual is activating and deploying his/her energy in professional practices that generate value added. *A contrario,* when the compatibility level is low, the individual commits him/herself to a lesser degree in his/her professional activity. Thus he/she generates, in interaction with his/her partners, more dysfunctions and hidden costs. So, his/her energy that would otherwise be devoted to one's vocation finds an outlet elsewhere, effectively robbing the organization of that productivity. The management and leadership role is a priori for accompanying the organizational actors, individually and collectively, in activating and deploying their collective energy.

Professional Behaviors

They are essential in the socioeconomic theory of organization (SEAM). Observable human behaviors have impacts on social and economic performance. Actors' needs in professional situations are *multiform* and composed of psychological, physiological, sociological and economical dimensions. The activation of professional behaviors depends on factors such as recognition, thriving, professional evolution and monetary retribution. The analysis of the *conflict-cooperation* couple, at the core of socioeconomic theory, highlights behavioral dialectics observed: involvement *versus* escape, commitment versus disobedience, creation of value versus destruction of value, teamwork versus egoist competition. The criteria of professional behaviors tend to be more discriminative than those of professional competencies, in the human resource management of today's organizations. Indeed, the transformation of professional competencies appears to be easier than changing professional behaviors. In addition, professional competencies are actually mobilized only if actors have the *will* and adopt active behaviors.

Professional Competencies

Their level results from the knowledge mobilized that serves to do the activities. One could distinguish two types of knowledge: *living* and current knowledge developed by individuals in thoughts and actions versus the *inert* knowledge from the past, stored, formalized and represented by symbols or signs on a written support *reminder*. Knowledge is mobilized according to a *cognitive interactivity* mechanism. The exchange is *interpersonal* between two or more human subjects, but it could consist of animating inert knowledge; when reading a text, seeing a picture is inspiring to an actor or a group to engage with some living ideas, opinions or feelings. The professional competencies are put into practice when this cognitive interactivity generates its effects, when the activities entrusted to persons activate the knowledge they have acquired by *experience*. One understands the harmful effect of **TFW virus** (taylorism-fayolism-weberism), which limits strongly the range of activities entrusted to an actor. The latter loses quickly his or her knowledge, which stays in the inert state for lack of implementation. *The obsolescence of knowledge and competencies, often* observed, is one of the major sources of dysfunctions and hidden costs.

Human Potential Life Cycle

Observing organizations shows that human potential is suffering from a life cycle phenomena. Thus, the energy tends toward *erosion*, which requires maintenance. If not, it will decrease over time according to the *entropy* phenomenon. The behaviors very frequently evolve at the whim of situations and professional or extra-professional events. This requires a great attention

from management for engaging in more listening, dialoging and contractu-
alizing performances with colleagues. The competencies are equally vulner-
able to erosion and degradation; this implies maintenance and preventive
acts in order to ensure their availability.

From Master-Slave Relationship to Proximity Democracy in the Enterprise

Jérôme Ballet, Aurélie Carimentrand and Patrick Jolivet (*L'entreprise et
l'éthique* [*Enterprise and ethic*], 2011) assert that a master-slave relationship
dates back to antiquity and endures in the twenty-first century. This is not
astonishing if we recall what Bernard de Mandeville wrote in the eighteenth
century, that *it is manifest that in a free nation where slavery is forbidden,
the more reliable wealth consists in a multitude of industrious poor.* At the
same time, Marivaux let play an actual theater production: "Slave's Island",
a social utopia where the valets were recycling their masters. Yet, Fernand
Braudel (1986) affirms that there is no clear rupture between slavery, servitude and the wage system. In fact, Pope Leon XIII in his encyclique "*rerum
novarum*" exhorted employers not to treat workers as slaves and to respect
human dignity (Beaud, 2010). Pope François, by talking to the worshiping
people gathered in the place St Pierre, in Roma, has deplored several times
the rise of slavery in this start of the twenty-first century. The UN outdis-
tanced him by sending out to states a warning concerning the recrudescence
of human trafficking across the world. TV documentaries have reiterated
this warning about the fate of modern slaves. Some NGOs are tackling these
inhuman working conditions and have made a complaint against "forced
labor" and "reduction to servitude".

As was rightly written by Andrew Crane in an article entitled "Modern
Slavery as a Management Practice: exploring the conditions and capabilities for human exploitation" (*Academy of Management Review*, 2013,
pp. 49–69) "slavery is not simply a line of economic history: it persists under
various forms and contexts in today's business world". Therefore, an edito-
rial of the *International New York Times* (June 2014, 3rd), entitled "The
Fruits of Forced Labor", recalls the report of United Nations International
Labor Organization, dedicated to this problem: "It debunks any notion that
forced labor is a problem restricted to the most depressed places on earth.
On the contrary, the world's most developed ones, including European
Union, account for nearly a third of the profits from illegal forced labor".

Public opinion is warned of the drift of such *unleashed and perverted* capitalism. Recall that in the twelvth century, a man could be bought as a merchandise, and a score was attributed to him based on his health and physical
conditions. More generally, William Petty has calculated the capital value of
an individual or a category several times, with sometimes very considerable
gaps (Hull, 1899, p. 265). For this economist, the score of individual value is
also linked to a kind of classification for *social utilities* (Pierre Rosanvallon,

Le capitalisme utopique [Utopian capitalism], 1979) to the notion of power, as Thomas Hobbes expresses with confidence in his *Leviathan* (1651) "*The Value or Worth of a man is as of all other things, his Price, that is to say, so much as would be given for the use of his Power: and therefore is not absolute, but a thing dependent on the need and judgment of another*". The mercantilists contradicted before Kant, for whom things have prices but no value, while humans get a value but no price. The word *worth* used by Hobbes is not redundant; quite the opposite. It expresses the degree of utility and financial value. According to Hobbes, "*a man's labor also is a commodity exchangeable for benefit as well as any other thing*". It is the "*commodization*" of individuals that we observe today (Hobbes, 1651, 1964, p. 174) and is reification. We note that at this period, the word *value* stands as the sense of exchange value. Use value was more specifically evoked, as for Hobbes, by the word *worth*. Marx puts it this way: "In the XVIIth century, we find often in British writers the word worth for use value and the word value for exchange value, following the mind of a language that loves to examine the immediate thing in German terms and the reflected thing in Roman terms" (Marx, 1967, p. 562). William Petty, as Adam Smith would do later, based value on three criteria: workload (labor), qualification (art) and accountability (trust) (Hull, 1899, p. 25). A slave who belongs, according to Petty, to the category of people of great labor and little expense (Hull, 1899, p. 303) is defined as a person under the absolute dependence of a master who could dispose of him/her as any other goods. His/her value is not estimated in terms of labor but as utility because it is really reduced to the state of a commodity. This impossibility for the slave to escape from their condition could be observed unfortunately in these times of unemployment where the employer could practice a coercive power by the possibility, which he/she has to use more or less violence to the psychological ascendancy, which consists of putting forward as a threat the unemployability of workers outside their actual frame.

This notion of **employability**, which is omnipresent nowadays in discourses on the insertion possibilities of the labor community, was earlier evoked by Adam Smith in his *Wealth of Nations*:

> The property which every man has in his own labor, as it is the original foundation of all other property, so it is the most sacred and inviolable. The patrimony of a poor man lies in the strength and dexterity of his hands; and to hinder him from employing this strength and dexterity in what manner he thinks proper without injury to his neighbor is a plain violation of this most sacred property. It is a manifest encroachment upon the just liberty both of the worker, and of those who might be disposed to employ him. As it hinders the one from working at what he thinks proper, so it hinders other people from employing whom they think proper. To judge whether he fits to be employed, may surely be trusted to the discretion of the employers whose interest it so much

concerns. The affected anxiety of the law-giver lest they should employ an improper person, is evidently as impertinent as it is oppressive.

(1776, p. 109)

Illiteracy represents a high degree of a worker's *dependence*, as well in his/her professional environment as in his/her family life. In addition, the lack of numeric competencies constitutes today a new form of illiteracy. There is an incompatibility between workers and the market. A statistical inquiry should present that only a few groups of persons are occupied in necessary works (Hull, 1899, p. 396). Among the causes of unemployment, Petty distinguishes *"a want of proper work"*: *"proper"*, i.e., adapted to the level of the existing workforce, a structural cause in some way, often put forward nowadays with this notion of employability (Péron, 2003, Chômage et emploi au dix-septième siècle [Employment and Unemployment in 17th century] *in Travail et emploi* [Labor and Employment], p. 56–60). It is necessary to adapt by the training the workers to the market and not create jobs adapted to over numbered workers, as Thomas Mun said in 1664 (*England's Treasure by Foreign Trade*).

Judging by the high number of job opportunities, which remain unsatisfied, the situation stays unchanged. In the framework of a SRC, we think, as William Petty, that *one has to get a deepened vision of the labor market with statistical inquiries and search for the genuine "employment areas" in order to avoid the massive arrival of a workforce without any qualifications.* Our intervention-research within a great variety of enterprises and organizations has shown through our competency grids that a lack of requirement in this domain could lead to sudden dismissal decisions. Because competitiveness necessitates training and adaptive recycling of human resources. Such compressions of workforce or relocation could be thus avoided. Anyway, we have observed that a lot of serious conflicts in enterprises could be attributed to organizational types or management models, which have evolved very little regarding the evolution of expectations of employees. For the active workforce, this situation ends on "social" hidden costs, which convey a deep disorder between organizational structures and human behaviors.

The issue has to be treated in the framework of socially responsible capitalism. We also observe that the social treatment of unemployment, as we are describing it today, was considered in the sixteenth century as particularly costly, from the social point of view, because the homeless, multiplied by the crisis of the wool industry, were in charge of the community, and therefore the parish and the local government. Spanish Juan Luis Vives' book *"De Subventione Pauperum"* published in 1526 (Translation Casanova and Caby, *De l'assistance aux pauvres* [Assisting the poor's], 1943) sums up perfectly the attitude that it was suitable to adopt facing the idleness of naked workers: giving a job instead of rescuing (*Travail et Emploi* [Labor and employement], *op.cit.* p. 22). In the framework of a socially responsible capitalism, the anticipated regulation of supply and demand of work should be unavoidable.

A *serf* (the intermediate condition between the slave and the salaried) is a person who does not have personal and complete freedom, related to a land, struck down by diverse incapacities, subjected to certain obligations and living under the dependence of a lord in the feudal system. There is an exchange tainted by certain *equity* between the lord and the serf, the first granted its protection in exchange for obedience and work from the second. In the perverted capitalist system, the wage-earner is a person remunerated by an employer for whom he/she sold his/her workforce, until swapping his/her status of human being for the one of commodity on the labor market. In this conception of the classical school of salaried condition, there is the renouncement from the salaried to its power of organization and its decision power. Its protection is in part ensured by the state with the social security system and in part with personal insurance that he/she has to pay him/herself. He/she relies on the organizational power of the employer by divesting of any responsibility in a labor world where one always considers there to be discriminate deciders and executors. That is to say, the basic worker who is economically exploited and underpaid has his/her decision power withdrawn. He/she is transformed into a dehumanized robot, such as in the admirable *Metropolis* from Fritz Lang. The worker does not have to think and can just execute the tasks according to prescribed methods, which we have called the *Scientific Organization of Work* since the time of Taylor. As Michel Beaud (2010, p. 263) wrote, "*The progress of productivity between the two world wars results at the same time from the mechanization/motorization/ rationalization of production and from the intensification of work under the pressure of diverse organizational methods and remunerations*".

In this century of outrageous computerization of human activity "*the different modes of constraints for overwork which the capitalism sets up during its development*" mentioned by Beaud (2010, p. 290) are no longer accurate. Reorganizing the job design and rationalizing working time to avoid dead times in production remain important worries of leading teams. Managers could no longer legitimately deprive the workers of their liberty at their workstations by expecting from them a higher and more and more intensive yield. All this is in conformity with the scientific organization of work, initiated by Taylor and pushed to the limit in order to respond to the expectations unleashed by a perverted and socially irresponsible capitalism, which has been favored by globalization. If we accept the idea that democracy is a not dissociable concept of the enterprise as supported by Olivier Voyant (Voyant, 2003), it would be suitable at this stage to question the implementation of democratic intentions by carrying forward a reflection on the break between the democratic intentions of society and democratic reality of companies.

We consider here **democracy** in its directly participative form and not the elective one. This latter is not basically *intrinsic* to the particular type of organization that the enterprise constitutes. In its usual configuration, its structures do not work in that sense of a governance model as *vox populi vox dei*. In a contribution to the 3rd congress of the Association for the Development of Education and Research on Corporate Social Responsibility (ADERSE) entitled "Approche philosophique de la Responsabilité Sociale de l'Entreprise (RSE): pour une nouvelle éthique du pouvoir du plus grand nombre" [Philosophical approach of Corporate Social Responsibility: for a new ethic of majority power], Loïck Roche notices that "*each member knows very well that he/she does not command—he/she feels that democracy is a swindle*" (ADERSE, *Responsabilité Sociale de l'Entreprise* [Corporate Social Responsibility], 2008, p. 2103). In the framework of a socially responsible capitalism, the question is not who gets the power but who knows better when it comes to managing. Thus, as Voyant states, the picture given by the enterprises appears to be more and more brutal, and not translating a democratic will.

Socioeconomic management (SEAM) with its insistence on proximity's dialogues, is searching to better integrate the minority to the decision-making process in the framework of a *collaborative* and participative process on the field *democracy*. It aims to reduce in parallel the opposition between permanent political dispute, which the press is echoing, and a non-oriented participation in social and economic development with the strong conviction to avoid all forms of **demagogy**. In Bangladesh, the collapsing of a building that housed workshops of the textile industry brought about the death of a thousand workers. This is a tragic illustration, all the more so as they were working at an untenable pace on behalf of important occidental firms, which are now constrained to ask for better working conditions for the employees who are threatened when it comes to their safety, their health and even in their existence. Compensation funds have been created with the support of Bangladeshian authorities and the ILO, but the distributors are considering gathering in order to improve working conditions in industry without evoking the lesser negligence of their own acts.

Democracy inside of the enterprise and more largely in the economic sphere remains flouted on several planes as demonstrating an example of this "unhealthy break" between economic and social concerns, which is mentioned by Jacques Delors in his foreword to Henri Savall's book *Enrichir le travail humain* [Work and people: An Economic evaluation of Job-Enrichment]. There are, of course, organizations whose objective is to ensure the defense of labor rights in general, for example the *International Labor Rights Forum (ILFR)*, more commonly referred to as *Clean Clothes Campaign*, which aims at the clandestine workshops. The *China Labor Watch* is an association of defense for Chinese workers based in New York, which denounces the pressures exerted by Apple on its subcontractors for whom competitiveness lays on infringement of worker rights.

The **negotiation spirit** is vital for the *non-elective* democracy inside of the enterprise, which is materialized only by the **day-to-day dialog** that allows one to collect opinions, but in any case, the final decision belongs only to higher authorities. The negotiation spirit is supposed to prevail according to the new reform of the French labor market, with the competitiveness pact between employers and trade unions, but it seems to surface rarely if we judge by the proceedings of company failures or the brutality of certain downsizing measures, which are explained by the incapacity of actors in negotiating, in an anticipative way and with the lack of courage from the hierarchy when it is an opportunity to anticipate inevitable hard decisions. The spirit of negotiation is totally absent to the upholders of the wild capitalism whose fatal weapon is the simple liquidation of unprofitable companies without looking for the causes or caring to remedy them.

In the course of our numerous interventions within enterprises, we observed that the drastic restructurations were often ineffective because they were undertaken too late. We could conclude that the opposition to change and protection of the *status quo* that have been created either by the myopia of the company and social actors, or by the seeking of a social peace in the short term, is brutally enacting a restructuration that affects the workforce in considerable proportion.

> If in the new methods of organization the stress is put on employees' motivation, their commitment and their empowerment, any "tool" which could make these objectives cross from the state of vain wishes to the status of inevitable factors in the new organizational strategies was not put forward. The socioeconomic approach fills this lack by proposing management tools such as competency grid, priority action plan, and piloting logbook. These tools allow one to think about the evolution of companies and to proceed if needed from soft and progressive micro-restructurings to evolutions by successive touches of the actual contents of jobs, to yield a better performance from each individuals' potential, to prepare them for products, jobs, technological evolution . . . .
>
> (Savall & Zardet, 2005b, p. 39)

That is to say integrating them into the framework of socially and sustainably responsible capitalism.

In a *resolutely* democratic view, the recycling of hidden costs into value added is operating with a participative method, as in the actions' conception phase rather than in their implementation when steered by a manager. Those actions focus on different domains: working conditions, work organization, time management, communication-coordination-cooperation, integrated training and strategic implementation. Innovative organizations allow, in one part, for actively soliciting the employees to search for *improvement solutions* for their company, and in another part, for soliciting the evolution of actors' human resources, given the fact that competencies and human potentials constitute the first strategic lever of sustainable improvement for economic performance (Savall & Zardet, 2005b). The company actors are far from being **passive** and **contemplative** of their organization's evolution. They have the capacity to struggle against the *exogenous* determination of their future because they are considered by the socioeconomic approach as plentiful members of an organization whose interests are merging with their own. The main issue for an organization is to create a performance, that could be obtained only through the *active cooperation* of individuals and teams. The stress is placed on creation of *synergies* in the company instead of the systematic search for compromise. *Human potential* is highlighted as the sole active principle in the business world and the key factor of the *democratic reflex* of collective commitment.

We have previously mentioned the protestant ethics of labor (Gervais, Azuelos & Esposito *Travail et emploi* [Labor and employment], 2003, p. 18). This should lead us to adopt a system of **values** that the founding fathers developed in a business world where the probity of behaviors is a necessity in order to ensure the fair application of former constructs. A severe hit had been given to this system of values by the successive scandals, which had splashed both the business and financial worlds onto the international scenery. Nevertheless, the business world is considered to be reflection of the society in which it operates. Socially responsible capitalism and the democratic enterprise are equally founded on values. The latter contributes to the creation and maintenance of benevolent and human organizations where candidates are rushing, attracted by the existence of moral rules and duties that contribute to ensure the permanency of the institution. As pinpointed by David Chandler (*Academy of Management Review*, 2014, p. 398) "*values underpin our daily actions and, in the aggregate, help constitute the society in which we live*". The market society in the USA symbolizes the way of life in that frame where the market's values permeate the way to be and to behave as responsible citizens. Socially responsible capitalism does not only subscribe to this affirmation because, by nature, it is led to define acceptable and unacceptable behaviors, which favor or, on the contrary, destroy **cohesion** and **social well-being.**

The notion of **interdependence** that is a key factor of socioeconomic management is also at the very foundation of the collective characteristics of enterprise strategies. This has to benefit to all stakeholders from the economic and social performance point of view. This is not the case of a *cynical* capitalism, which leads large companies to be acclaimed for their ethics and immediately thereafter denounced for their scandalous and criminal practices. Implementing a system with complex values belongs to socioeconomic management. It includes possible negative impacts and needs consensus. Max Weber asserted that the development of capitalism owed a lot to moral qualities from religious expectations of Protestantism. What remains of this today? Among the basic values, we could quote freedom, human dignity and democracy, components therefore of the founding principles of the only nation in the world that was born from a commercial compact—the *Mayflower Compact*. In its constitution, the young nation pointed out freedom and pursuit of happiness. Freedom is an important concept in our representation of a SRC. Let us note besides that capitalism is sometimes simply described as an economic system of freedom. But this liberty should not be practiced outside the scope of values such as trust, commitment, respect and business honesty, which are so-called relational or mutual values and expect **reciprocity.**

Socially responsible capitalism highlights the concept of **dignity**, which starts with self-respect. It refuses each situation where human beings, transformed into dehumanized robots, lose their dignity. Our **socioeconomic productivity** concept, which is both legitimate and beneficial, refers to human dignity, which stokes up sustainable autonomy. SRC has to foster the development of a society in which rules, institutions, circuits and structures foster the respect and development of human dignity by imposing sanctions on behaviors that degrade dignity. A staff treated with dignity is bound to show more cooperation. Cultivating, promoting and preserving dignity are **both ethical and profitable.** Nevertheless, this point of view is part of the socioeconomic reasoning only by coincidence. The dignity dimension in SRC is based on the very foundation of socioeconomic management, in other words shared and common work with a view to create shared value added. Personal profit to the detriment of collective profit, whatever it is, is not acceptable. It would be contrary to the values of altruism and empathy. Especially in times of crisis, enterprises are cornerstones of the society from which they expect commitments in exchange of their economically and socially structuring roles that allow for ethics and moral values which preside over the creation of major organizations.

A recent pamphlet made by the organization "*Great place to Work*" focused on ranking enterprises where it feels good to work. This illustrates the point of view that we have shared since 1973 in this period of disaffection regarding the business world. It is not enough to entrench itself or to face stormy periods. It is in the equitable value distribution and not on its simple predation that the respect of the other dignity lies. Depriving the stakeholders of the value that they had contributed to create comes to attack their dignity because production and creation are themselves demonstrations of human dignity. Dignity is absent in the parasite, predator and unproductive *speculator*.

Proximity and Stress Management

Since the publication of the annual barometer on employment elaborated by the *Confédération française démocratique du travail (CFDT)* [French Democratic Confederation or Work], which concerns quality and access to training, autonomy conditions, self-expressions in workspaces, integration in the workplace, talent acquisition and professional assessment, it emerges according to the secretary in charge of labor that "*70% of salaried people estimate getting the means to execute a quality job, enough autonomy to realize it and satisfying responsibilities. This is the proof that today work is not a synonym of suffering"* (Le Figaro Économique, 4 novembre 2011). However, this same periodic notice indicates that millions of workers from all over the world feel suffering in work, which reminds us what our encyclopedists were expressing (*Encyclopédie ou Dictionnaire raisonné des sciences, des arts et des métiers*, 1751–1772) in the article dedicated to work: "Man looks at labor as a pain, and then as the foe of his rest. On the contrary, this is the source of all pleasures and the safest remedy against boredom. The labor of body which delivers the mind from sorrows, is what makes the poor happy". Even if they are only manual laborers, this remark should not be obliterated because it concerns a large number of individuals reduced by unemployment to accept small jobs, *hamburger-flipping jobs* as is said in the USA.

We must emphasize that the optimistic results from the inquiry of CFDT union are tempered by the fear that 47 percent of interviewed workers have for their futures, that of facing the risk of unemployment. They are feeling unable to get back into the employment market. It is essential to present the conditions of a socially and sustainably responsible capitalism because it is admitted that the pressure does not increase performance and also that the feeling of a worker gets at his own workstation has a strong impact on his creativity, productivity, quality of work, commitment and team spirit. In the framework of a socially and sustainably responsible capitalism, there are crucial domains in which one has to obtain the means in order to activate or reactivate them. Not doing that should be contributing to the lack of attractiveness of professional life that we deplore nowadays.

The stress factor is largely analyzed in the press and specialized books. It has to be **refocused**. Of course, stress has a negative impact on individual and collective performance. However, its origin cannot be blamed on the so-called infernal pace imposed by hierarchies that indeed fail to take into consideration labor rights from the twenty-first century. In Italy, the Swedish household equipment company Electrolux had, in January 2014, proposed to its employees a wage decrease that trade unions estimate to be 40 percent against the abandonment of an eventual relocation project in Poland. It was the only way to manage the stress and the most reasonable solution for avoiding the closing of an industrial plant. It seems that his perception of a source of stress in enterprises just feeds political debates in which actors forget that there is **no dichotomy between professional and personal life**. The stress exists in the enterprise, but it is not only engendered by such category of actors or other, but each individual also creates his or her own stress. The reasons for employees' suicides in large groups in France, as in China, have not been clearly established. Saying that each worker gets the right to both sure and ethical working conditions refers to an incantation and a statement of the obvious.

What should be the object of particular attention is the quality of transversal **cooperation** between individuals within different departments, clients, suppliers, etc. In addition, if we consider a company as a web of interconnections, we have to be precise that it might be a network tending toward a sustainable result with the objective of creating values. The **entrepreneur** does not content himself to be a creator of economic wealth because he has to be a *sense-maker* (values) and creator of social links, as labor is conceived as a factor of collective and individual self-accomplishment. In the framework of a socially and sustainably responsible capitalism, the socioeconomic model (SEAM), by stressing a close managerial approach, prevents *burnout* or the syndrome of professional exhaustion that leads those who suffer from it to become withdrawn and to seek remedy, instead of antidepressants and anxiolytics. One has, in fact, to rethink the organization not as a closed system but as an **open system** with *porous* borders where professional and personal problems are cross-interacting.

Our works since 1973 show that the reduction of the dichotomy between man at work and man outside work entails the improvement of the professional quality of life and contributes to an increase human performance. *"Being unaware of the extra-professional life of an employee, establishing a tight seal as recommended by the classical management school is source of errors, tensions, erroneous interpretations and behaviors in the field of professional life"* (Savall & Zardet, 2005a, p. 168). We do not deposit our external mental charge at the front door of the company when coming to work. The **management of proximity, which is at the core of our socioeconomic approach,** answers concretely the need of work recognition which, if not satisfied, leads one to lose interest in its objectives. It also leads one to be inhabited by a feeling of frustration and injustice. Therefore, it is in the proximity of actors and the insurance of a better participation that lay the ferments of **democracy in enterprise**. In order to struggle against dehumanization, which leads to speculative capitalism, we stress the high importance of teamwork and the necessity to constantly reinforce the relationships between all the company members at work. Hence our insistence on the decompartmentalization of work spaces, this latter being more and more collaborative, in an opposite view from a Taylorist management model, where the design of narrow jobs should be prioritized over their inter-connection in order to facilitate the professional and social relationships in the company.

Socially responsible capitalism recognizes the benefits of the *natural capacity of autonomy* of individuals and teams that allows them, by cooperating with others, to cultivate dignity in professional and personal life. Socially responsible capitalism favors **subsidiarity**. Activities become more pertinent, effective and efficient when they are managed and realized closer to the spaces of life, action and use. That is why SRC opposes itself to distant, centralized and abstract concepts, which are causes of harmful dysfunctions at the field level. SRC **energizes** everybody, individual, team, company and territorial organization (local, regional, national, and international), by the decentralized creation of companies, associations, jobs, products (goods and services), artistic activities and cultural and spiritual activities. SRC is opposed to centralized forms of planned, distant and bureaucratic management practices. The *periodically negotiable activity contracts* set up during the interventions we carry out within enterprises which desire to apply SEAM model allow even for jobs, which traditionally do not have any perspective of career evolution, a strategy of personalized evolution avoiding any feeling of support failure from the hierarchy, and so loss of self-confidence, which generates "emotional, cognitive and physical disorders" (Elisabeth Grebot, *Stress et burn out au travail* [Stress and burnout at work], 2008).

It is this incapacity or impossibility of self-achievement at the workplace, often blamed on badly scheduled restructuration, which shackles each learning from thriving, coming to a feeling of *"uneasiness"*, denounced more by employees than managers, leads sometimes to suicide while their expectation at their workstation might be, at first, satisfied by an empowerment that is better explained and assumed. Labor is not by itself a torture, which is due to its unsuitability to the responsibilities and charges it contains. Labor is even considered as an effective therapeutic regarding the psychosocial disorders. Thus, each individual has and gets capacities and competencies, so that he/she is able to *create economic value*. The notion of human capital is **incoherent**, because this capital is inalienable and pertains intrinsically to each person. Therefore, its value remains potential as long as it is not transformed into real value added, and appreciated for its utility in the public sphere or by market demand. Man holds a development project and not only a survival one. He/she has at his/her disposal a potential for self-achievement, quite surpassing his/herself in ways that the actual economic game does not give to him/her the opportunity to realize. The acknowledgment of failure of the emergency plan for preventing professional stress, which has been elaborated three years after its implementation by the French Conseil Économique, Social et Environnemental (CESE) [*Economic, Social and Environmental Council*], told in a prospective report *"the economic context has just amplified the psychosocial risks"*. Therefore, both labor as and unemployment are vectors of psychological disorders.

The tools of socioeconomic method have been conceived with the objective to face this problem always in mind. In the socioeconomic approach (SEAM), each person in the company could communicate on points that are not owing to the company. As pinpointed by Samuel Rouvillois (Collomb et al, 2011, p. 29) *"the central question is to decrypt in our new labyrinths of means where the good for humanity is! Today, we know how to make Man effective, but with the loss of the horizon of Goodness"*. Michel Crozier in a book with an illuminating title *"Attentive Enterprise. Learning the post-industrial management"* (1994) expressed the same concerns when he advocated that relationships at work might not be founded on suspicion and that the centralizing authoritarianism of decisions from a so-called hierarchical system might be tempered by more collegiality. If top management teams could naturally determine the objective to reach for such a production unit, the means in order to be successful (excluding the financial ones) in terms of operational performance should be under the responsibility of negotiations with trade unions at the local stage, where they have more chances not to remain dead letters. At the national scale, Michelin engaged itself into this direction for its 16 industrial plants (*Le Figaro Économique*, May 2015, 20th). Our concept of **decentralized synchronization** addresses this concern. A management called socioeconomic is structured around architectures of decentralized synchronization, which allows improvement of the management of the enterprise's social responsibility.

The fact remains that a group of individuals cannot sustainably self-organize or self-manage by granting exemption from any subordination to one form of authority or another. In the book they dedicate to *Tetranormalization*, Savall & Zardet note, "*Capitalism and Marxism consider that humanity is exerting its activities in situations of subordination or submission and that it accepts without dispute either the authoritarianism of hierarchy inside enterprises, organizations and democratic institutions, either the dictator of party in other regimes*". However, we notice that today there is no adhesion without limits to the interests of the company as it is currently conceptualized. An individual adhering without negotiation to the rules established by the management runs the risk of being manipulated (François Grima et Renaud Muller, Responsabiliser sans manipuler, *in* ADERSE, *Responsabilité Sociale de l'Entreprise*, 2008, p. 2441).

The collective ownership of production means by workers in equalitarian association is not a guarantee of success, as the failure at varying lengths of existence of cooperative movements advocated by Charles Fournier (1772–1837) shows. His ideas aiming at reforming the industrial capitalist society of the first part of nineteenth century would find, according to him, no favorable echo without the financial support and the supervision of *industrial knights*. Such a debate remains nowadays absolutely pertinent when the giants of the Silicon Valley dream of working-class neighborhoods in a fit of paternalism. *Le Figaro* (April 2, 2015) quotes the estate projects manager of Facebook who declares "*we think that one could not content oneself to build a business campus, it has to be integrated to the 'community'* ".

Nowadays, the conflict between empowerment and **authority** is very accurate, referring to the emergence of *"flexible" workshops* supposed to benefit from certain autonomy and whose direct supervision is made very difficult. In a collective book dedicated to psychosocial risks at work (2008, p. 133), Sabrina Rouat in her chapter "*Mal-être et stress*" [Uneasiness and stress] defines autonomy as "*an important resource in adapting its rhythm and workcharge, and also a recognition and trust expression granted to wageworkers*". However, she takes care not to forget that "*when the autonomy is not accompanied by a minimal frame, it could only put the person in incertitude and anxiety*". One could, in truth, apply word for word what Christian Merlin wrote in an article entitled "*Les anonymes des grands* *orchestres"* [Famous orchestras anonymous people] (*Le Figaro*, February, 2012, 11–12th) in order to illustrate these reciprocal relations of power and trust in enterprise: "*The best directors are those who trust the orchestra and give to each one the feeling to exist*". This is what he wrote in one part, without forgetting to emphasize in another part that "*beyond the sense of collective interpretation, the orchestra musician has to get used to being managed early*". The orchestration and orientation are essential factors to ensure the good walk of each organization, in a trust climate opposed to one of anxiety at work, which is this "*communicational distortion*" so well analyzed by Guiddens (*Les conséquences de la modernité* [Modernity consequences], 1994, p. 106).

The enterprise's spirit, forecasting capacity, organizational sense and self-confidence, are part of the essential characteristics of the *Schumpeterian entrepreneur* whose role is, according to Henri Savall (*La roue du gouvernail* [The steering wheel], 2013), that of the director of team activities, leader of collaborators who benefit from more audacious and effective delegations, capacity of initiative on a par with the aspirations of most of them. The role of accomplishing together could thus define power. **Actually, economic power is not the prerogative of those who own the capital.** Thus, for example, it is not genuinely in the attribution of hedge funds, which capitalize companies in order to ensure their management but simply to make sure of the optimal distribution of dividends. The latter do not contribute in any case to the entrepreneurial and intrapreneurial dynamics that the entrepreneur injects in his/her company and which represents the intangible investment mentioned by Oliver Torrès in a book entitled "*La santé des dirigeants. De la souffrance patronale à l'entrepreneuriat salutaire*" [Employers health. From managerial suffering to salutary entrepreneurship] (2012). The massive arrival of hedge funds (whose ethical funds represent solidarity saving) in the capital of enterprises lead companies to noticeably modify their management objectives. The quest for economic profitability is curtailed and toppled by equity capital yield when the only thing that matters is value added on invested money. The sales argument of ethical and ecological hedge funds lies, however, in their financial performance and not on their conformity regarding environmental corporate responsibility. The perspectives of growth are taken into account before the degree of conformity within social responsibilities. Sometimes, even administrators of funds identified as ethical refuse this label and declare that they are not here to be good or noxious for humanity but simply to do business in industries that benefit from complete reputations. However, it is in general judged very positive for a fund to present itself in a socially and environmentally acceptable light in a public relations campaign. One could also notice that, in principle, companies and organizations have to conform to new reporting obligations and to communicate openly on the negative and positive impacts that their activities should have regarding stakeholders and society.

One could not neglect, both on the macroeconomic and microeconomic scales, the analyses made by corporate social responsibility (CSR) partisans. Angie B. Carrol (1991) represents it under the form of a four levels pyramid which has economic responsibilities as its base, followed by legal ones then ethical with, at the top level, philanthropic responsibilities. But he ended by merging the latter with the ethical preoccupations. Strong and Meyer (1992) suggest deleting this factor, which, in truth, is not as we heretofore mentioned such a genuine component of CSR, even if the CEO of LVMH company decided to contribute toward saving employees of the last workshop of Lejaby.

> We advocate for a concept of bearable and sustainable corporate social responsibility which we make the hypothesis that only it could reinforce the capacity of survival and sustainable economic development both of companies, their industries, their employment areas and, as a consequence, for their nation.
>
> (Savall & Zardet, 2005a)

Human Resource or Human Potential?

After emphasizing the increase of productive capacities due to work division, by taking the example of the pin factory, inspired by an article from *L'Encyclopédie* of Diderot and Alembert, Adam Smith (1776, p. 6) highlighted, however, the negative impact of this repartition because it dazes the worker, who becomes as ignorant and stupid as it is possible to be for a human creature (1776, p. 264). One should not forget that physical suffering engendered by repetitive tasks as well as psychological suffering from a mind-numbing activity were first evoked by Smith long before they were considered as the result of *Taylorism's excesses* (Pierre Bardelli et José Allouche, *La souffrance au travail. Quelle responsabilité pour l'entreprise* [Suffering at work. What responsibility for enterprise], 2012). In opposition, William Petty, by addressing the same topic in taking for example the fabrication of a watch, does not express compassion for the victims of repetitive work. Moreover, both wish that this human material could be kept in a good condition even while at work. We notice however that Petty and Smith both advocate taking into account traineeship and apprenticeship. It was convenient to improve the yield through rationalization of such actions. Petty also saw in the seeking of new working methods the possibility to improve the quality of products put into a more and more competitive market. Nevertheless, his preoccupations were essentially quantitative. As for today, the parceling out of tasks, which we propose to avoid by multiqualification, does not lead to the empowerment of workers, nor to their *value creation*.

Our experience in enterprises where we carried out interventions research convinced us of the noxiousness of several models always applied in those companies. In order to improve performance, Taylor (*The Principles of*

Scientific Management, 1911) recommended the division of labor. This concept, when pushed to the extreme by Fayol (1916), entailed the dichotomy between the project conceptor and executor. This split lies in its acceptance and its realization with the consequence of depersonalization of workstations, preeminence of impersonal rules and opposition between conceptors and executors (following the overtaking or the distortion of the original thought of these authors and their followers). In order to attenuate the perverse effects of such an evolution, we developed a *vaccine* (SEAM) against what we called *TFW virus* (taylorism-fayolism-weberism). This is our socio-economic approach of management which, once again, reintroduces the concept of human potential at each level, as the only active factor in the company allowing the creation of qualitative and quantitative value added for the stakeholders, the necessity of dialoguing and advocating communication and cooperation without forgetting the *empowerment of each one* at each activity stage.

In order to implement socially responsible capitalism, it would be necessary to conceive of a system that gives back to the employees a **power of operational autonomy elaborated with the hierarchy** at work, and also not only attribute **an economic value.** Of course we are no longer at that period where Jean-Jacques Rousseau could pretend "*one would say to you that a man is worth, in such a nation, the amount that we would expect in Algers; another, by following this calculation would find countries where the man is worth nothing and others where this man is worth less than nothing. They evaluate men as cattle herds*". Taylor takes over the picture of *beast of burden* by saying that a worker "*a worker more nearly resembles in his mental make-up the ox than any other type*" (*The Principles of Scientific Management*, 1911, p. 56).

In the nomenclature of tasks, the complexity of the latter constituted the determining factor at the guild level where salaried people's relationships were collectively accepted with an exception, which concerned the apprentices. The *naked worker*, for himself, was entrusted the most tiresome tasks as a genuine beast of burden. It is curious to notice that we had to reach 2008 before seeing the difficulty of workers' tasks that has gone unacknowledged be taken into account in an approach as scientific as it is possible of work, especially for unpackers and forklift truck operators, where one will have to measure the time spent in holding weights from more than 15 kilos. The employer would not forget to classify the postures judged tiresome on working sites.

In our socioeconomic approach of enterprises, it has taken a long time to catch the attention of public and organization authorities concerning the importance of not neglecting the increasing number of muscle-skeletal disorders and their consequences on the good running of companies. In a report given to the French *Agence Nationale pour l'Amélioration des Conditions de Travail* (ANACT), we highlighted these dysfunctions, far from being inevitable, which result and the financial negative consequences illustrated by our interventions on the field which constitute recyclable hidden costs. Concerning the measure of specific work tasks, a feeling of preparedness dominated because the four main criteria retained were still ignored and that a mission for simplifying has to adapt the devices already in use to be less individualized. We mention that according to Smith the *hardship* justifies higher salaries yet than those guaranteed to most *skillful artificers* (*the Wealth of Nations*, 1776, p. 93).

One could, in this case, talk about an essential social innovation, which marks a considerable advance for laborers' rights in order to reiterate the words of a communication from the concerned ministers. But here again, at this moment where companies feel the effects of the first efforts of "simplification breakdown", their CEOs are facing administrative and financial problems in order to implement the new dispositions (even if this is only the first draft) and also a probable loss of competitiveness in certain industries, such as chemistry, because of the over-costs incurred. As says Jean-François Roubaud, CGPME president: *"we cannot afford the means to grant costly social improvements, we are on bones"* (Le Figaro, July 2014, 7th). One could deny there is here a brake to employment, which remains the absolute priority. One seems to be aware of the issues created by this new regulation because the charge of responsibility for evaluating workers' exposure to hardship would not only be attributed to companies but to professional sectors. In our sense, each *external evaluation* from the company, according to an already established standard level of difficulty, would not fail to generate disagreement. A well-prepared social dialog has to be preferred to a sporadic application of new regulations.

It is necessary to prefer the phrase *human potential* to that of *human resources* in order to clearly mark that in an effort to achieve socially responsible capitalism, it is convenient to empower the workforce. That would allow employees to become development project stakeholders and so forth in the future. François Hauter, in an article from *Le Figaro* (July 2011, 28th) entitled *"Chez Michelin, l'intelligence du capitalisme français"* ["Among Michelin, French capitalism intelligence"], reports the following declaration: *"employees are not a resource in our company, they are the company"*. Unfortunately, two years later, in an interview given to the same newspaper, Jean-Dominique Sénart, Michelin's CEO, was obliged to justify the deletion of 730 jobs on a plant. As usual in this kind of situation, the stress is laid on the mutation of the industrial tool in order to improve competitiveness and ensure its sustainability. Once again, technology overshadows humanity. One sacrifices a plant in order to make another one the new competitive flag. Michelin's head affirms that the new decisions of investment in 2019 horizon *"have to allow the hiring of 1 700 persons in France during the period"*. Regarding the workers concerned by the restructuration of Joué-Lès-Tours factory, *"our objective is not to be obliged to proceed to forced departures"*.

In our notion of *socially and sustainably responsible capitalism*, the human is not a resource of the same nature as other economic resources.

Moreover, humans own their proper capital made by their competencies and capacities, which have to allow the creation of economic value. In the expression of human capital, the stress is placed on a notion of collective capital for the company, which is susceptible to acquire a value on market. By talking about human potential, we highlight the **freedom** that each individual has to use, as good as it seems, a capital (defined as the capacity to generate the value calculated by an income flow) belonging to him/her and which the individual decides to use in order to yield profit or not. The inalienable responsibility of capitalists should be to highlight this intrinsic capital of each individual, to help him/her to exploit it to his/her benefit and to that of the company in which he/she works. Robert Boyer (*Du rapport salarial fordiste à la diversité des relations salariales* [From Fordian salaried relationship to diversity of salaried relationships], 2009, p. 24) underlines that in the Anglo-Saxon world has been developed the notion of *selfish entrepreneur*, in virtue of which "*each one should be considered to be the seller of their talents and competencies*".

In a socially and sustainably responsible capitalist environment, the enterprise has to make sure that its different actors use and develop their own potential in *societally useful* activities in order to create value, shared by the stakeholders. This approach represents the cornerstone of a socially and sustainably responsible capitalism, which would characterize to our eyes the creation of sustainable and shareable value. While with this actual financing process of economy, talking about value-added creation by playing with words comes to restrict itself to the often artificial increasing of capital, which not only creates egoist profits that do not benefit the whole array of actors but also finds their origins in this unacceptable situation that represents capital dismissals. Human resources should no longer be considered as expenses, but as investments.

5 Challenging the Socially Responsible Capitalism Organization

The Enterprise Facing "Tetranormalization" in a More and More Complex and Changing Environment

Intervention research carried out within companies has made an exogenous factor of emergent *hidden costs exacerbation*: the tetranormalized environment, i.e., the proliferation of contradictory norms, concerning each domain of company activity and running (Savall & Zardet, 2005b) in a context of globalization (Datry & Savall, 2015) and serious crises. Thus, successive real estate crises from 1990 to 2008 and the one of "new economy" in early 2000 were the forerunners of the extraordinary financial worldwide 2008 crisis. This discovery of the *tetranormalized universe* has revived the original objective of socioeconomic theory (SEAM), namely to consolidate *entrepreneurial and intrapreneurial capitalism,* by dissociating it from the speculative financial capitalism, in the line with our research in macro economies (Savall, 1973, 1975). This research was based on the innovative, visionary and prophetic works of the unknown Spanish economist Germán Bernácer (see Part 1). Therefore, two colloquiums were organized by the Association François Perroux (2002, 2008) founded by Gilbert Blardone with the support of Raymond Barre and presided over by Henri Savall (Barre et al., 2004).

Tetranormalization Phenomena

Tetranormalization refers to four main poles of standards and norms that harass organizations daily, the norm being understood as the larger meaning of *social and economic rules of the game.* A norm should be applied to an intra or inter-organizational, intra or inter-territorial scope. Norms are derived from world trade (ex: WTO), accounting and financial (ex: IAS-IFRS), social and human resources (ex: ILO) and the three-part quality-security-environment (ex: ISO). The phenomena related to tetranormalization have two facets, as for strategic analysis. These norms constitute *constraints* or threats, but also *opportunities.* The first published version of our tetranormalization theory was entitled *Tétranormalisation: défis et dynamiques* (Savall & Zardet, 2005b). The English translation *The Dynamics and Challenges of*

Tetranormalization was published in the USA in 2011, followed by a book coordinated by David Boje in 2015.

Some companies, which are practicing socioeconomic management, have discovered some obstacles in the growth of their performance, due to the flood of contradictory norms. Tetranormalization has first been studied from perspective of the decider/CEO by setting up the basic *dialectics* of: conflict/cooperation, constraint-threat/opportunity-innovation. Indeed, new norms are creating barriers for companies' functioning, some of them expressing a kind of protectionism through barriers to entry. However, tetranormalization could also be a source of innovation and proactive strategies when the decider steers the integration of norms that affect his/her organization in order to make the corporate strategy compatible with its new normative environment and so avoid additional hidden costs and benefit from the *innovative dynamics* that arouse the new norms challenge.

Indeed, when tetranormalization is *badly integrated* in the enterprise, it generates a surfeit of dysfunctions and hidden costs endured by the enterprise and its stakeholders. Nevertheless, when it is *carefully integrated*, it is a source of performance and economic, social and societal progress because it allows recycling of hidden costs into value added. It appears that the level of overall and sustainable performance of the company depends on the quality of norms integration and compliance. Policies of *social responsibility development* financing action find their origin in the proper potential resources of the company, constituted by its deposit of hidden costs, the amount of which accounts for €20,000 to €70,000 per person per year, according to ISEOR's database, which includes 1854 enterprises and organizations.

The strategies that better integrate the norms of the tetranormalized environment are profitable for the company and its stakeholders, if their convergences are managed, in part at the exterior of the organization and in other part within the enterprise. This convergence expects the development of periodic negotiation knowhow on behalf of stakeholders.

The Hidden Face of Tetranormalization and Emergent Dynamics

Table 5.1 identifies 16 different categories that demarcate the outline of tetranormalization:

- the seven firsts categories take an inventory of observed *dysfunctions* and constitute the descriptive dimension of tetranormalization phenomena;
- the items 8 to 10 propose an explicative *analysis*;
- the items 11 to 16 spot innovative *solutions* which modify the economic and social rules of the game.

The meticulous observation of tetranormalization phenomena (1 to 7) underlines the intensification of any kind of standards and norms (labels,

1: Production, proliferation of standards and norms
Public/private (ideologies or political choices)
IFRS standards
Standard/nonstandard dilemma
Labels, brands, identifiers

2: Proliferation of institutions and standard organizations on the standard and norms market
Standards and norms compliance control institutions
Research institutes and sources of standards and norms
Rating agencies
Universities (role/citizenship)
Privatization of institutions and organizations
Accreditation/certification organisms
"Lobbying" organizations

3: Conflict/competition of standards and norms
Concentration of firms
Language(s)
Contradiction of political regimes and economics of transition
Technological changes and productivity
International disparities
Monetary struggles
Remuneration of executive officers
National protectionisms
Barriers to entry (industries, companies)
Inter-institutional competition
Competition and development of emerging countries
Intercompany competition: value-added sharing
Competition of religions
Fluctuation of exchange rates and destabilizing markets changes
Scientific and technical controversies

9: Acceptable and sustainable social responsibility of companies and organizations
States' insolvency
Social responsibility of public organizations
Social responsibility of companies
Inequality and poverty (political responsibility)
Public safety (asbestos, flu, etc.)
Food security
Labor market and unemployment regulation by the state
Welfare, retirement, etc.

10: Forecasting and warning signs
New scientific concepts and paradigms
Major inventions
Mutating professions
Geopolitical mutations
Norms evolution

11: Convergences and cooperation
Cooperation between nations (globalization)
Inter-institutional cooperation
Interorganizational cooperation (public/private)
Contractualization of performance
Cooperation between actors (other stakeholders)

(Continued)

Table 5.1 (Continued)

4: **Conflict/hierarchy of standards and norms (legality)**
Territoriality
Public/private (for given territory)
Geopolitical disparities (negotiations, etc.)
Controversial arbitration of national policies

5: **Effective application of standards and norms**
Safety/transports
Complying workers' rights
Legal practice
Account audits
Inspections of the application of labor regulations (laws, agreements, etc.)

6: **Fraud**
Insubordination to political power, legality
Swindles
Respect of copyrights and patents
Doping
Corruption
Fraud/public service
Tax havens
Piracy
Spying (industrial, etc.)
Public/private collusion

7: **Sanctions (financial or penal)**
Taxes
Application of sanctions
Resources available/means of implementation

12: **Obsolete standards and norms cleaning up**
Laws and regulations deletion and simplification
Norms and standards restructuration
Regulation of norms and standards market
Sanitation of markets (other)

13: **Monitoring Indicators**
Increase of transparency and reliability of shared information
Audit of public institutions and organizations

14: **Structuring Innovations**
Innovative public policies
Reforms and restructuration of public services
Development of public organizations' social responsibility
Effective intervention of public authorities in labor conflicts
Managerial innovations (businesses and organizations)
Extended assumption of corporate social responsibility
Renaissance of professions (businesses, professionals)
Renaissance of professions' revalorization rites
New markets and products

15: **Development of entrepreneurship and intrapreneurship**
Creating business
Entrepreneurship among public actors
Succession and transfer of businesses
Incentives to SMEs

8: TSIT theory of stock-in-trade
Compensation market
Research and innovation
Grants market
Sports market
Financial bubble (speculation, hegemony of financial sector)
Crisis of capitalism
Industrial "yoyo" speculation on energy, raw materials, works of art
Housing market
Ecological bubble and "green" markets
Health market
Humanitarian market
Market of credit for SMEs
Unmet needs (market failures)
Shortages of jobs without applicants (market failures)

16: Major innovative concepts of the socioeconomic theory (SEAM model)
Citizen science and socially responsible research
Macro-hidden costs
Vital sales function and interactive marketing (Internet vigilance)
Theory of the person of many parts (citizen, consumer, producer)
Theory of intergenerational management (youth, seniors, retired)
Periodic assessment of workers

certificates and identities). Those norms come from the increasing multiplication of institutions and organizations that operate on the *norms market* as producer, trainer, controller, certifier, expert, etc. This tangle is all the more complex as these entities are situated at extremely diverse territorial levels and in activity domains and are not articulated to each other. Thus, the *conflicts and competitions* between standards and norms accumulate. Despite the laudable and benevolent ideas they convey, norms have a function of national or sectorial protectionism, as, for example, we observe the rough negotiation between France and the USA to withdraw the prohibition of Roquefort cheese, on behalf of supposed public health security. Polemics on scientific knowledge are increasing, as the controversy on the resistance of bacteria against antibiotic treatments or also the ambivalent effects of hormonal treatments for menopause.

Besides the issue of norm production, there is the question of their real application, sanctions, and intentional frauds and falsifications. Thus, fraud constitutes an infringement of the rules of the game and entails distortions of the economic and social game. In addition to its *ethical* dimension, it provokes an **unfair competition** between economic partners. Spying and hacking constitute infringements of the intellectual and industrial property rules; they have a moral and penal facet and a facet of deregulation of the economic and social systems. Indeed, investors are spoiled from the return on investment they expect, while the predators, who did not assume the real cost of innovation, make a profit from what they spoiled. Tax havens also constitute a fraud factor by playing on the territorial contradictions of norms.

Who really benefits from these norms among the different stakeholders? Besides the "good" practices suggested by standards and norms, a lucid analysis reveals the existence of *powerful stock-in-trades*. Norms are intangible products, which are emitted by producers and generate new development of professions, such as auditing, inspection, expertise, consulting, control, legal conflict, training, etc. Several intermediate agents between producers and users are emerging, especially as the normative texts are blurred. Several industries are developing such compensation grants, sport, humanitarian and SMEs loan or health markets. Thus, today depression is an expanding disease, which calls for advertising, medical consultations, drugs, preventive products and psychiatric restructuration.

The corporate social responsibility of public and private organizations and public authorities is being questioned more and more, and this carries weight in its financing actions. The concept of *sustainably bearable social responsibility* that we are proposing allows insisting on the double social and economic facet of these issues: public health, food security, employment market regulation, unemployment, foresight and the political responsibility in matters of inequity and poverty. Poverty shows two facets, one moral and the other one socioeconomic. It engenders hidden costs of *development opportunity losses* of poor and rich populations. Thus, wealth transfer alone could not be a solution for development because it constitutes a *macro-hidden cost*.

Our recent research revealed the intensification of dynamics based on initiatives taken by public authorities and other economic actors. The nomenclature is enriched from new themes (item 11 to 16—table 5.1):

New *coordinations, convergences, and cooperations* between nations, territories and institutions. For example, in France: the development of apprenticeship advocated in universities and national schools, including for PhD (see Fondation Nationale de l'Enseignement pour la Gestion des Entreprises FNEGE [National foundation for the teaching of management science]); good practices for preserving the activity and employment of seniors in companies; creation of new space of cooperation between nations, such as the Gulf Cooperation Council;

The *cleaning up of norms and rules*: for example late 2007, more than 130 French laws considered as obsolete have been abolished;

The development of *steering indicators* in order to increase the transparency of information, the auditing of institutions, from which they were previously exempted; thus, account certification is applied from now on public administrations;

The *structuring of innovations*, innovative public policies such as the spin-off creation of companies from public institutions (e.g.: l'Institut national de recherche en informatique et en automatique, INRIA [*the National Institute for Research on Informatics and Automatic*]) or the incentives for a better sharing of value added, development of public organization's social responsibility, such as the rediscovery of microcredit, managerial innovations and a better consideration of CSR (telework, strategies of prevention against Stock Exchange caprices, reflux from excessive practices of relocation), the rebirth and the innovation dynamic of craft professions or the ritual of rise in professions.

Entrepreneurship and intrapreneurship development, including creation of enterprises and the success of corporate transmission, see for example the creation of the self-entrepreneur status elaborated in France whose results show that it meets actual expectations.

Liberalism and Tetranormalization

The *Robert* dictionary gives **liberalism** as a synonym for capitalism. It is the same for the *Dictionary of Economics* from Sloan and Zurcher (1970). It is sometimes described as a system of freedom economy. In the frame of a debate with Natacha Polony (*Ce pays qu'on abat* [This country we slaughter], Plon, 2015) on "*how could* one be liberal?", Gaspard Koenig (*Le Révolutionnaire, l'Expert et le Geek. Combats pour l'autonomie* [The Revolutionary, the Expert and the Geek. Fights for autonomy], 2015) remarks accurately "*in liberal thought, market is not a starting principle but the consequence of individual rights that we recognize to each one. The individual* *has to get the freedom for entrepreneurship. We instituati*onalize *a regulation and a market which guarantee the effectivity of this right"* (Le Figaro, 26 mars 2015).

Liberalism is not a simple *ideological* addition of socially and sustainably responsible capitalism, it is *fundamental*. In an interventionism and centralization state, *"the capitalist logic is staying in default"*, as François Perroux told us rightly. One should not, however, make wrong accusations to the proponents of a certain form of protectionism and reaffirm, on the contrary, with Maurice Allais, Nobel Prize Awarded of Economy in 1988 that the *"genuine fundament of protectionism, its justification and its necessity, is the protection against disorders and difficulties in any forms engendered by lack of each regulation at the worldwide scale"* (Allais, *L'Europe en crise? Que faire? Réponses à quelques questions. Pour une autre Europe* [Europe in crisis? What are we doing? Answers to same questions. For another Europe], 2005, p. 74). The pertinence of this observation takes all its sense at this moment where the partisans of all-liberalism wish to delete *all the brakes* to free competition and free trade in a globalized market.

In the so-called mercantilist period, one perceives yet in neo-mercantilists (Dudley North, Roger Coke, Joshua Child, Charles Davenant, etc.) a strong liberal stream which is favorable to the opening of an entrepreneurial mindset of the capitalist type. Davenant affirmed, for example, that *"Industry has its first foundation on liberty"* (Petty, 1771, p. 35). William Petty was not denying that the civil law might be necessary to order, but he had no idea that the excess of laws and decrees represented an infringement of individual freedom and also an obstacle to the good functioning of the national economy (Petty, Lansdowne & Southwell, 1927, p. 59). As a good physician, he thought that it was more suitable to seek for the cause of economic difficulties than merely apply some remedies empirically.

Entrepreneurship has always constituted the **proactive** response to regulation, to "tetranormalized rigidity" of regulations, standards and norms, which Henri Savall and Véronique Zardet denounce in their book *Challenges and Dynamics of Tetranormalization*. They indicate that

> A norm of general or universal interest can only be applied after it has been transformed, acclimatized, assimilated and adopted. It includes participants in the economic and social 'game' within teams, organizations, institutions and territories that adapt the standards and norms to the geopolitical and historical contexts, customs and mindsets.
>
> (Savall & Zardet, 2012, p. 138)

This feeling is shared by Pascal Salin in his article of the *Monde de l'Entreprise* dated 10 June 2009, and entitled "Crises: les libéraux plaident non-coupable" [*"Crises: liberals plead not-guilty"*] when we writes: *"we are in a very perverse system, where millions of regulations exist. If we could add these, we would perceive that we are living in a totalitarian world"*.

Totalitarianism, don't look, is therefore more endogenous than exogenous. It is true that the French Labor Code includes some 3,600 pages, which testifies to such complexity, all corbertist, compared to the 70 pages of the Swiss Code. We mentioned herein above the investor's role for the entrepreneur. About this issue, there are in France so many shackles, which are obstacles to investment and break the entrepreneurs in their decision-making process, by constituting a violation of individual freedom.

Besides a tetranormalization that is badly integrated by the company, due to internal polemics that it engenders, an **accumulation of chronic hidden costs** is also produced, which reduce the enterprise's economic performance. So we witness the destruction of real and potential value added, which is neither supervised nor measured by the organizational information and management system (Savall & Zardet, 2005a, p. 12). Catherine Mathieu and Henri Sterdyniak remind us in an article focused on strength and weaknesses of Anglo-Saxon capitalism (2009, p. 36) that, with Reagan and Thatcher, capitalism was revived by policies of deregulation and privatization and also that the liberal counter-revolution of 1980s was made possible by the ideological victory of liberalism over Statism, on the extravagant regulation, centralization and redistributing policies, interventionism and excess regulating. In France, one estimate making a great step in the improvement of companies' situation with the *administrative simplification*, which transfers to the establishment of fix deadlines in order to force the application of decrees and order that concern them, so their CEOs simply avoid being caught unawares by untimely modifications of rules or norms. We notice, however, that an impact study could be required before the application of these norms.

In France, with the term of office of the last elections at its conclusion, things have not evolved much. The actual government expects to carry out the same battle against norms as the former one and give *rendezvous* to CEOs for the "*breakdown of simplification*" which is meant to be a breath of fresh air for companies. However, once more, one must ask of the dialog, "Will it become law before the potential implications have been studied?"

"Norms which are really applied and integrated by a company are those which combine a general, universal and specific norm with its application to a local context such as the company, the social group, the ethnicity and the country" (Savall & Zardet, 2005b, p. 37). There is the unavoidable shaping of proximity for norms engendered by a centralized approach if, in the domain of territorial collectives, there seems to be an understanding on the necessary abrogation of a former norm when it is important to create a new one. In the company sector, we always stand on an attack against the administrative paperwork and the slowness it incurs. However, since the seventeenth century, Petty wished that, in terms of regulation, the superfluous, supernumerary and antiquated should be abrogated (Hull, 1899, p. 25). One should hope that the setting up of a simplification council (with ten workgroups) would be effective in domains where the state could lighten the administrative procedures and put an end to the troubles due to too finicky rules, by responding to an expectation of MEDEF. The concrete results should necessarily be translated in new texts, new regulations, but they could also be engendered at least from constructive dialog with the small entrepreneurs. The two leaders of this working site should in addition create, as in Great Britain, an entrepreneurs' committee, which would evaluate all new measures touching the enterprises (Le Figaro, March 2014, 29/30th). Reducing the burden of the regulations which weigh on companies is also a worry of the White House, which, according to *Wall Street Journal* from August 2011, 23th, envisages to update, make lean, or delete costly regulations.

The same approach is a part of the EU preoccupations in order to address the renewed expectations of employment and growth. The EU's Commission proposes the deletion of not-useful standards and norms edited at a European scale, which constitute barriers to the good running of companies. In Italy, a decree from 27 January 2012 just abolishes 333 important laws considered as useless and penalizing to enterprises and individuals. Richard Heuzé, who gives precisions in an article from *Le Figaro Économique* (June 2011, 28/29th) states that "*the decree holds already an emblematic name: Free Italy*". Even if changes are well perceived, they are not considered to be pushing far enough. One should not forget that negotiations, officially started in July 2013, are still ongoing with the objectives of creating the biggest free-trade area between USA an EU which aims to delete the maximum of customs, regulated barriers to the profit of the transatlantic trade, while Americans seem to play the card of protectionism with their *Buy American Act*.

The American government would also remove the financial services from negotiations: France refuses to abandon the measures for supporting the audiovisual industry. It has a lot to do with technical, social and environmental norms as much of non-tariff barriers, which are effective against free trade. It is interesting to notice that this project agreement, well known under the logo TAFTA (*Transatlantic Free Trade Agreement*) has been also named *Transatlantic Trade and Investment Partnership* without any allusion to any form of free trade. By the way, one could legitimately think that the objective is on the contrary the possibility to corner markets through mastering norms and standards. There are also fears in the frame of TAFTA that the setting up of supranational authorities should only increase the lack of transparency in norms establishment and implementation.

Our assumption is that the four poles that gather the whole of sustainable development norms are not always compatible, wherever they be—at the company, regional, nation and international scales: world trade (ex: WTO), accounting and financial (ex: IAS-IFRS), social and human resource (ex: ILO) or the three-part quality-security-environment (ex: ISO). Each effort of cooperation and coordination is thus made inoperable by the important differences in their interpretation and implementation. A setting up of those exogenous norms is considered essential for companies in order to avoid, specifically in the technical domain, their fatal obsolescence on the financial scale because of the rising number of dysfunctions and the hidden costs entailed by such situations. To make this wish exist not only on solely paper, the socioeconomic approach has to facilitate both the appropriation and interpretation of exogenous norms by the company in order that they still not be disconnected from the imperatives of local environment reality and become in some way endogenous norms applicable to the specific needs of the organization.

Nowadays one could not pretend that liberalism constitutes a threat to capitalism. Because our conception of socially and sustainably responsible capitalism leads us to consider that, liberalism is the *unmovable bedrock* of capitalism. Such an ounce of Statism, centralization and regulation should not crack capitalism because throughout history, it never ceases to struggle against interventionist policies. This is its liberal dimension that makes capitalism effective and efficient. It has allowed development as social as it is economic by fostering *creativity* and *entrepreneurial spirit* in a climate of trust, which is not convenient to stifle under a torrent of standards and norms. Nicolas Lecaussin, director of *Institut de Recherches Économiques et Fiscales* (French Institute on Economics and Taxes Research) *(IREF)* in a book entitled *L'Obsession anti-libérale française. Ses causes et ses conséquences* [The French Anti-Liberal Obsession. Causes and consequences] (2014) notes that countries on the path of improvement are those which have adopted liberal reforms.

Even at the height of the mercantilist period, the economic world does not seem to be led by only an arsenal of laws and regulations enacted by the public authorities. "*So many problems had been regulated by laws*", wrote William Petty (Hull, 1899, p. 243). While they should be dependent upon the public's general contentment, even Hobbes himself, whom no one would suspect to be a great liberal, affirmed that it is the individual who is the engine of economic activity (Hobbes, 1651, 1964, p. 174). We notice, in addition, that against the complex or contradictory rules and norms proliferation, the concept of **managerial and entrepreneurial abstentionism** that we define as the lack or delay in strategic and operational decision making, aims at showing what the excesses of a modern form of French Colbertism could lead to.

There are the recent abuses that ended tintechnological, estate, trading, etc., bubbles, which could lead one to arrive at such a conclusion, but only in the case of what the anti-globalists, by considering the USA in particular, shout down under the name *ultraliberalism*, that we choose to call **unleashed or without moral liberalism**. One should exercise care in assimilating the *laisser-faire* to a *lack of attention*. Alain-Gérard Slama in his column of *Le Figaro* (July 2012, 4th) on "*Le renouveau programmé de l'économie libérale* [The scheduled renewal of liberal economy]" underlines wisely that "*the word freedom in its root has never meant the law of the free fox in the free henhouse*". The word *ultraliberalism* is used by the sworn enemies

122 Socially Responsible Enterprises

of the liberal ideology whose ethical considerations are not, however, banished as testimonies, the analysis made by Adam Smith in his prologue to the *Wealth of Nations* (1776), in which, he refines the principles highlighted in his *Theory of Moral Sentiments* without contradicting them. Emmannuel Toniutti in his book of interviews, *"L'urgence éthique. Une autre vision pour le monde des affaires"* [Ethical emergency. Another sight for business world] (2010) regrets *"an interpretation of liberal thought exacerbated by American culture"*. We think that the utilitarian and pragmatic approach inherited by the Pilgrims of the *Mayflower* would make this drift impossible were it not for some badly intentioned CEOs. Thus, ethical codes and good practice charters are here only for restraining excesses in terms of corporate misbehavior and do not constitute smoke screens. Of course, at the top of the list of principles one could find the necessity to make profits, but this is not a unique objective, as Milton Friedman highlighted ("The Social Responsibility of Business is to Increase its Profits", *The New York Times Magazine*, September 1970, 13th).

Human potential (all company actors) becomes the masterpiece of enterprises. Entrepreneurial capitalism is an *"adventurous regime"* according to Nicolas Berdiaeff (Berdiaeff, 1927) quoted by Perroux, who likens it to a **"regime of adventurers"** unlike the world of "traders" we see nowadays. What appears to be essential to us is the entrepreneurial freedom reclaimed in the face of an excessive and permanent intervention from the state and other inspection agencies.

The notion of **risk** is inseparable from each entrepreneurial adventure and could not be ignored in the framework of a socially and sustainably responsible capitalism. Accepting a risk is refusing the opposition to change and goes hand in hand with each gamble on the future. Being able to imagine the future developments of his/her company is part of the genuine CEO's obligations. As Charles Beigbeder rightly writes (*Le Figaro*, November 12, 2013) *"the key toeconomic success lies in audacious projects, which conjugate innovation and risk taking and are held with the will of a conqueror"*. The issue of risk-sharing has never been highlighted, but it should be the object of a deepened examination from the viewpoint of socially and sustainably responsible capitalism. The risk is the very basis of the company. Without going so far as to consider the wage worker as his/her own employer, it should seem normal that he/she accepts a part of the risk in the framework of CSR. It is again the role of the firm to procure a certain form of assurance to its workforce throughout the stability of employment. However, the latter depends on the **flexibility** factor, which only allows rapid reactions to the moving conditions of the market. On other hand, it is in the socioeconomic *approach to management for enterprises and organizations* (SEAM), which aims at sharing the value created by the whole spectrum of actors, that it would appear as normal that this convergence of interests goes hand to hand with a sharing of responsibilities whose risk factor is a component.

Three Synthetic Indicators for Revealing and "Forecasting" Organizational Health

It is imperative to develop a social and economic strategy at the heart of which "there is a conception of the individual as active unit, by transposing the concept of **active unit company**" created by Perroux. This is the individual capacity to act upon on his/her environment and his/her energy that it matters to highlight. In our concept of socioeconomic corporate strategy, we recognize a preeminent place for actors' strategies, considered in their voluntarism, conscious and prospective dimensions (Savall & Zardet, 2005a, p. 89, 2005b). **Hidden costs** are not detected in the accountability and financial information systems of a company or an organization—budget, income statement, balance sheet, financial and cost accounting—or in the balanced scorecards (Savall, 1974b, 1975; Savall & Zardet, 1987, 1992). The visible costs that indicate the categories of charges indexed in information system, help in measuring the evolution of financial resources but not in analyzing the deep causes of deficits. On the contrary, hidden costs are of a phenomenological nature and help to explain the quality of an organization's functioning. Thus, a high level of hidden costs related to absenteeism brings to light how the organization suffers from a negative impact in its current functioning and in its resource management, and to identify the regulating actions set up in order to address the effects of these absences. The expression *hidden costs* is the abbreviation of the completed denomination of **hidden cost-performance**. Indeed, the reduction of costs constitutes a type of performance and a reduction of performance constitutes a cost.

Regulation is the action of *correcting* dysfunctions' effects. For example, a manager informed of the absence of a staff member, could either replace him/her by a temporary worker, or make the present ones doing extra-hours. These two choices represent two types of regulation for the *same dysfunction*, the absence. The cost of the dysfunction depends on the corrective action (so-called "regulations" in SEAM theory) chosen by managers. "Regulations" require *time* and provoke *loss* of production and *overconsumption* of raw materials and external services, financial charges, remuneration and wastes. The organization spontaneously reproduces those dysfunctions in a recurrent manner, and those regulations absorb increasingly more resources. Hidden costs constitute the **destruction of real and potential value added**, often unintentionally. The regulation of dysfunctions mobilizes two sorts of resources, human activities and the consumption of bought goods or services. The human activities of regulation are expressed in time units (hours, minutes) and then translated into monetary units (euro, dollar). The time included in overtime and *non-production* is measured by multiplying it with the ratio of *hourly contribution to value added on variable costs (HCVAVC)*. This indicator measures the average value added of one activity hour in the whole company or organization. It is calculated by dividing the value added of the global number of hours from the whole of the organization's manpower, including the CEO or the volunteers in a nonprofit organization. The global value added is obtained by subtracting the variable costs from turnover in companies or global budget in nonprofit organizations.

Hidden costs are from two categories: those which are integrated into visible costs but still diluted inside different charge accounts—*overcharges*—and those that do not appear in accountability—*non-products*. Hidden costs constitute a potential deposit of resources, which are partly *recyclable* and, further **budgetary wiggle room** for improving the financial results. Considering this dynamic of hidden costs inside the organization, such a global approach is necessary for explaining the mechanism of financial performance genesis.

Value-Added Destruction

The socioeconomic theory of organizations and territories establishes a link between the individual, organizational and macroeconomic levels of value creation, according to a principle of *isomorphism*. The **value added** is the *raison d'être* of a public or private organization, being useful to the societal environment. It is measured in accounting: sales or incomes *minus* supplies and external services. Inside the organization, the value added per person corresponds to the average contribution of each individual to collective performance. The level of hidden costs is a **predictive** variable for the level of organizational performance, measured by the value added to share with shareholders and stakeholders. At the macroeconomic scale, **the GDP** accounts for the nation's creation of value that aggregates the GDP of all domestic industries. The GDP of an industry integrates the value added of each company. The *hidden costs* constitute a destruction of value added which is partly or totally ignored in national or company accounting. This waste of economic resources results from useless expenses and the voluntary or involuntary creation of value-added *abstention* on behalf of internal actors. The destruction of value added could be measured at different economic or geopolitical scales: individual, organizational, industry, regional and national.

The HCVAVC is a relevant indicator of the sustainable overall economic performance of an organization. Its increase shows a reduction of value-added destruction, regardless of the organizational economic or strategic situation. The reduction of dysfunctions produces a decrease of hidden costs and the *rise of HCVAVC*, either by the growth of value added on variable cost (VAVC) amount according to the same quantity of expected hours; either by the reduction of worked hours for a same amount of VAVC, either by the combination of both.

Sustainable Economic Performance of the Organization

The sustainable economic performance of an organization comes from the rational utilization of its resources over short and long-term intervals, by taking into account *anthropological criteria* (physiological, psychological, sociological and economical) in its economic activity. Two elements comprise sustainable economic performance: immediate results and creation of potential. *Immediate results* depend on visible costs and performances spotted and evaluated by the company actors. They are short-term economic results, as they appear in annual financial statements. *Creation of potential* is the *self-financed investment*, which will have a positive impact on future periods' economic performance.

Three Synthetic Ratios Which Constitute Predictors

Three strategic ratios express the variations of observed performance and allow anticipation of future performance: (a) hidden costs/visible costs; (b) externalized costs/internalized costs; (c) creation of potential time/directly productive time. They explain the level of performance for the organization by means of quantitative financial variables. Nevertheless, these variables represent only the impacts of fundamental causes of performance, for which the complexity is such that they could only be expressed through qualitative variables.

Hidden costs on visible costs ratio (HC/VC): the increase of hidden costs reported to visible costs means that the dysfunctions and the loss of human energy of the organization are increasing. This is a warning indicator.

Externalized costs on internalized costs ratio (EC/IC): The externalized costs are those organization expulses in order to discharge certain costs or financial obligations. Traditionally, a good practice consists of thinking that all things paid by a third party (outsider) constitute an advantage for the company or the organization. This is not true because of the *boomerang effect*. When an organization externalizes charges to its environment, the latter "seeks revenge" later by forcing this organization to internalize back the costs previously externalized. This constitutes a phenomenon of contagion such as one could spot, for example, in downsizing restructuration.

Time dedicated to the creation of potential on directly productive time ratio (CPT/DPT): the creation of potential represents the current actions, which will realize their effects in future years. The *directly productive time* is the human time dedicated to realize tasks, operations or activities, which directly impact the operational activity of the organization and its *immediate results*. According to the socioeconomic theory of organizations, directly productive time is only efficient when it is coupled with a suitable dose of indirectly productive time, called *time for creation of potential*. Some intangible investments are dedicated to *dysfunctions prevention*, i.e., actions aimed at improving organizational functioning by avoiding dysfunctions. A decrease in this ratio is a warning indicator, because it signifies that the organization is losing its professionalism.

The ratio (CPT/DPT) allows prediction of the forecast level of future economic performance. When it is low, it means that the proportion of hours dedicated to creation of potential is insufficient. When it is high, the organization fairly allocates its resources to both activities: time for creation of potential and directly productive time. Time and financial resources aimed at increasing human potential are a genuine *intangible investment in qualitative development of human potential (IIQDHP)*, the ROI of which could be calculated with the same method as for corporeal investment. This intangible investment includes integrated training sessions and strategic and operational focus groups. Unlike the current accounting norms, they have to be considered as a highly **profitable investment** and not like a recurrent charge imputable to the operating result.

These three predictors are meaningful in regard to organizational economic health and constitute indicators of sustainable overall performance.

Cyclic Resurgence of Dysfunctions

Dysfunctions have a spontaneous propensity for self-developing and follow a life cycle logic. The correction of a dysfunction temporarily reduces its negative effects. Nevertheless, the dysfunction might reappear during next period and should provoke once more two negative effects, the dissatisfaction of stakeholders and destruction of value added. Dysfunctions are cyclical phenomena, as the activity of organization engenders a periodic resurgence of dysfunctions that generate recurring hidden costs. Thus competencies and human behaviors need steering, as evidenced by problems related to the dysfunctions of repeated absences, quality of work and management of persons, work and social climate or communication and cooperation among managers and staff.

Somewhere along the line, the structure of organizational economic performance, represented by its three strategic indicators, has an impact on the cyclical resurgence of dysfunctions and allows predicting the following period performance. The lower the ratio of hidden costs to visible costs (HC/VC) and externalized costs to internalized costs (EC/IC), and the more time that the creation of potential to directly productive time (CPT/DPT) ratio is *high*, the more the economic performance will be *high*, all things being equal. The propensity for a resurgence of dysfunctions engenders a new cycle of hidden costs that influences the level of organizational economic performance in the following period.

Part III

Socially Responsible Individuals

Value(s) Producers and Consumers

6 The Citizen-Producer-Consumer of Social Values and Economic Value

It appears from the two previous parts of the book that our conception of socially responsible capitalism entails the elimination of withdrawal positions or refocusing for organizations, whose survival has been ensured since 1973 by socioeconomic management model (SEAM), which implies the loss of *status quo* in favor of change, even more precisely from a **metamorphosis**, endogenous by nature.

Socioeconomic management, as we believe we have demonstrated, refuses to see in the level of workforce, the essential adjustment variable in crisis period, which results in not only staff downsizing, but also reduced working hours, a decrease in training budgets or the stopping of remuneration. Our experience shows that such a policy could only lead one to discourage the "surviving" staff and cause its demobilization. Time lags between the labor supply, market expectations and job seekers are often blamed on training programs taught by specialized institutions, which are often accused of having caused such situations. This could be explained by the insufficient inclusion of the individual producers' interests, a lack of meeting their empowerment expectations in current managerial practices and working conditions improvement.

Responsibility of the Citizen-Consumer-Producer Individual

In exchange for more participative behavior, we propose a genuine internal professional training policy implemented through management proximity including participation by top management, which tangibly and sustainably mobilizes actors. Socially responsible capitalism recognizes, on one hand, the requirement to match technical and operational skills expected for vacant jobs with employees' and workers' expectations, as human persons. Thus, we propose a better coupling between the lives of **citizen-human** *"overindulged, considered and solicited"* (Savall, 1979; Savall & Zardet, 1995, 2005a, p. 74), and those of the *producer-*hu*man*, neglected and pushed aside. We also underline that *"the individual nature is both physic-chemical and socioeconomic. So he/she has multidimensional needs in four domains: physiology, psychology, sociology, economy"* (Savall & Zardet, 2005b, p. 115).

The socioeconomic approach to management is a model that fosters initiative and empowerment. Of course, such a policy could lead; as our detractors might suggest, to the implosion of many corporate structures. However, this fear is why we insist on the necessity to build and rebuild constantly an area of operating consensus.

It is convenient at first to proceed to an analysis of behaviors, acts and practices of actors in and around an organization. The term *actor* seems to cause a problem for some of our interlocutors. However, its utilization appears to fairly highlight the frame of the metaphor we often make when assimilating the enterprise and theater. Our *"interactive and evolving polygon of actors"* concept highlights the complexity of relations and exchanges between **"actors"**, who, on stages as well as in offices, could not avoid interacting more or less openly. Our theory of human behavior (Savall & Zardet, 2005b, p. 165) tends to demonstrate that the latter results in a dialectic movement between conflict and cooperation, attraction and repulsion, scenarios well known from theatrical productions. The denouement, to carry further the metaphor, should consist of reducing or eliminating the disequilibrium in the dosages of conflict and cooperation in human behavior, that the socioeconomic approach to management, as like the demiurge of plays, allows the actors and audience to do (Savall & Zardet, 2011). It is the responsibility of top management to know the current state, at any given time, between conflict and cooperation, in order to undertake the corrective actions that will reestablish an effective dosage of both conflict and cooperation. Multiple dysfunctions could thus be avoided by a better appreciation of **unvoiced comments** of communication and the real motivations of each one.

When we titled one of our publications *"Observing the complex object"* (Savall & Zardet, 2004), it was to stress on the fact that a multitude of actors are intervening in the enterprise, whose facets and dimensions are numerous and consequently contain a lot of stakes. When Taylor considered the consumer as the most important person, he forgot the multiplicity of roles of all persons who participate in company activity, and that the so-called "beast of burden", by this author, for the basic worker is also a **consumer**.

In the framework of socially responsible capitalism, it is especially fecund to develop

> The awareness of producer-man's conditions of working life, compared to those of citizen-man, who benefited from numerous laws that facilitated his/her democratic advantages and development as a responsible actor of political life. As well the consumer-man, who is the object of all attentions from marketing companies or advertisers which bring into play a lot of money in order to keep him/her informed and solicited.
>
> (Savall & Zardet, 2005b, p. 8)

Our competency grid tool answers this need, by highlighting the know-how and the qualifications of the individual as competitive advantages. This latter is completed by the self-analysis of time tool, which aims at seeking a more effective structure for the development of individual scheduling collaboration with his/her partners in activity.

That is how the ethnologist Maurice Godelier, while distinguishing social relations in their collective form, also takes an interest in the individual in all contexts of his/her existence and forms of his/her activity—material, social, symbolic. As for us, in the same spirit, we have sought the means to improve the individual's adhesion to the corporate strategy. One of those means and far from least is the **rehabilitation of enterprises** in mind-sets. These must cease to be considered as corruption factors to become the unavoidable and salutary **crucibles** of value creation, and foster the exemplary daily behavior of individuals in the workplace.

In the frame of another essential principle that we evoked herein above, that of strategic vigilance, the individual is a masterpiece, a genuine internal sensor of external information and so, he/she does represent a potential change agent for the enterprise. That is why it appears essential to us to involve and commit individuals, at all responsibility levels, in decision-making *processes* and action, thus leading to a better promotion of human resources.

Some Philosophical Considerations

At this stage, we have to introduce some philosophical considerations, which allow us to find the deep roots of humanism that some wrongly accuse the capitalist system of forgetting. One just has to considerer the themes retained for not-so-old annual conferences of *Academy of Management* in order to be aware of the important rank occupied by factors, other than financial in the challenges faced by companies: *Doing Well by Doing Good* in 2007, *Green Management Matters* in 2009, *Dare to Care: Passion and Compassion in Management Practice and Research* in 2010, the objective being to better contribute to the well-being of the society where we live in, by going against Taylorian world of labor and dehumanized, and logic of profit maximization. The *utilitarian moral* proposed by Jeremy Bentham (1748–1832), whose great principles were taken again by John Stuart Mill (1806–1873) in a book *Utilitarianism* (1863) always constitutes the theoretical base of the research of a greatest happiness for the greatest number. This is one of the main objectives for socially and sustainably responsible capitalism, as the *Conscious Capitalism Institute of Bentley University, seems willing to reach, since 2009.*

The concept of *sympathy* which Adam Smith (1723–1790) analyzes in the first chapter of *The Theory of Moral Sentiments* (1759) and that is not without relation to his famous principle of **invisible hand** (which is mentioned only once in the *The Wealth of Nations* in 1776), remains an essential criterion in order to better identify the link between social responsibility and entrepreneurial ethics. Francis Hutcheson (1694–1746), whose student was Adam Smith, opened the way with his concept closely related to *benevolence*, to which David Hume (1711–1776) had already dedicated a whole section of his essay entitled *An Inquiry Concerning the Principles of Moral*. For Hume, "*a benevolent man . . . invigorates and supports the surrounding world*" and "*the utility which stems from social virtues is constituting at less a part of their merit*" (1741–1742, p. 413) and he exclaims with emphasis, "*Which praise implies the simple useful epithet*". He put as principle that "*the merit of benevolent sentiment comes from its tendency to promote the interests of our species and bring happiness to Man society*" *(p. 415)*. The individual **well-being** cedes to the total sum of **happiness** while remaining the essential component of this latter. Individuals and society are considered sheltered from the consequences of the unrestrained pursuit of personal interests for some of them. If the quest of one's own interest is inherent to humankind, he does not necessarily have to play against the collective interest. If egoist preoccupations constitute an important lever at each stage of the enterprise, it is convenient that the CEOs, by evaluating the issues faced inside the company, are examining the way that diverse actors could succeed in harmonizing their interests. By promoting everyone's benefit, one automatically promotes oneself (Carr, E.H., *The Twenty Years Crisis, 1919–1939*, 2001). Adam Smith also noticed in his *The Wealth of Nations*: the common good is the sum of personal interests.

President of Association pour la Liberté Économique et le Progrès Social [Association for promoting Economic Freedom and Social Progress] (ALEPS) Jacques Garello, in an article entitled "Après l'échec du socialisme, si on essayait enfin le libéralisme?" [After failure of socialism, would we try at least liberalism?] testifies to the persistent topicality of this information when he writes

> The capitalist system is that which allows one to restore the creativity of the human-being, his property and his responsibility in order to develop the service orientation of the community, because no one could succeed in it without satisfying the needs of others, choosing the trust and the faith in the given word instead of suspicion and constraint.
>
> (Le Figaro, November 15, 2013)

Labor humanizes when it conveys meaning. By assimilating benevolence (or beneficence) with utility, Hume could legitimately wonder: "Could one make more vigorous praise of a profession as such of trade or manufacture, thanobserving the advantages they produce for society?". Such observation remains topical in the USA, where enterprises are perceived as essential to the cohesion of the fabric of society. The same vocabulary is still employed nowadays. David Packard, for example, mentions in his HP Way that William Hewlett and he had created the "concept of modern and benevolent company in which the bottom-line consisted in treating people rightly" (HP Way, 1993). Pierre-Yves Gomez, a member of the stream for a human ecology, comes back to this theme in his book Le Travail invisible: enquêtes sur une disparition [Invisible Labor: investigations on a disappearance] (2013) and in an article (Le Figaro, December 2014, 5th) entitled "Pourquoi beaucoup disparaissent au travail" [Why so many persons disappear at work]. After advocating that rather than being considered as a cost, the worker asks to be treated with **benevolence,** he joins Hume by insisting on the link between benevolence and utility, which is the preoccupation of the teams aligned with human ecology. The latter put the stress on the benevolent role of management.

> Being benevolent it is assurance of well-done work, to consider it as a good. Being benevolent, it is to see others as co-responsible for this work. A company which puts benevolence at the heart of its management considers that at each scale, salaried employees could define their own and collective activity with respect to utility and quality of what they are producing together.
>
> (Desjaques, Le Figaro, June 8, 2015)

Yves Desjaques, HRM of Groupe Casino, explains that benevolent management "consists of restoring the meaning and also the sensibility in enterprise, and to be interested by the other". In the introduction to 2014 edition of the book *Reconstuire l'entreprise* [*Rebuilding the enterprise*], Henri Savall and Véronique Zardet echo Jeremy Bentham when he "admits that the finality of economic activity, at leastin a democratic regime, is to ensure the social progress for the happiness of the greatest number". The word **ethics** recovers all the reality of enterprise in so far that we distinguish in ethical trends of companies, philosophical ethics (inviting one to think on what is morally acceptable and what is not), CSR defined as the voluntary actions of companies in order to take into account their impacts on the social domain and on environmental protection. That is to say the **firm contribution to sustainable economy** (Andreas Rasche, Dark Ulrich Gilbert, et Inso Schedel, Cross-Disciplinary Ethics Education in MBA programs: Rhetoric or Reality?, Academy of Management Learning and Education, 2013, pp. 71–85).

With this in mind, socially and sustainably responsible capitalism invites one not to neglect the microeconomic, even "infra-microeconomic", in favor of an analysis focused on the macroeconomic scale. In that sense it is significant to see that in a current book coordinated by Lucie Davoine (2012) entitled *Économie du Bonheur* [Happiness economy], the central topic is *well-being in enterprise*. The devastating economic crisis, which we have just undergone, leads one inescapably to think about the role that is convenient to attribute to the entrepreneurial sphere. The playwright Yasmina Reza in his book *Heureux les heureux* [Happy are the Happy] (2014) regrets *"this time that, unfortunately, does not exist yet, where managers were not technocrats but builders, where the State was not the conservatism but the progress, where the bank was not the mad money of a globalized casino but the stubborn financing action of production system"*. Bertrand Collomb and Samuel Rouvillois (*L'entreprise humainement responsable* [Humanely responsible corporate], 2011) strongly insist on the necessity to conceive of the enterprise as *"major social actor, a place where the responsibility of persons toward others is a sine qua none condition for defeating the power of alienation that exercise the economic competitiveness on individuals and teams"* (Collomb & Rouvillois, 2011, p. 44). According to them, one has to conceive of it either as *"a place in where we do not have the right to use human energy without bringing as compensation genuine growth or personal development possibilities"* (Collomb & Rouvillois, 2011, p. 45).

Inquiries in this domain show that the highest performing companies are those which most are concerned about the flourishing of the staff and also with team work As Laurent Cappelleti underlines in an article on *"la macroéconomie et l'imposture"* [macroeconomy and duplicity] (*les Échos*, December 2012, 19th), *"development factors have to be searched for at the heart of organizations and in the quality of their management"* following Henri Savall and Véronique Zardet's assertion that *"the only active factor of value creation is situated in the management of organizations whether they be macro, or micro"*. The *only genuine creation of wealth depends on the human being*, whose potential it is convenient to reveal with the socioeconomic management method. Human potential is fundamental to a proactive approach to enterprise. It is the only source of value-added creation, financial and technical capital remaining without a doubt precious tools but still inert when they are not activated by human potential. We define this latter as an ensemble of resources whose upsurge requires an individual or a human group, a capacity of action, production, innovation, creation, development and transformation on its environment. On that observation lays our theory of human potential conceived of as the way to redeploy the active factors, **active units** according to François Perroux, and to clearly distinguish them from passive factors. The socioeconomic theory (SEAM) establishes a distinction between the visible structure of a company and the hidden and intangible infrastructure, which depends on human potential. The **proximity management** proposed by a socioeconomic approach to management allows for better change management because it facilitates the staffing of salaried positions and better communication at each level of the company, which results in a reduction of dysfunctions, an increase of performance and the improvement of working conditions.

In the framework of socially and sustainably responsible capitalism, which could be summarized as a cumulative process of economic and social development, *stagnation* of productive capacity is impossible. It is matter for the company to go further or disappear because, by definition, it is a place for movement and **metamorphosis** encouraged by an exogenous stimulation such as external strategic threat. We prefer the word *metamorphosis* to that of change because it better expresses the importance of internal develop-ment, modifications of structures and behaviors in the frame of the com-pany. The permanent and complex interaction creates activity beats, which constitute the functioning of companies. It is essentially an endogenous and scheduled transformation of the inside. Of course, scientific and techno-logic advances play an indispensable role, but what is making them in one part possible and in another part, operational are first the investments in "human resources". Technical capital and investments dedicated to techni-cal innovation are of course essential for the survival and the future of the company, by improving products and production and so the economic and social progress. But each technological step has to be accompanied by the development of human potential, which is necessary to the progression of performance and to the increasing of **competitiveness** by applying the prin-ciples of socioeconomic management.

It is convenient to train the workers who are at the helm of the new machine. A lack of vigilance or knowhow on their part would risk cost-ing much more than what the technological advance could represent in terms of potential savings. On this last point, Patrick Artus, economist from NATIXIS, rightly remarks, in *Le Monde* (July 2014, 1st), that one has to maintain full teams of server maintenance, systems and networks, guard-ians of informatics security . . . whose costs are absorbing a large part of the potential savings. It is only by taking in mind the training needs on one hand, and the new conditions entailed by massive production on other hand, that Karl Marx could notice "the inept contradiction that comes from what one forgets in the fact that modern industry is more and more replac-ing the complex labor by simple labor, which requires no training" (Marx, 1963, p. 158). In a time of disruptions in production processes, the worker could not be considered as "conscious accessory" of the machine but as the only person able to master new methods and new tools.

Since the seventeenth century, we have underlined that only the evolution of competencies and skills would allow technology to yield its full potential. William Petty comes back to this theme several times in his works. In chapter one of his *Political Arithmetic* he compares, for example, the results obtained by a man working with a mill and 20 others equipped only with a mortar (Hull, 1899, p. 249), or those of a printer and 100 scribes. This clearly shows an attempt to raise a kind of values ladder for labor founded, not only on its level of difficulty, but also rather on its degree of complexity (more or less). Petty put the *projector*, the inventor-conceiver in pole position. Later on, in the eighteenth century, J. Tucker in his *"Instructions"* (1757, pp. 21–22), commented on the benefits of mechanization as reducing the costs of labor and merchandise prices, laying the blame on those who see a threat to employ-ment, by highlighting the variety of necessary types of knowhow in matters of the building, manipulation and maintenance of machines.

The same applies today in terms of adaptation to the challenge of the numerical revolution and regarding artificial intelligence, which would always be a reproductive intelligence incapable of rivaling the creative intelligence of the human being: "*The so-called intelligent machines have been conceived and maintained by humans who incorporated some of the knowledge that only they are able to create, produce, reproduce, diffuse, transfer, perfect, and question*" (Savall, H. & Zardet, V. in Association François Perroux *Comment vivre ensemble: conditions économiques de la démocratie* [Living together: economic conditions of democracy], 2008b, p. 129). One does not have to inventory the list of cell phones, tablets, computers and smartphones or to salute the unmeasured influence of social networks such as *Twitter* or *Facebook* without proposing solutions in order to address the associated disruptions in structures and behaviors at each scale of the company. It is necessary to impose a new managerial approach and the learning process of a more and more collaborative style of work and the exigency of numerical enterprise. It could not be enough, only a technological revolution impulse through the rise of numerical technology. Christian Saint-Etienne in his book entitled *l'iconomie pour sortir de la crise. France: arrêtons la débandade* [the economy in order to overcome the crisis. France: stop this stampede] (2013) brushes an interesting portrait of the entrepreneurial economy and shows how the radical transformation of management modes is necessary for the improvement of both industrial economy and the development of social dialogue.

However, this situation is the status of **apprenticeship** that we have advocated since 1973 when an economic and social crisis was outlined that was likely similar to those we cross today, excluding the mutation that today one holds the Internet as responsible. We notice, therefore, that this latter is accused of favoring long hours of work outside the standards without regard to the legal duration of work time and constituting an additional factor of stress. Being reachable at each time by email, SMS and other technical means of communication is not a source of thriving but rather spawning organizational flaws (time management, etc.) that lead to a poorly mastered utilization of the numerical tool. With the extension of IT techniques, costly dysfunctions have been multiplied in the numerical enterprises, which entail *plethoric* hidden costs. The deep roots are apparent not only in unsuitable material investments but also in the lack of commitment or training for the teams that have to take in charge of communication and information techniques, concerning the implementation of tools that, thanks to high-speed networks facilitating their interactions, are vital for the good companies' functioning.

"*Cloud computing*" is supposed to have a beneficial influence on the quality of the working life of individuals, because of the distant access to all functionalities of their computing, which gives more flexibility to working methods and improves their conditions. However, would this not be another case of favoring productivity efficiencies *at the expense of* a supposed quality of life by creating a workplace without any limits? Rather than complaining about **technological idolatry**, it is convenient to be ensured that each new technique has to be perfectly mastered at this time of the supposed post-industrial and post-service society. Our research shows, once again, that it is the lack of intangible investments, which causes many dysfunctions and a high level of hidden costs. The time spent to resolve dysfunctions ends up extracting a lot from those dedicated to train users. Each recourse to a material investment should be entailed in the budgeting of intangible investments, by costing out the alternatives before decision and implementation.

Material investment represents only the visible part of the iceberg in the decision-making process. It does not generate economic performance. Neglecting the intangible aspect of the investment is extremely prejudicial to the quality of decision making because it remains the only possibility for companies to reinvent their business and management models. In no case does technology replace human intelligence. More and more sophisticated tasks should be possible because of fully autonomous machines, with man always still being the guarantor of their optimal functioning, even though some persons call into doubt the reliability of man in the production process and even in urgent decision-making. This is the point of view that CEO Charles-Édouard Bouée develops in a book co-authored with journalist François Roche "*Confucius et les automates*" [Confucius and the automaton] (2014), while not disparaging the intrinsic wisdom of humanity in order to keep the invasion of machines and robots within reasonable limits. When a company is not sensitive to the importance of the necessary intangible investment in order to ensure the profitability of information and communication technology, it suffers from severe dysfunctions because the costs, which ensue from their blindness, cancel the potential benefits of material investments.

Coupling material investment with intangible investment means adapting working conditions, ensuring the development of new qualifications in order to facilitate the utilization of new equipment, modifying work procedures when a previously manual activity is computerized, adjusting the distribution of tasks between employees, animating training sessions to new operational modes for users, valorizing knowhow and ensuring a tight communication-coordination-cooperation between computing specialists and users (Zardet & Harbi, 2007). Even in fully automated Japanese plants, humans remain essential at the operation center. If one could be tempted to assimilate economy and manufacturing tangible products, it remains true at least that the essential aspects of value added are due to intangible components that are outside of accounting documents, but should be in good ranking when valuing the asset. For Petty, what is sold is not so much the product than the value added by knowhow of the inventive mind of humans.

7 Conclusion

This book endeavors to answer these questions: Why do we need a socially responsible capitalism? What is the use of a new book on capitalism?

Considering the ambient falling out of love with the *enterprise*, we think that this book allows us to get out of the moroseness, which emerges from the major part of current publications, in order to give a fresh boost to capitalism. Of course, it concerns a capitalism that has to be reinvented, full of *creation, innovation* and *evolution*. We rethink capitalism in another way, constrained and forced by the disappearance or the bankruptcy of other systems and by the distress aroused. *Capitalism, as it currently exists, is its own worst enemy.*

We need an economic system that will last. The notion of *sustainability* is intrinsic to the notion of **individual and collective responsibility**. The latter should not be ephemeral and has to be maintained by day-to-day practices, in the proximity of actors.

All the book shows that one has to replace humans at the core of action, in order to produce economic *value* and anthropological *values*, which are inseparable. Therefore, it was to show that socially responsible capitalism is not a utopia. It has already been inscribed in the history of economic and social facts, and it is *viable* nowadays.

The Entrepreneur Is a Creator

From this perspective, we recall that *socioeconomic management (SEAM)* started in 1973, but it has not lived self-contained. It has evolved, faithful to its basic *leitmotiv*: management is a synonym of **change**. The enterprise and the organization are living beings; they are not fixed, and only a dynamic approach, that shows them in movement is likely to highlight the path of prosperity for the greatest number and sustainable economic and social performance. The notion of *creation* is intrinsic to the company. *The entrepreneur is a creator.* A company is also a group of humans who produce economic value and anthropologic values. It is the **crucible** in which the salutary socioeconomic value is forged and elaborated. An essential engine of social and economic activity is the **project**, the movement, the creation embodied by the *individual* and his capacity to *include* others. We do adhere to Perroux's thought, according to whom a man is not a simple subject but a *project in movement*. The enterprise or organization is the proximity environment, which favors stimulation, development and thriving of the individual contribution to the creation of value(s).

Interaction with Democracy

SRC serves *democracy's* recognized universal value, or at least its practices. SRC constitutes an economic system, which contributes to the *democracy* and feeds from it. Democracy does not have to be lived in a so-called corporate "culture". Being eminently virtual, it is played out and built every day in the reality of human relationships, productive or not. That is the requirement for the enterprise be an exemplary "*institution*". Socioeconomic management, by means of its concept of *daily and proximity democracy*, not elective democracy per the usual political meaning, contributes to extend, root and reinforce both practices and political democracy devices.

Greatness and Servitude of State

The state has an irreplaceable role to play through its great missions, here where capitalism, were it socially responsible, should be neither legitimate, nor effective and efficient. It is a question of the sovereign missions, such as education, justice, security and health. The eminently economic mission of the state consists of enacting economic and social rules of the game, by means of democratic dialog and taking the leadership in steering and financing the *fundamental economic infrastructures*, either entirely with its own public resources or with the concourse of private partners, in the frame of a peculiarly efficient *hybrid economic system*.

By the way, the seductive attempts to draw the attention of some from anti-globalism partisans do not lead anywhere; do not propose an organized system, which could be used as a framework and offer rules of the game to the countless initiatives of responsible actors, individuals, enterprises, associations, territorial communities and institutions.

The servitude of the state lies principally on the principle of a state that is *respectful* of the individual and private, associative and public socially decentralized groups. Its bill of charter is to ensure the respect of everyone: freedom, his/her *dignity*, his/her personal or collective development.

Eminent Educative Role of the Media

The *press* played an *historical, educative role* in the advent and progresses of democracy, thus in its opening to the world. Today, media risks the "*irresponsible*" overflowing of social networks. This threat is also an opportunity for media to retrieve its educative function of channeling and assuming its responsibilities in this cacophonic concert, by contributing to the enhancement of democracy. The condition for this renewal of the media comes back to cultivate the critical spirit of the citizen reader and to avoid the drift toward a kind of *clientelistic demagogy* of poor quality, a source of exacerbation for society's struggles.

The Tamed Technology, Immanent Creation of Man to Man

History spanning more than two centuries has revealed a phenomenon of *technological idolatry*. One could spot it under the form of losing critical-mindedess facing technological investment decisions where each machine acquisition appears to be a rational decision, which fits within the usual historic patterns. Economic models, which have been followed for two centuries, have never put into question the fact that technology is *not naturally* complementary to human action and that it could be diverted from its intended purpose. Technology is a creation of humanity (man and woman). Its legitimacy is proved when it serves humanity because this is its *raison d'être*.

Technology should not be autarkic and pretend to self-suffice and self-support its development. The myth of the *sorcerer's apprentice* looms on the horizon when we observe some excesses of robotic. Yet, the well-mastered technology is a precious tool, which has a multiplicative effect in terms of economic value and social values. For example, information and communication technologies facilitate the access to information and education over and over. The technological investment is rational from the socioeconomic point of view, *on the condition* that one dedicates resources (intangible investments in qualitative development of human potential) to integrated training of producers, users or clients.

Socially responsible capitalism must favor this mastering of **citizen technology**, the fruit of individual and collective human genius, by means of debate, dialogue and reconstructive criticism.

Build Instead of Destroy

The resolving of issues and economic and social challenges has fluctuated, throughout history, between two options and propositions which are diametrically opposed: *struggle* or social dialogue founded on *negotiation*. Some theories and ideologies have chosen and favored the struggle in their recommendations. Recent history has shown that their effects are no longer accurate. One just has to observe and analyze the global state of crisis, never-ending actually, since 1973 in order to be convinced. The constructive way of negotiation, which creates the need to be better highlighted at each scale of society and at each step of projects. It is convenient to oppose the observed failure of communist utopia and the **hope** that socially responsible capitalism arouses, pared down from its sclerosis speculative pollution.

This book lies on a multidisciplinary approach and more than half a century of research in economy, management science and human and social sciences. Offered to any kind of reader, it presents key ideas from some fundamental authors who have proposed constructive theories that are liable to support the concept of socially responsible capitalism: Petty, Bernácer, Keynes, Schumpeter, Perroux and Allais. This book endeavors to situate itself with respect to the unavoidable and well-known Marx, who proposed a solution based on the struggle (of classes).

Our objective was not to propose small and fast remedies to the acuity of the crisis. The *sustainable* character of solutions *to be invented* for the future is found, indeed watermarked, in the whole book. This is not also a *pro domo* appeal but a roadmap for enterprises, consultants, teachers and researchers. For all that, politicians, journalists and all civil life actors will find substance and tools for a constructive, generative, *hopeful* reflection.

The reader would forgive us to think that a discourse on moroseness was not appropriate anyway.

Bibliography

Allais, M. (1943). *Traité d'Économie pure*, Paris: Imp. Nationale.

Allais, M. (1989). Discours de réception du Prix Nobel d'Économie, *Annales des Mines*, mars, 876–891.

Allais, M. (2005). *L'Europe en crise? Que faire? Réponses à quelques questions. Pour une autre Europe*, Paris: Ed Clément Juglar.

Allais, M. (2008). Comment vivre ensemble: conditions économiques et sociales pour la démocratie, in Association François Perroux (Ed.), *Comment vivre ensemble: conditions économiques de la démocratie*, pp. 19–32. Écully: ISEOR éditeur.

Amabile, T., & Kramer, S. Opinion, *New York Times*, 3 septembre 2011.

Association François Perroux (2002). *Une mondialisation apprivoisée?* Écully: ISEOR éditeur.

Association François Perroux (2008). *Comment vivre ensemble: conditions économiques de la démocratie*, Écully: ISEOR éditeur.

Azuelos, M. (2001). *Travail et Emploi: L'Expérience Anglo-Saxonne, Aspects Historiques*, Paris: Sorbonne Nouvelle éditions.

Bacon, F. X. (1597). *Essais*, traduction française, Paris: Éditions Aubier-Montaigne.

Ballet, J., Carimentrand, A., & Jolivet, P. (2001, 2011). *L'entreprise et l'éthique*, Paris: Seuil.

Barad, K. (2007). *Meeting the Universe Halfway: Quantum Physics and the Entanglement of Matter and Meaning*, Durham: Duke University Press.

Bardelli, P., & Allouche, J. (2012). La souffrance au travail. Quelle responsabilité pour l'entreprise, Paris: Armand Colin.

Barre, R., Blardone, G., & Savall, H. (2004). *François Perroux, le Centenaire d'un grand économiste*, Paris: Economica.

Baumol, W., Litan, R. E., & Schramm, C. (2007). *Good Capitalism, Bad Capitalism*, New Haven, CT: Yale Press.

Beaud, M. (2010). *Histoire du capitalisme: 1500–2010*, Paris: Seuil 1981, nouvelle édition avril 2010.

Benedict, XVI. (2009). *Caritas in Veritate*, Paris: L'es Editions Blanche de Peuterey.

Berdiaeff, N. (1927). *Un nouveau moyen âge*, Paris: Librarie Plon.

Bernácer, G. (1916). *Sociedad y felicidad. Ensayo de mecanicá social*, Madrid: Ed. Beltrán.

Bernácer, G. (1922). La teoría de las disponibilidades como interpretación de las crisis y del problema social, *Revista nacional de economía*, 3(40), 267–303.

Bernácer, G. (1945a). *La teoría funcional del dinero*, Madrid: Consejo Superior de Investigaciones Científicas, 2nd édition en 1956.

Bernácer, G. (1945b). *Una economía libre sin crisis y sin paro*, Madrid: Aguilar.

Bichot, J. (2004). Monnaie, religion et croissance, in I. Barth & M. Pothier (dir.), *Le commerce peut il être éthique? Du passeur des mondes au commis voyageur*. Actes des 4èmes assises de la Vente, avril; ISEOR, IAE Lyon, Université Jean Moulin, Écully: ISEOR Éditeur.

Blardone, G. (2013). Un nouveau monde et les zones d'échanges organisés, in Association des Amis de François Perroux (Ed.), *Agir dans nouveau monde: le développement et les coûts de l'Homme*, pp. 168–179. Écully: ISEOR éditeur.

Boje, D. (2004). Préface, in H. Savall & V. Zardet (Eds.), *Recherche en sciences de gestion: approche qualimétrique. Observer l'objet complexe*, pp. 7–22. Paris: Economica.

Boje, D. M. (2014). *Storytelling Organizational Practices: Managing in the Quantum Age*, London: Routledge.

Boje, D. (ed.) (2015). *Organizational Change and Global Standardization: Solutions to Standards and Norms Overhelming Organizations*, London: Routledge.

Boje, D. M., & Henderson, T. L. (eds.) (2014). *Being Quantum: Ontological Storytelling in the Age of Antenarrative*, Cambridge: Cambridge Scholars Publishing.

Boje, D., & Rosile, G. A. (2003). Comparison of socioeconomic and other transorganizational development methods, *Journal of Organizational Change Management*, Emerald, (États-Unis), 16(1), 17–34.

Bonnet, M. (1988). Expériences du traitement de l'illettrisme en entreprise indutrielle. Cas d'une intervention socio-économique dans une verrerie, *Actualité de la Formation Permanente*, (96), septembre–octobre, 298–331.

Bonnet, M. (1996). Entreprises et illettrisme, *Bulletin du Groupe Permanent de Lutte contre l'Illettrisme*, (34), octobre, 179–201.

Bouée, C.-E., & Roche, F. (2014). *Confucius et les automates*, Paris: éditions Bernard Grasset.

Boyer, R. (2009). Du rapport salarial fordiste à la diversité des relations salariales, *Cahier français*, (349), mars–avril, 298–330.

Braudel, F. (1986). *Civilisation matérielle, économie et capitalisme XVe-XVIIIe siècle*, Paris: Armand Collin.

Brundtland, G. H. (1987). *Report of the World Commission on Environment and Development: "Our Common Future,"* New York: United Nations.

Buono, A.F. (2001). *International Development of the Management Consulting Division of the Academy of Management*, in *Knowledge and Value Development in Management Consulting*, Écully: ISEOR Éditeur.

Buono, A.F. (2003). SEAM-less post-merger integration strategies: A cause for concern, *Journal of Organizational Change Management*, 16(1), 90–98.

Buono, A. F., & Savall, H. (eds.) (2007). ISEOR's Socioeconomic Method: A Case of Scientific Consultancy, in Socioeconomic Intervention in Organizations (Ed.), *The Intervener-Researcher and the SEAM Approach to Organizational Analysis*, pp. 20–51. Charlotte, NC: Information Age Publishing.

Buono, A. F., & Savall, H. (eds.) (2015*). The Socioeconomic Approach to Management Revisited: The Evolving Nature of SEAM in the 21st Century*, Charlotte, NC: Information Age Publishing.

Cantillon, R. (1755, 1931, 1952). *Essai sur la Nature du Commerce en Général*, Paris: Institut National d'Études Démographiques.

Cappelletti, L. (2012). La macroéconomie et l'imposture, *Les Échos*, 19 décembre, p. 27.

Carr, E. H. (2001). *The Twenty Years Crisis, 1919–1939*, New York: Perrenial.

Carré, J. J., Dubois, P., & Malinvaud, E. (1972). *La croissance française. Un essai d'analyse économique causale de l'après-guerre*, Paris: Seuil.

Carrol, A. B. (1991). The pyramid of corporate social responsibility: Toward the moral management of organizational stakeholders, *Business Horizons*, 34, 39–48.

Chandler, D. (2014). Morals, markets and values-based businesses, *Academy of Management Review*, 39(3), 396–406.

Chappel, T. (1993). *The Soul of a Business*, New York: Bentham Books.

Chen, M.-J., & Miller, D. (2011). The relational perspective as a business mindset, *Academy of Management Perspective*, 25(3), 143–160.

Coase, W. (1937). The nature of the firm, *Revue Economica*, novembre, 386–405.

Collins, E., & Kearins, K. (2010). Delivering on sustainability's global and local orientation, *Academy of Management Learning and Education*, 9(3), 132–158.

Collomb, B., & Rouvillois, S. (2011). *L'entreprise humainement responsable, sous la direction de Francis Mathieu et de Marianne de Boisredon*, Bruxelles: Desclée de Brouwer.

Collomb, B., Rouvillois, S., Mathieu, F., & de Boisredon, M. (2011). *L'entreprise humainement responsable*, Paris: Desclée De Brouwer.

Crane, A. (2013). Modern slavery as a management practice: Exploring the conditions and capabilities for human exploitation, *Academy of Management Review*, 38(1), 49–69.

Crozier, M. (1994). *L'entreprise à l'écoute. Apprendre le management post-industriel*, Seuil.

Davenant, C. (1771), London: Works, p. 35.

Datry, F., & Savall, A. (2015). Global-Local (Glocal) Creation of Value Added, in A. Buono & H. Savall (Eds.), *The Socioeconomic Approach to Management Revisited: The Evolving Nature of SEAM in the 21st Century*, pp. 57–81. Charlotte, NC: Information Age Publishing.

Davoine, L. (2012). *Économie du bonheur*, Paris: La Découverte.

Delors, J. (1975). Préface, in H. Savall (Ed.), *Enrichir le travail humain: l'évaluation économique*, pp. 17. Paris: Dunod.

Desné, J. (2012). Jack Ma, un ancien professeur d'anglais devenu milliardaire, *Le Figaro*, 21 May 2012.

Diemer, A., & Laurier, P. (2013). Hommage à Maurice Allais, in G. Blardone & H. Savall (Eds.), *Association des Amis de François Perroux: Agir dans un monde nouveau: le développement et les coûts de l'homme*, pp. 63–70. Écully: ISEOR éditeur.

Di Maggio, P., & Powel, W. (1989). The iron cage revisited: Institutional isomorphism and collective rationality in organizational fields, *American Sociological Review*, 28(3), 179–198.

Encyclopédie ou Dictionnaire raisonné des sciences, des arts et des métiers, Paris: Larousse, 1751–1772.

Faber, E. (2012). *Chemins de traverse: Vivre l'économie autrement*, Paris: Albin Michel.

Fayol, H. (1916). *Administration générale et industrielle*, Paris: Gauthiers Villars.

Fayolle, A., & Verstraete, T. (2005). Paradigmes et entrepreneuriat, *Revue de l'Entrepreneuriat*, 4(1), 33–52.

Ferry, L. (2012). Chronique, *Le Figaro*, 18 octobre 2012.

Financial Times (2011). Financial amnesia: A factor behind crisis, capitalism in crisis: The code that forms a bar to harmony, 27 December, p. 29.

Frère, B. (2011). *Économie sociale et solidaire: béquille du capitalisme*, Paris: Édition Textuel.

Fried, B., & Tosi, H. (2005). Pay without performance, *Administrative Science Quarterly*, 50(3), 483–487.

Friedman, M. (1970). The social responsibility of business is to increase its profits, *New York Times Magazine*, 13 September 1970.

Friedmann, G. (1956). *Le travail en miettes*, Paris: Gallimard.

Galbraith, J. K. (1958, 1961). *L'ère de l'opulence*, Paris: Calmann-Lévy.

Gervais, P., Azuelos, M., & Esposito, M.-C. (coord.) (2003). *Travail et Emploi: l'expérience anglo-saxonne*, vol. 1, *Aspects historiques*, Paris: Presses de la Sorbonne Nouvelle.

Gilpin, R., & Gilpin, J. M. (2000). *The Challenge of Global Capitalism: The World Economy in the 21st Century*, vol. 5, Princeton, NJ: Princeton University Press.

Gomez, P. Y. (2013). *Le Travail invisible: enquêtes sur une disparition*, Paris: François Bourin.

Grebot, E. (2008). *Stress et burn out au travail*, Paris : Éditions d'Organisation.

Grima, F. & Muller, R. (2008). Responsabiliser sans manipuler, in ADERSE (Ed.), *Responsabilité Sociale de l'Entreprise*, Écully: ISEOR Éditeur.

Guénois, J.-M. (2013). Le Pape dénonce le "fétichisme de l'argent", *Le Figaro*, 17 mai 2013.

Guiddens, A. (1994). *Les conséquences de la modernité*, Paris: L'Harmattan.

Hardt, M., & Negri, A. (2001). *Empire*, Boston, MA: Harvard University Press.

Hayes R. B., (2001). Using real option concepts to guide the nature and measured benefits of consulting interventions involving investment analysis, in *Knowledge and Value Development in Management Consulting*, Écully: ISEOR Éditeur.

Heidegger, M. (1962). *Being and Time*, trans. J. Macquarrie and E. Robinson, New York: Harper & Row.

Henderson, T., & Boje, D. M. (2015). *Organizational Development and Change Theory: Managing Fractal Organizing Processes*, vol. 11, London: Routledge.

Heorhiadi, A., Conbere, J., & Hazelbaker, C. (2014). Virtue vs. virus can OD overcome the heritage of scientific management?, *OD Practitioner*, 46(3), 28.

Hobbes, T. (1651, 1964). *Leviathan*, Washington: Washington Square Press.

Hull, C. H. (ed.) (1899). *The Economic Writings of Sir William Petty ("Wrote Probably by Captain John Graunt")*, vol. 1, Cambridge: Cambridge University Press.

Hume, D., & Beauchamp, T. L. (2006). *An Enquiry Concerning the Principles of Morals 4*, Oxford: Oxford University Press.

Josephson, M. (1972). *The Money Lords: The Great Finance Capitalists 1925–1950*, New York: Weybridge & Talley.

Kees Van Kersbergen (1995). *Social Capitalism: A Study of Christian Democracy and the Welfare State*, London: Routledge.

Keynes, J. M. (1936). *Théorie générale de l'emploi, de l'intérêt et de la monnaie*, Paris: Payot.

Koenig, G. (2015). *Le Révolutionnaire, l'Expert et le Geek. Combats pour l'autonomie*, Paris: Plon.

Krupicka A., & Dreveton B. (2015). Les rôles des collectivités locales dans l'adaptation d'un projet relatif à la responsabilité sociale des entreprises, in H. Savall, M.Bonnet, V. Zardet, & M. Péron (Eds.), *Actes du 3ème Congrès de l'ADERSE*, Écully: ISEOR Éditeur.

Lagarde, X. (2012). La valeur travail en question, *Le Figaro*, 23 fevrier 2012.

Lawson, T. W. (1905). *Frenzied Finance*, New York: Ridgway-Thayer Co.

Lecaussin, N. (2014). *L'Obsession anti-libérale française. Ses causes et conséquences,* Paris: édition Libre échange.

Le Goff, J. (1986). *La bourse ou la vie: Économie et religion au Moyen-Âge,* Paris: Hachette.

Leter, M. (2015). *Le Capital,* Paris: Les Belles Lettres.

Lipson, E. (1958). *The Economic History of England,* London: A&C Black.

Llau, P. (1961). *La détermination des taux d'intérêt,* Paris: Cujas.

Locke, J. (1740). *Treatise on Interest,* London: Folio.

Lussato, B. (1972). *Introduction critique aux théories d'organisation: modèles cybernétiques, hommes, entreprises,* Paris: Dunod.

Mackey, J. & Sisodia, R. (2013). *"Conscious Capitalism" Is Not an Oxymoron,* Cambridge: Harvard Business Review Press.

Marchesnay, M. (2005). Qui a peur de ses responsabilités sociales, in H. Savall, M. Bonnet, V. Zardet, & M. Péron (Eds.), *Actes du 3ème Congrès de l'ADERSE,* vol. 3, pp. 78–109. Écully, France: ISEOR Éditeur.

Marcuse, H. (1970). *L'homme unidimensionnel,* Paris: Le Seuil.

Marschak, J., & Radner, R. (1972). *Economic Theory of Teams,* New Haven and London: Yale University Press.

Marx, K. (1867a). *Das Kapital,* Bd. 1. *MEW, Bd, 23,* 405.

Marx, K. (1867b). *Le capital,* traduction française dans la collection Folio en 2014, Paris: Folio.

Marx, K. (1963, 1968). *Œuvres,* Paris: La Pléiade.

Mathieu, F.-R. (1997). *William Petty, fondateur de l'économie,* Paris: Economica.

Merleau-Ponty, M. (1955). *Les aventures de la dialectique,* Paris: Gallimard.

Mill, J. S. (1863). *Utilitarianism,* London: Penguin Books.

Muller, A. R., Pfarrer, M. D., & Little, L. M. (2014). A theory of collective empathy in corporate philanthropy decisions, *Academy of Management Review,* 39(1), 1–21.

Misselden, E. (1622). *Free Trade, or the Means to Make Trade Flourish,* New York: A. M. Kelley.

Montmollin, M. (1981). *Le taylorisme à visage humain,* Paris: Presses Universitaires de France.

Morin, F. (2011). *Monde sans Wall Street,* Paris: Seuil.

Mun, T. (1664, 1713). *England's Treasure by Foreign Trade: Or the Balance of Our Foreign Trade Is the Rule of Our Treasure,* London: J. Morphew.

Péron, M. (1982). *Sir William Petty, sa pensée économique et sociale,* 3 vols., Thèse d'État Lyon: Université Lyon II.

Péron, M. (ed.) (2002). *La Transdisciplinarité: Fondement de la Pensée Managériale Anglo-Saxone,* Paris: Economica.

Péron, M. (2003). Chômage et emploi au dix-septième siècle, in Gervais, I. Azuelos & M. Esposito (Eds.), *Travail et emploi,* pp. 56–60. Paris: Presses de la Sorbonne Nouvelle.

Péron, M., & Péron, M. (2003). Post-modernism and socioeconomic approach to organizations, *Journal of Organizational Change Management,* Emerald, (Etats-Unis), 16(1), 49–55.

Perroux, F. (1935). Introduction à l'ouvrage de Joseph Schumpeter "théorie de l'évolution économique. Recherches sur le profit, le crédit, l'intérêt et le cycle de la conjoncture", traduction française, pp. 148, Paris: Dalloz.

Perroux, F. (1935, 1965). *La pensée économique de Joseph Schumpeter. Les dynamiques du capitalisme,* Genève: Droz.

Perroux, F. (1936). Les paternalistes contre la personne humaine, *Esprit,* 3, 854–866.

148 *Bibliography*

Perroux, F. (1948). Esquisse d'une théorie de l'économie dominante, *Économie Appliquée*, 1(2–3), 345–371.

Perroux, F. (1950). La généralisation de la théorie de l'intérêt de Keynes, *revue Banque*, 3, 43–62.

Perroux, F. (1955). *Note Sur la Notion de Pôle de Croissance: l'Économie du XXème Siècle*, Paris: Presses Universitaires de France.

Perroux, F. (1963, 1968). *Préface Oeuvres de Karl Marx*, Paris: La Pléiade.

Perroux, F. (1975). *Unités actives et mathématiques nouvelles-Révision de la théorie de l'équilibre économique général*, Paris: Dunod.

Perroux, F. (1979). L'entreprise, l'équilibre rénové et les coûts "cachés", Préface, in H. Savall (Ed.), *Reconstruire l'entreprise. Analyse socio-économique des conditions de travail*, Paris: Dunod.

Petty, W. (1662). *A treatise on taxes and contributions*, vol. 1, London: Brooke.

Petty, W., & Graunt, J. (1899). *The Economic Writings of Sir William Petty*, vol. 1, Cambridge: Cambridge University Press.

Petty, W., Lansdowne, H. W., & Southwell, R. (1927). *The Collected Works of Sir William Petty*, "Correspondence," London: Routledge/Thommes.

Peyrefitte, A. (1995). *La Société de confiance*, Paris: Odile Jacob.

Polony, N. (2015). *Ce pays qu'on abat*, Paris: Plon.

Porter, M. E., & Kramer, M. R. (2011). Creating shared value, *Harvard Business Review*, 89(1/2), 62–77.

Rasche, A., Dark Ulrich, G., & Schedel, I. (2013). Cross-disciplinary ethics education in MBA programs: Rhetoric or reality? *Academy of Management Learning and Education*, 12(1), 71–85.

Reich, R. X. (2008). Supercapitalism: The transformation of business, democracy and everyday life, *Society and Business Review*, 3(3), 256–258.

Reinhart, C. M., & Rogoff, K. S. (2010). *Cette fois, c'est différent: huit siècles de folie financière*. Paris: Pearson Education France.

Reza, Y. (2014). *Heureux les heureux*, Paris: Gallimard.

Robertson, D. H. (1940). A Spanish contribution to the theory of fluctuations, *Economica*, fevrier, 50–65.

Roche, L. (2008). Approche philosophique de la RSE: pour une nouvelle éthique du pouvoir du plus grand nombre, in H. Savall, M. Bonnet, V. Zardet, & M. Péron (Eds.), *Actes du 3ème Congrès de l'ADERSE*, vol. 3, pp. 292–315. Écully: ISEOR éditeur.

Rosanvallon, P. (1979). *Le capitalisme utopique*, Paris: Seuil.

Rouat, S. (2008). Mal-être et stress, in Y. Grasset & M. Debout (Eds.), *Risques psychosociaux au travail: vraies questions et bonnes réponses*, pp. 125–140. Paris: Éditions Liaisons sociales.

Saint-Etienne, C. (2013). *L'Iconomie pour sortir de la crise. France: arrêtons la débandade*, Paris: Odile Jacob.

Salin, P. (2000). *Libéralisme 2000*, Paris: Odile Jacob.

Savall, H. (1973a). À la recherche des coûts cachés. Une méthode de diagnostic socio—économique de l'entreprise, *Revue Française de Gestion*, (18), 96–108.

Savall, H. (1973b). Germán Bernácer, économiste espagnol 1883–1965. Une théorie générale de l'emploi, de la rente et de la thésaurisation, Thèse de doctorat d'État en sciences économiques, Paris II, p. 602.

Savall, H. (1974a). *Avant Keynes et au-delà: Germán Bernácer, Mondes en développement*, Paris: Éditions Techniques et Économiques.

Savall, H. (1974b). Enrichir le travail humain: l'évaluation économique, thèse Université Paris-Dauphine, publiée chez Dunod (1975) préface de Jacques Delors; 4

édition, Economica, 1989. Traduit en espagnol: *Por un trabajo más humano*, Tecniban, Madrid, 1977 et en anglais; *Work and People—An Economic Evaluation of Job-Enrichment* (Oxford University Press, New York, 1981), préface de H.I. Ansoff; 2 édition (IAP, États-Unis, 2010).

Savall, H. (1975). *Germán Bernácer: L'hétérodoxie en science économique*: Collection *Les grands économistes*, Paris: Dalloz.

Savall, H. (1978). Perroux, in A. Brignone, J. Lambert, & H. Savall (Eds.), *Encyclopédie de l'économie; le présent en question*, pp. 139–153. Paris: Larousse.

Savall, H. (1979). *Reconstruire l'entreprise. Analyse socio-économique des conditions de travail*, Paris: Dunod.

Savall, H. (1981). *Work and People: An Economic Evaluation of Job Enrichment*, London: Oxford University Press.

Savall, H. (2003). An update presentation of the socioeconomic management model, *Journal of Organizational Change Management*, Emerald, (États-Unis), 16(1), 33–48.

Savall, H. (2010). Allocution d'ouverture, in H. Savall & V. Zardet (Eds.), *Réussir en temps de crise. Stratégies proactives des entreprises*, pp. 3–6. Paris: Economica.

Savall, H. (2013). Individu, entreprise et nation. Comment créer le PIB? dans Agir dans un nouveau monde: le développement et les coûts de l'homme, Écully, France: ISEOR éditeur.

Savall, H., & Bonnet, M. (1996). Recommandations de la méthode socio-économique pour la politique de développement des entreprises d'insertion et associations intermédiaires, communication au Conseil Économique et Social, Paris, p. 26.

Savall, H., & Zardet, V. (1987). *Maîtriser les coûts et les performances cachés. Le contrat d'activité périodiquement négociable*, Cambridge: Prix Harvard l'Expansion de Management Stratégique.

Savall, H., & Zardet, V. (1992). *Le nouveau contrôle de gestion*, Paris: Editions comptables Malesherbes-Eyrolles.

Savall, H., & Zardet, V. (1995, 2005a). *Ingénierie stratégique du roseau, souple et enracinée*, Paris: Economica.

Savall, H., & Zardet, V. (2004). *Recherche en sciences de gestion: approche qualimétrique. Observer l'objet complexe*, Paris: Economica.

Savall, H., & Zardet, V. (2005b). *Tétranormalisation: défis et dynamiques*, Paris: Economica.

Savall, H., & Zardet, V. (2006b). Théorie socio-économique des organisations: impacts sur quelques concepts dominants dans les théories et pratiques managériales, communication au Colloque Academy of Management (ODC) & ISEOR, Lyon, France; Avril, 267–302.

Savall, H., & Zardet, V. (2007). *L'importance stratégique de l'investissement incorporel: résultats qualimétriques de cas d'entreprises, Actes du 1er congrès Transatlantique de Comptabilité, Audit, Contrôle de gestion, Gestion des Coûts et Mondialisation. IIC-ISEOR-AAA*, Écully, France: ISEOR éditeur.

Savall, H., & Zardet, V. (2008a). Le concept de coût-valeur des activités. Contribution de la théorie socio-économique des organisations, *Revue Sciences de Gestion-Management Sciences-Ciencias de Gestión*, (64), 61–90.

Savall, H., & Zardet, V. (2008b). Tétranormalisation et nouvelles règles du jeu: contribution de la théorie socio-économique, in Association des Amis de François Perroux (Ed.), *Comment vivre ensemble: conditions économiques de la démocratie*, pp. 99–150. Écully: ISEOR éditeur.

Savall, H., & Zardet, V. (2010b). Le non-dit dans la théorie socio-économique des organisations: situations de management et pièces de théâtre, in R. Ocler (Ed.),

Fantasmes, mythes, non-dits et quiproquo: Analyse de discours et organisation, pp. 113–134. Paris: L'Harmattan.

Savall, H., & Zardet, V. (2011). La RSE, lien entre l'individu, l'organisation et la société: nouvel énoncé de la théorie socio-économique; Actes, ADERSE Conference, Brest, France, mars. Published in *Management et sciences sociales*, 2013.

Savall, H., & Zardet, V. (2014a). La théorie du socle stratégique et l'effet de levier de la cohésion. Communication au *5ème colloque et séminaire doctoral international de l'ISEOR—AOM*, Juin 2014, France. p. 27.

Savall, H., & Zardet, V. (2014b). *Reconstruire l'entreprise; les fondements du management socio-économique*, Paris: Dunod.

Savall, H., Zardet, V., & Bonnet, M. (2000, 2008). *Libérer les coûts et les performances cachés à travers un management socio-économique*, Genève: ILO-BIT.

Savall, H., Zardet, V., & Bonnet, M. (2002). *Prévention des troubles musculo-squelettiques*, Rapport, Lyon: ANACT.

Savall, H., Zardet, V., & Bonnet, M. (2006). Isomorphisme dysfonctionnel de la petite à la grande entreprise, in C. Fourcade, G. Paché, & R. Pérez (Eds.), *La stratégie dans tous ses états, Mélanges en l'honneur du Professeur Michel Marchesnay*, pp. 231–243. Paris: Éditions EMS.

Savall, H., Zardet, V., & Bonnet, M. (eds.) (2009a). *Management socio-économique, une méthode innovante*, Paris: Economica.

Savall, H., Zardet, V., & Bonnet, M. (2009b). Théorie socio-économique des organisations et tétranormalisation: perpétuer l'œuvre de François Perroux, in M. Kalika (Ed.), *Les hommes et le management: des réponses à la crise*, pp. 122–140. Paris: Economica.

Say, J.-B. (1953). *Cours complet d'économie politique 1828–1829*, textes choisis, Paris: Dalloz.

Schumpeter, J. (1911). *Théorie de L'évolution Économique*, Paris, Dalloz.

Schumpeter, J. A. (1939). *Business Cycles*, vol. 1, New York: McGraw-Hill.

Schumpeter, J. A. (1942). *Capitalisme, socialisme et démocratie*, France: Editions Payot.

Schumpeter, J. A. (1954). *History of Economic Analysis*, UK: Psychology Press.

Schumpeter, J. A., & Anstett, J. J. (1935). *Théorie de l'évolution économique: recherches sur le profit, le crédit, l'intérêt et le cycle de la conjoncture*, Paris: Dalloz.

Seghers, V. (2009). *La nouvelle Philanthropie réinvente-t-elle un capitalisme solidaire*, Paris: Autrement.

Servet, J.-M. (1979). Le Prince Masqué, formation de l'économie politique et occultation du politique: l'exemple de l'argent, *Procès* (4), 37–59.

Sloan, H., & Zurcher, A. (1970). *Dictionary of Economics*, New York: Barnes and Noble Books.

Smith, A. (1759). *The Theory of Moral Sentiments*, New York: Garland, 1971.

Smith, A. (1776). *The Wealth of Nations*, vol. 1, London: Everyman's Library.

Smith, R. (2013). Capitalism and the Destruction of Life on Earth: Six Theses on Saving the Humans, *Truthout*, 10 November 2013.

Stiglitz, J. E. (2012a). *Le prix de l'inégalité*, Luxembourg City: Babel.

Stiglitz, J. E. (2012b). Interview de Joseph Stiglitz, *Journal du Dimanche*, 2 septembre, p. 17.

Strauss, E. (1954). Sir William Petty: Portrait of a genius, *Population*, 9(4), 773–774.

Strong, K. C., & Meyer, G. D. (1992). An integrative descriptive model of ethical decision making, *Journal of Business Ethics*, 11(2), 89–94.

Tarbell, I. M. (1916). *New Ideals in Business: An Account of Their Practice and Their Effects Upon Men and Profits*, London: Macmillan.

Tawney, R. H. (1922). *Religion and the Rise of Capitalism*, London: Penguin Books.

Taylor, F. (1911, 1957). *Principes d'organisation scientifique des usines, traduit en français de The principles of scientific management*, Paris: Dunod.

Toniutti, E. (2010). *L'urgence éthique. Une autre vision pour le monde des affaires*, Paris: Ed Je Publie.

Torrès, O. (2012). *La santé des dirigeants. De la souffrance patronale à l'entrepreneuriat salutaire*, Bruxelles: De Boeck.

Tucker, J. (1757). *Instructions for Travellers*, London: William Watson.

Turse, N. (2007) Baghdad 2025: The Pentagon Solution to a Planet of Slums, *Truthout*, 8 January 2007.

Van Marrewijk, M. (2003). Concepts and definitions of CSR and corporate sustainability: Between agency and communion, *Journal of Business Ethics*, 44(2/3), 95–105.

Villey, D., & Nême, C. (1973). *Petite histoire des grandes doctrines économiques, nouvelle édition revue et complétée*, Paris: M. T. Génin.

Vives, J. L. (1943). *De Subventione Pauperum*, publié en 1526, Traduction R. A. Casanova et L. Caby, *De l'assistance aux pauvres*, Bruxelles: Valéro et fils.

Voelcker, J. (2014). 1.2 Billion Vehicles On World's Roads Now, 2 Billion By 2035, online report. Accessed 14 April 2017, www.greencarreports.com/news/1093560_1-2-billion-vehicles-on-worlds-roads-now-2-billion-by-2035-report

Voyant, O. (2003). La démocratie est un concept indissociable de l'entreprise, AOM Conference, Seattle.

Wang, H., & Qian, C. (2001). Corporate philanthropy and corporate financial performance: The role of stakeholders response and political access, *Academy of Management Journal*, 54(6), 1159–1181.

Weber, M. (1924–1964). *The Theory of Social and Economic Organization*, New York, NY: Free Press.

Wuthnow, R. (1982). The moral crisis in American capitalism, *Harvard Business Review*, 60(2), mars–avril, 206.

Yunus, M. (2007). *Vers un nouveau capitalisme*, p. 74, traduction française, 2008, Paris: Jean-Claude Lattès.

Yunus, M. (2010). *Building Social Business: The New Kind of Capitalism That Serves Humanity's Most Pressing Needs*, Philadelphia: Public Affairs.

Zardet, V. (2010). Développement du potentiel humain et création de valeur économique dans l'entreprise, in Association des Amis de François Perroux (Ed.), *Agir dans nouveau monde: le développement et les coûts de l'Homme*, pp. 85–90. Écully: ISEOR éditeur.

Zardet, V., & Harbi, N. (2007). Mastering Computer Technologies: Contributing to Research-Experimentation with Users and Computer Specialists, in A. Buono & H. Savall (Eds.), *Socioeconomic Intervention in Organizations*, pp. 33–42. Charlotte, USA: Information Age Publishing.

Zardet, V., & Voyant, O. (2003). Organizational transformation through the socio-economic approach in an industrial context, *Journal of Organizational Change Management*, Emerald, (Etats-Unis), 16(1), 56–71.

Index

For Product Safety Concerns and Information please contact our EU
representative GPSR@taylorandfrancis.com
Taylor & Francis Verlag GmbH, Kaufingerstraße 24, 80331 München, Germany